CHINA'S GROWING MILITARY POWER: PERPECTIVES ON SECURITY, BALLISTIC MISSILES, AND CONVENTIONAL CAPABILITIES

Edited by
Andrew Scobell
and
Larry M. Wortzel

September 2002

*****

The views expressed in this report are those of the authors and do not necessarily reflect the official policy or position of the Department of the Army, the Department of Defense, or the U.S. Government. This report is cleared for public release; distribution is unlimited.

*****

Comments pertaining to this report are invited and should be forwarded to: Director, Strategic Studies Institute, U.S. Army War College, 122 Forbes Ave., Carlisle, PA 17013-5244. Copies of this report may be obtained from the Publications Office by calling (717) 245-4133, FAX (717) 245-3820, or via the Internet at Rita.Rummel@carlisle. army.mil

*****

Most 1993, 1994, and all later Strategic Studies Institute (SSI) monographs are available on the SSI Homepage for electronic dissemination. SSI's Homepage address is: http://www.carlisle.army. mil/usassi/welcome.htm

*****

The Strategic Studies Institute publishes a monthly e-mail newsletter to update the national security community on the research of our analysts, recent and forthcoming publications, and upcoming conferences sponsored by the Institute. Each newsletter also provides a strategic commentary by one of our research analysts. If you are interested in receiving this newsletter, please let us know by e-mail at outreach@carlisle.army.mil or by calling (717) 245-3133.

ISBN 1-58487-093-1

CONTENTS

FOREWORD

The tenor of U.S.-China relations for much of the first year of the administration of President George W. Bush was set by a crisis that need not have occurred. How the situation was handled and eventually resolved is instructive. It tells us about a beleaguered communist leadership in the buildup to major generational transition (scheduled for late 2002 and early 2003) and the mettle of a democratically elected U.S. government tested early in its tenure by a series of foreign policy crises and a carefully coordinated set of devastating terrorist strikes against the continental United States.

The way the April 2001 crisis on Hainan Island was resolved must be chalked up as a success for the United States. The key was Washington's ability to convince Beijing that holding the air crew was hurting, and not advancing, Chinese interests. That is something Beijing seems not to have grasped when, without warning, the EP-3 suddenly swept down onto the runway in Haikou, bringing a treasure trove of super-secret electronics and 24 Americans, who looked at first to be valuable bargaining chips. With the plane and the crew, China seemed to hold the best cards and behaved accordingly. The top leaders who Ambassador Joseph Prueher had tried to cultivate did not return his calls, and Chinese President Jiang Zemin, after demanding an apology from Washington, left for a Latin American tour. Let the Americans stew in this for awhile, Jiang's message seemed to be.

But Washington managed to reduce the value of those bargaining chips. This was done, first, by making clear that no substantive concessions would be made to secure their release; and, second, by persuading Beijing that continuing to hold the Americans would bring real damage to Chinese interests. As indignation mounted in the United States, economic dangers began to loom on China's horizon. The Beijing government, after all, counts on a rising standard of living to limit dissent, and even a brief loss of access to the American market could be damaging. Nor did Asian neighbors rally to support China. They worry, mostly in private, about Beijing's growing military strength and assertiveness. The State Department boycotted Chinese embassy functions and Secretary of State Colin Powell, while offering regrets and condolences—even eventually sorrow over the loss of the Chinese pilot—showed no inclination to consider the apology China demanded.

The most sensitive nerve in Beijing, however, may have been the Olympics. Having the games in their capital is a cherished Chinese aspiration, and when members of Congress began organizing against it as the crisis developed, the Chinese embassy took the unusual step of sending rather snippy letters to the offenders. Only releasing the hostages could possibly remove the very real threat, and even then not with certainty. Hence Beijing's decision to send the crew home, which, once made, began the search for a linguistic formula to explain it. Washington had not, in fact, apologized, but we could not prevent Beijing from pulling some of what we had said out of context and presenting it through state-controlled media as being, in fact, the apology China's leaders sought. That, plus the usual "humanitarian considerations," provided sufficient cover to end the crisis.

Americans were reminded that the Chinese are not always their friends. Despite some real economic progress, the regime still often becomes confrontational with its own people and with other countries. The United States must treat it with prudence and respect, hedging against dangers even as it seeks to promote positive development. By the same token, China has been reminded that Washington cannot be relied upon to yield when the two states collide. Our growing economic interests in China and our hopes for a future positive relationship with China would be negatively affected if our fundamental American national interests or our commitments to democratic friends and allies in Asia are challenged by China.

During the period that the Chinese changed course, from seeking concessions to seeking an exit, the United States calmly followed procedures. First the Ambassador, then the Secretary of State—and briefly the Vice President—took the spotlight to deliver an authoritative "no" to the demand for apology. Skilled State Department wordsmiths cobbled together a precisely crafted letter that gave China cover, but no more. President Bush choreographed all of this, mostly behind the scenes, and earned our applause. President Jiang seems to have concluded that the matter should be handled expeditiously with civilians, not the PLA taking the lead in the negotiations. Once the Hainan Island Incident was resolved and strategic clarity was emphasized on Taiwan, the U.S. moved swifly to put economics at the top of our agenda, and China's entry into the WTO become the first priority.

This volume, comprised of papers originally presented at a conference held at Carlisle Barracks in September 2001, helps to put the Hainan Island incident in the broader context of China's strategic aspirations and its growing military capabilities. I am proud to be a prime initiator of this conference on the People's Liberation Army, which has been an annual event for more than a decade. Last year's conference's co-sponsors were the American Enterprise Institute, the Heritage Foundation, and the U.S. Army War College. For the fourth consecutive year, the War College's Strategic Studies Institute is publishing the proceedings. The nine chapters in this volume, all written by leading experts, cover a diverse set of important topics: East Asian perspectives on China's security ambitions, the status of the Chinese ballistic missile program and regional reactions to U.S. missile defense initiatives, and China's ever-improving conventional military capabilities. I commend *China's Growing Military Power* to you.

AMBASSADOR JAMES R. LILLEY
Senior Fellow
American Enterprise Institute

CHAPTER 1

CHINA'S RESPONSE
TO A FIRMER AMERICA

Andrew Scobell
Larry M. Wortzel

President George W. Bush made it clear as a candidate for office that U.S. policy toward China "will require tough realism." Presidential Candidate Bush's speech on September 23, 1999, at the Citadel, the military college of South Carolina, foreshadowed his firm approach to Beijing.[1] In that speech, Candidate Bush recalled for the American people that "in 1996, after some tension over Taiwan, a Chinese general reminded America that China possesses the means to incinerate Los Angeles with nuclear missiles."[2] Bush followed up in a speech in Simi Valley, California, with the warning to China that it is a "competitor, not a strategic partner," that the United States would deny the right of Beijing to impose their rule on a free people (Taiwan), and that the United States would help Taiwan defend itself.[3] He also made clear early in the campaign that he would pursue ballistic missile defense for the United States.[4] Thus, the leadership of the Chinese Communist Party in Beijing had early notice that they would not be dealing with a President William J. Clinton who considered China to be a "strategic partner" of the United States.

For Beijing, this was a very different America. Under Clinton, U.S. foreign policy was generally more solicitous of Beijing. Defense officials ran off to China with packages of "deliverables" that the Chinese had come to expect out of meetings in which the United States sought more dialogue

1

and cooperation between the armed forces of each country. Clinton responded to China's March 1996 missile launches off Taiwan with two American aircraft carrier battle groups.[5] However, once the Taiwan elections were over later that month, Clinton dispatched National Security Council and State Department officials to Taiwan to encourage the leaders of that island to work harder at getting along with the People's Republic of China (PRC). Thus policy seemed to vacillate between a firm foreign policy line toward China and one that sought to placate the Chinese leadership when it complained about the U.S. position.[6]

Once Bush took office, Beijing dispatched successively higher-level diplomats to Washington—former ambassadors, foreign ministry officials, and advisers to Chinese President Jiang Zemin—to gauge the White House's position on China and Taiwan. This culminated in the visit to Washington of Vice Premier Qian Qichen on March 20, 2001. The Chinese were clear on one major point: they worked hard to deliver the message that the sale of the Aegis-class guided-missile destroyer to Taiwan by the United States was "unacceptable" and, in Beijing's eyes, amounted to the creation of a new alliance among the United States, Taiwan, and Japan.

The Bush position on Taiwan was clear. He did not back away from his campaign position that "we'll help Taiwan defend itself." The President and his appointees at the Departments of State and Defense, pointing to the large-scale buildup of ballistic missiles on the Chinese coast opposite Taiwan, also made sure that Beijing understood that the United States would meet its commitments under the Taiwan Relations Act (Public Law 98-6) to provide Taiwan adequate defensive arms and services to respond to the Chinese threat.

On April 1, 2001, during a mid-air intercept by the Chinese Navy, a Chinese F-8II fighter aircraft collided with an unarmed American EP-3 reconnaissance aircraft operating in international airspace in the South China Sea.

The American aircrew was detained by China for 11 days and subjected to lengthy and unpleasant interrogation. China made expansive claims about its sovereign territory, insisting that the entire exclusive economic zone, 200 miles off the Chinese coast, was its own. The United States insisted that China's territorial waters and seas extended out 12 miles, consistent with international law. This incident, and the treatment of the aircrew, probably did more to convince the President and the American people that firmness was the only way to deal with Beijing than any other action or statement from either capital. From the perspective of many in the United States, the actions and rhetoric of the Chinese government were confirmation that Beijing did not have friendly intentions toward Washington. The release of the crew and, eventually, the aircraft is seen as the successful outcome of firmness coupled with flexibility and superb interagency coordination from the most senior officials in Washington to the members of the actual negotiating team on Hainan Island. In the face of this, Chinese truculence gave way to Chinese pragmatism.[7]

On April 25, 2001, after 100 days in office, President Bush restated that the United States will help Taiwan defend itself, and in a television broadcast went further, saying that the United States will "do whatever it takes" to defend Taiwan against Chinese aggression. Lest anyone misinterpret just how serious President Bush was about that statement, it was repeated for emphasis. In St. Petersburg, Florida, on March 11, 2002, Deputy Secretary of Defense Paul Wolfowitz, speaking to an audience that included Taiwan's Defense Minister Tang Yao-ming, reiterated Bush's pledge.

Security Policy.

Under the Clinton administration, military-to-military contacts between China and the United States were treated as routine matters. In a number of ways, the "Engagement

3

Policy" of the United States Pacific Command also treated military contacts with China as more or less routine, even desirable, despite concerns expressed in the Congress. From Capitol Hill, many conservatives expressed concerns that such contacts were only helping the People's Liberation Army (PLA) learn more about U.S. defense establishment plans and systems, with no reciprocity from the Chinese side. That, too, changed with the Bush administration.

Soon after assuming his post, Secretary of Defense Donald Rumsfeld conducted a review of military contacts with China. That review concluded that the United States should cease pursuing military contacts or engagement with China as a matter of routine practice. Instead, future U.S.-China military contacts and exchanges would be conducted on a case-by-case basis, with decisions in line with U.S. interests. Contacts should benefit the United States and should not strengthen the PLA.

Ballistic Missile Defense.

One of Candidate Bush's strongest foreign policy and defense positions during his presidential campaign was to call for a ballistic missile system that would defend forward-deployed American forces, U.S. allies, and the homeland of the United States. In Simi, California, he said: "We still, however, need missile defense systems—both theater and national. If I am commander-in-chief, we will develop and deploy them."[8] Of course, the implicit message in this was that the Anti-Ballistic Missile (ABM) Treaty with the Soviet Union had to be reexamined. Two years later, in December 2001 at the Citadel, President Bush made it explicitly clear that the United States must move beyond the ABM Treaty.[9] Since June 13, 2002, the United States is no longer be constrained by that treaty. This means that ABM testing can go ahead against warheads of any speed and with interceptors of full capability. The United States can also work on cooperative programs with friends and allies as well as conduct testing at sea; things that were prohibited under the ABM treaty.

China saw this coming, and Beijing's security planners were not happy about the turn of events. At a conference on arms control in Beijing, China, September 14-15, 2000, representatives from China's arms control community argued that any attempt at developing a ballistic missile defense system in the United States "is inherently destabilizing and will foster a world-wide arms race."[10] The Chinese attendees argued that China was the primary target of ballistic missile defenses, and a United States goal was to seek "absolute security and military superiority."[11] U.S. ballistic missile defenses have never been "aimed" at another country. They are aimed at incoming missiles. Nonetheless, from the time that the U.S. Congress directed the Department of Defense (DoD) to explore ballistic missile defenses in Asia in the Fiscal Year 1998 "Strom Thurmond" Defense Authorization Act, to the time that President Bush assumed office, Beijing repeated these arguments in nearly every international and bilateral forum it could. A year after Bush assumed the presidency, China's representatives continued to argue that the ABM Treaty constitutes "the cornerstone of international strategic stability."[12]

From the time of the Presidential campaign, the incoming Bush administration made it clear that its approach to China would differ from Clinton's and perhaps even differ from that of Bush's father, the 41st President of the United States. After the election, to the surprise of some in China and the United States, President Bush actually followed through on the principles he had expounded in his campaign speeches. This surprise was the result of a failure to recognize the firm commitment to principles on the part of President Bush and senior members of his administration stemming from their deeply-held conservative Realpolitik beliefs.[13] China's reaction is the focus of the chapters in this book.

China's Reaction.

This book was developed against the backdrop outlined in the first section of this introduction. The conference organizers sought to capture the changes in China, not only in terms of rhetoric, but also in military doctrine, training, and hardware purchases, in response to Bush's firmer tone. Of course, we recognize that Beijing had already taken note of the deployment of two U.S. aircraft carrier battle groups to the vicinity of Taiwan during the 1996 Strait Crisis. But as noted above, this strong message was soon diluted by more conciliatory moves from the Clinton administration toward Beijing. As a result, the firmness displayed by Washington in early 1996 was not perceived as a permanent shift in institutionalized approaches to American security policy on China.

Then there was the accident in Belgrade. Despite all of the U.S. apologies, investigations, and fact-finding commissions, many in Beijing, particularly in the PLA and the intelligence community, remain suspicious that the bombing of the Chinese embassy in Belgrade in 1998 was not an accident.[14]

In this volume, some of the best analysts of contemporary China assess how Beijing has reacted, and can be expected to react, to the changes in United States foreign policy. The authors examine Chinese perceptions of the United States, American security and foreign policies in Asia, and the effects of those policies on the Asia-Pacific region.

In chapter 2, Dr. David Finkelstein, Director of Project Asia at the Center for Naval Analyses, examines security relations between China and the United States from the events in Kosovo though America's reaction to the attack on the United States by terrorist forces of the al-Qaeda network. Finkelstein argues that the United States has serious worries about China's activities in four vital areas: Taiwan, the proliferation of weapons of mass destruction

6

and delivery means, the intentions of China's military modernization programs, and whether China is attempting through diplomacy to push the United States out of the Asia-Pacific region.

In Finkelstein's view, although Bush and Jiang were able to improve U.S.-China relations, and to convey the impression that in the war on terrorism at least, Washington and Beijing see eye-to-eye, there was not much substance in the Bush visit to China in October 2001.[15] But a reduction in tension has some value in and of itself, according to Finkelstein, because increased tensions between the United States and China complicate such other key U.S. security concerns as stability on the Korean Peninsula and the prosecution of the war on terrorism.

Finkelstein concludes that there remains deep-seated mutual distrust between China and the United States, particularly among members of the security establishment in both countries. In Beijing, a number of influential security thinkers appear to have concluded that the ultimate objective of United States policies is to obstruct China's rise as a more rich and powerful nation. Therefore, "U.S. policies in the region are increasingly filtered through a set of lenses [in Beijing] that are already calibrated to ensure some distortion." More and more Chinese security thinkers are concluding that the United States wants to "change China," to "deter China," and to "collect intelligence on China." Finkelstein argues that the depth of this mistrust, which is to a certain extent mutual, is reason enough to maintain some sort of security dialogue aimed at dispelling misperceptions and avoiding conflict.

In Chapter 3, Hideaki Kaneda, a retired Vice Admiral in Japan's Maritime Self Defense Forces, addresses China's growing military power and its significance for Japan's national security. Kaneda makes the point that China has used its own military strength to advance territorial claims, while ignoring the sovereignty and jurisdiction of other nations in the East China Sea and South China Sea. He outlines what he characterizes as a methodical effort by China's navy to eventually control "biological and nonbiological resources in China's peripheral waters." The resources Kaneda sees as the object of China's goals are primarily undersea gas and petroleum deposits, but also fishing grounds to secure food supplies.

The major security component of Beijing's strategy is a "near-water defense" of the "first island chain" stretching from the Aleutian Islands, across to the Kuriles, the Japanese Islands, the Ryukyu Islands, Taiwan, the Philippine Islands, and Borneo. Kaneda notes that many of China's territorial claims, the Senkaku Islands in the East China Sea, and the Spratly and Paracel Islands in the South China Sea, fall within the perimeter of this "first island chain." He also argues that control of the waters within this area gives Beijing not only the resources it needs, but also the strategic position to bring military power to bear on Taiwan with reduced fear of outside intervention.

Kaneda believes Japan must call for more transparency in Chinese defense policy. He also argues that China must be prepared to come to agreements that permit joint exploitation of undersea resources by the countries with competing claims. As early confidence-building measures, Kaneda seeks to involve China in regional efforts to provide for maritime safety, combat piracy, stop drug transfers, control and end the trade in persons, and work to control environmental pollution. He takes a firm position on resisting any expansion by China, and insists that Japan must be ready to counter any illegal reconnaissance efforts by the Chinese navy in Japan's territorial waters. Finally, he calls for a firm U.S.-Japan alliance as a counter to China's expansionary tendencies.

In Chapter 4, Anatoly Bolyatko of the Institute of Far Eastern Studies in Russia discusses how in military doctrine and exercises the PLA has reacted to the incoming Bush administration. Bolyatko predicts that, as joint military exercises are conducted between the United States and its East Asian allies in Korea and Japan, and as the United States moves forward with a "missile defense shield," China will react by producing thousands of missiles, aircraft, and tanks. He believes that such production will stress China's military-industrial base, but that such stresses can be tolerated by the Chinese economy. His conclusion is that China will seek to be more effective at force projection and defense in the Asia-Pacific region and will strengthen its forces against Taiwan, but will not seek to become a world military power, as was the Soviet Union, with the capability to conduct military operations outside East Asia.

Lieutenant Colonel Mark Stokes of the U.S. Air Force explains China's reactions to the Bush administration's plans for developing a ballistic missile defense system to protect deployed U.S. military forces, American friends and allies, and the U.S. homeland. As Stokes notes in Chapter 5, China's campaign against the U.S. withdrawal from the 1972 ABM Treaty dates to well before the Bush administration took office. But as a candidate for office, Bush and his security advisers made it clear that the United States would pursue these defenses. Stokes sees China's development and modernization of its own strategic missile forces as "an integral part of PRC coercive strategies." Whether discussing China's theater-level missile programs, short-range missiles, or intercontinental missiles, Stokes believes that any American missile defenses, however modest, are perceived by Beijing as having "serious implications for the viability of its nuclear deterrent and for its expanding inventory of conventional short and medium range ballistic missiles."

Beijing's ballistic missile forces are a political and military "trump card" intended to stem any moves for more autonomy and international recognition from Taiwan, and also limit the freedom of action of the United States to respond to contingencies not only in the Taiwan Strait, but in the Asia-Pacific region. Moreover, Stokes notes, Beijing fears that, if viable ballistic missile defenses are deployed, the command and control architecture for these systems could turn into a "de-facto" alliance if Japan, South Korea, the United States, and Taiwan integrate their missile defense programs.

Stokes predicts that Taiwan will adopt a combination of passive defensive measures to complicate PRC targeting, while Chinese military planners will develop better plans to absorb and reconstitute forces after a PRC first strike. America's withdrawal from the ABM Treaty on June 13, 2002, hands China's diplomats a defeat of monumental proportions. Russia not only accepted the end of the ABM Treaty, but also agreed to major cuts in the numbers of its offensive weapons. Thus the predictions of not only China's arms control community but of the supporters of China's position in the United States ring hollow. Indeed, if there is a missile buildup in reaction to the end of the ABM Treaty, it will come from China, seeking to maintain what Stokes calls a "trump card."

In Chapter 6, Eric McVadon, a consultant on Asian security and former U.S. Defense Attache in Beijing, explains in great detail the positions China has taken in reaction to the Bush presidential campaign statements on missile defense and to the actions taken by the Bush administration in its first 6 months in office to address China's concerns over U.S. ballistic missile defense plans. McVadon outlines the efforts by the PRC arms control and diplomatic community to so limit any American defense efforts that they would have no practical effect on China's nuclear force. China's negotiators, according to McVadon, "could not tolerate" an American missile defense force of 250 interceptor missiles, but "might be able to tolerate 10 interceptors devoted to the defense of the American homeland." According to McVadon, China's negotiators argued that one factor forcing Jiang to take a firm position is "public opinion in China." McVadon opines that the United States must find ways to demonstrate that it "will not be hegemonic" and must continue a dialogue with China on the purpose and extent of any U.S. ballistic missile defense system.

Asia, too, has reacted to American ballistic missile defense plans, explains Dr. Taeho Kim, Senior China Analyst at the Korean Institute for Defense Analyses. In Chapter 7, Kim acknowledges the profound changes in the strategic environment produced by the September 11, 2001 terrorist attacks on the United States. Kim examines missile defenses as part of a more comprehensive effort to transform not only the U.S. military, but also American strategy. He notes that the Bush administration's approach to security represents a radical departure from that of the Clinton administration. Kim predicts an approach that has nuances in policy and missile defense deployments in East Asia, taking into account the political sensitivities in Japan, where some are wary of going beyond the research stage, and in Korea, where the popular focus is on North Korea and its conventional forces, not on China's or North Korea's ballistic missiles.

Colonel Susan Puska, currently U.S. Army Attaché at the American Embassy in Beijing, assesses Beijing's efforts at force projection in Chapter 8. She asserts that China is modeling its own military modernization and efforts to develop advanced capabilities based on the capabilities of the U.S. military. To increase military capabilities, China is focusing more on power projection in peripheral areas by its own military, while changing training methods to increase effectiveness. Puska documents new scenarios for Chinese military training that focus on meeting what Beijing sees as its main threat—the forces of the United States. The PLA also seems to be conscious of its own relative weaknesses in comparison to U.S. forces. Therefore it is focusing on what it sees is the main vulnerability of the United States, a dependence on the electromagnetic spectrum for communication and the exchange of intelligence and threat data.

Beijing is improving management in the PLA, improving the quality of its own military personnel by better educating them and recruiting more qualified personnel. The PLA is also increasingly able to coordinate and use effectively reserve and militia forces. The Central Military Commission, the Chinese Communist Party's leading military body, is also trying to reduce corruption and waste. Puska concludes that today Beijing has a "rough but ready" force projection capability that will improve over time and create greater risks and costs to any country that seeks to challenge China on its periphery.

In Chapter 9, Mr. Kenneth Allen, an expert on Chinese security at the Center for Naval Analyses, examines the changes in the PLA Air Force (PLAAF) as it modernizes and reforms its logistic systems in order to fight high-technology wars. In the 1990s the PLAAF began transforming itself from a force reliant upon single branch deployment to one able to utilize multiple branches in joint service campaigns, indicating a shift in the focus of the PLAAF from a primarily positional, defense oriented operation, to a more mobile, maneuverable, preventative force, able to address local concerns and strike quickly. Allen analyzes this shift through examination of the PLAAF operational theory, logistics structure and theory, and the types of training used to implement these changes. Allen then addresses the specific changes enacted by the PLAAF in preparation for a military confrontation with the United States. Over the last 50 years, China's PLAAF has engaged in only three external campaigns, in Korea, Taiwan Strait (1958) and Vietnam. Given recent military history, the PLAAF has realized the need for a transregional strike force and has initiated the training necessary to create one. While it is not yet clear how effective the PLAAF would be during a real conflict, particularly if facing anticipated U.S. strategies such as interior airfield destruction, the PLAAF has made significant strides in improving pilot proficiency, sortie generation and sustainability, logistical support, communications, and intelligence. Thus, Allen concludes that, while the PLAAF may not currently be able to field a rapid strike force of any threat to the United States, it is making definite progress in this direction.

Each of the authors has effectively captured the main trends in regional security in East Asia. The terrorist attacks on the United States, and the subsequent war on terrorism, only increased American resolve to deploy a ballistic missile defense. They also brought about the deployment of American forces on China's western periphery, something that was not foreseen in the days before the attack on the United States. The trends outlined in this book, therefore, have perhaps played themselves out over a more compressed time frame. But the assessments by each author hold up, and provide some framework for understanding how Beijing may react to the firmer positions taken by the United States.

ENDNOTES - CHAPTER 1

1. George W. Bush, "A Period of Consequences," Charleston: The Citadel, September 23, 1999. *http://citadel.edu/pao/address/pres_bush.html*.

2. The remarks, which have been attributed to General Xiong Guangkai, were made in a private conversation with a former U.S. government official, Ambassador Chas. W. Freeman, and should not carry the weight of an official Chinese statement. Moreover, according to Freeman, these words were not couched as a threat and should be evaluated in the context of an extended off-the-record discussion between himself and the Chinese military official. See Ambassador Chas. Freeman, "Did China Threaten to Bomb Los Angeles?" *Proliferation Brief*, Vol. 4, March 22, 2001, available at *www.ceip.org/files/publications/proliferationbrief404.asp?from=pubtype*; and Allen S. Whiting, "China's Use of Force, 1950-1996, and Taiwan," *International Security*, Vol. 26, Fall 2001, pp. 129-130. In Scobell's view, Xiong's comments should be seen as providing important insights into the mindset of Chinese military elite perceptions of U.S. strategic priorities and the existence of an "asymmetry of motivation" between Beijing and Washington on Taiwan. See Andrew Scobell, *China's Use of Military Force: Beyond the Great Wall and the Long March*, New York: Cambridge University Press, 2003, forthcoming, chapter 8. Zhu Chenghu, then a senior colonel in the PLA serving at China's National

Defense University and now a major general, repeated the warning that Americans face the threat of nuclear attack from China in the event of a response by the United States to an attack on Taiwan. See *Jiefangjun Bao*, February 28, 2000 and Larry M. Wortzel, "Should the United States Feel Threatened by China's Growing Role in the International Military-Political Arena?," *The Retired Officer*, December 2000, p. 35.

3. George W. Bush, "A Distinctly American Internationalism," Simi Valley, CA, November 19, 1999.

4. *http://www.pbs.org/newshour/bb/election/2000debates/2ndebate1.html*.

5. *Chinese Exercise Strait 961: 8-25 March 1996*, Washington, DC: Office of Naval Intelligence, May 1996.

6. For a detailed and comprehensive analysis of Clinton's China policy, see David M. Lampton, *Same Bed, Different Dreams*, Berkeley and Los Angeles: University of California Press, 2001.

7. John Keefe, "A Tale of 'Two Very Sorries'," *Far Eastern Economic Review*, March 21, 2002, pp. 30-33. Significantly, China also concluded that its handling of the incident was virtually exemplary. Chinese analysts insist that Beijing handled the situation in a mature, measured way and demonstrated the effectiveness of China's "crisis management ability." See, for example, the discussion in "Thinkers' Forum: Midair Collision and the Future of Sino-U.S. Relations," *Zhongguo Pinglun* (Hong Kong) June 1, 2001, translated in *Foreign Broadcast Information Service-China*, June 21, 2001.

8. Bush, "A Distinctly American Internationalism," November 19, 1999.

9. George W. Bush, "Bush at the Citadel," Charleston, SC, December 11, 2001. *www.cbsnews.com*.

10. Evan S. Medieros, Rapporteur, *US-China Arms Control and Nonproliferation Cooperation: Progress and Prospects*, Monterey: Monterey Institute of International Studies, October 2000, p. 19.

11. *Ibid.*, p. 20.

12. Li Daozhong, "An Interpretation of Challenges Imposed by U.S. Unilateralism on International Multilateral Arms Control Regime," *Peace*, No. 61, December 2001, p. 19.

13. See, for example, Andrew Scobell, "Crouching Korea, Hidden China: Bush Administration Policy Toward Pyongyang and Beijing," *Asian Survey*, Vol. XLII, No. 2, March/April 2002, pp. 344-345. Scobell contends that Bush appears to see China not so much as a strategic competitor but rather with uncertainty about whether it is a friend or foe. The President's thinking about China might be called "strategic ambivalence." *Ibid.*, pp. 363-364. This ambivalence was likely only reinforced as the result of the war on terrorism and the two face-to-face meetings in late 2001 and early 2002 with Jiang in Shanghai and Beijing, respectively.

14. On Chinese suspicions about the Belgrade bombing and Chinese suspicions about U.S. intentions generally, see Andrew Scobell, *China and Strategic Culture*, Carlisle Barracks, PA: Strategic Studies Institute, May 2002, pp. 18-19.

15. The authors of this introduction would add that, like the Bush-Jiang talks in Shanghai and Beijing, there was not much of substance that came out of the Hu Jintao visit to the United States at the invitation of Vice President Cheney in May 2002. On the Bush-Jiang talks, see, for example, Scobell, "Crouching Korea, Hidden China," p. 359.

PART I: PERSPECTIVES ON CHINA'S SECURITY AND MILITARY POWER

CHAPTER 2

THE VIEW FROM BEIJING:
U.S.-CHINA SECURITY RELATIONS
FROM KOSOVO TO SEPTEMBER 11, 2001

David M. Finkelstein

Introduction.

On October 19, 2001, Presidents George W. Bush of the United States and Jiang Zemin of the People's Republic of China (PRC) had their first face-to-face meeting on the fringes of the Asia-Pacific Economic Council (APEC) meeting in Shanghai after almost a year of increasingly strained bilateral relations. What was originally scheduled to be a full-blown summit meeting, to include a visit by Bush to Beijing, was curtailed to a half-day of talks due to the unforeseen and tragic terrorist attacks on the United States on September 11.[1]

By all accounts, the meetings went well enough. The official Chinese press characterized the discussions as "constructive and fruitful" and held in a "friendly and candid atmosphere."[2] In their joint press conference, Bush readily agreed with Jiang that the discussions were useful and that the two men had "a very good meeting."[3] Both men agreed to improve relations. Jiang called for "constructive and cooperative relations," as did Bush, who added the word "candid" to the construct.[4]

The usual "deliverables" that are associated with and often anticipated as a result of these types of U.S.-China summits were modest. But given many months of tense relations and the events of September 11, Bush and Jiang were able to accomplish two key objectives: establish a baseline dialogue from which to attempt to improve relations, especially security relations, and publicly present a "united front" on the issue of the war on terrorism. In the future, these two threads may become increasingly interwoven as operations in Afghanistan continue. Indeed, for both countries, the war against terrorism will only magnify the importance of placing U.S.-China relations, especially security relations, on an even keel.

For China, the next few years will witness a significant leadership succession—the accession to power of the "Fourth Generation" of leaders in 2002. These are the men who will have to grapple with the increasingly difficult task of pushing forward economic and structural reforms, while managing the social and political dislocations attendant to those reforms. They will have to move forward with the development of China's western region, tackle the internal problems plaguing the Chinese Communist Party (CCP), and manage the issues associated with World Trade Organization (WTO) entry. All of this will be going on while China will be increasingly placed under the international microscope in the lead-up to the 2008 Olympics. Moreover, the Taiwan issue is becoming more complex for Chinese leaders as political developments and domestic politics in Taipei become more complicated. And now that the United States is actually prosecuting military operations in a country with which China shares a land border—always a high order Chinese security concern—Beijing now has a serious stake in not being cut out by Washington. China simply cannot afford a confrontational relationship with the United States at this point in time if it can be avoided.

Needless to say, a confrontational relationship with China will not serve U.S. interests either. Especially because of the campaign in Afghanistan and the global nature of Washington's war on terrorism, stable bilateral relations between the United States and China are a must. The issue of terrorism notwithstanding, strained security relations with China serves no ends if it can be avoided.

Increased U.S.-China tensions will only unnerve Washington's allies and friends in the Asia-Pacific region. An unstable relationship could have a deleterious impact on U.S. business and trade interests at a time of economic uncertainty. Increased tensions could complicate key U.S. security concerns in East Asia, such as the maintenance of stability on the Korean Peninsula and especially across the Taiwan Strait. Overall, worsening bilateral relations with China could become an unending foreign policy distraction to a Bush White House that needs to focus its foreign policy energies on the war against terrorists.

At the same time, due to a growing mutual distrust that has evolved within the two security establishments over the past few years, security differences between the two nations will be the most challenging area in which to repair relations and move them forward.

U.S. concerns vis-à-vis China are well known. For the most part, U.S. worries on the security front have revolved around the following four key issues. First, growing concerns that Beijing is prepared to use force to resolve the Taiwan issue "sooner rather than later," based on a calculus that few in the West can claim to understand with any degree of certainty.[5] Second, U.S. concern about Chinese proliferation behavior. Third, given the lack of defense transparency in China, uncertainties in the United States as to the intentions behind China's military modernization programs—conventional and nuclear. And fourth, questions in the United States as to whether China would like to see the U.S. military pushed out of the Pacific, or at least pulled back.[6] All of these issues are critically important to the regional security interests of the United States. On a 4-tier scale of national interests—(1) survival, (2) vital, (3) major, (4) peripheral—they rate in the vital and major categories. This is not insignificant.

Likewise, in Beijing, the "U.S. factor" in the Chinese national security calculus appears to have grown even greater than in the past. Over the past few years, the perceived "challenges" to Chinese national sovereignty and security interests posed by the security policies of the United States—real or imagined on their part—are being viewed by a good number of Chinese security analysts with increasing alarm. Whereas, one could argue, U.S. security concerns about China range backwards from "vital" to "major," many Chinese see U.S. challenges as ranging upwards from "major" to "vital" and, in some cases, even "survival." This trend is extremely worrisome if true.

Because most American analysts are already well aware of the Chinese security policies that give pause in the United States, the assignment given this student by the conference organizers was to identify the Chinese concerns—which are not always self-evident. The author of this chapter, therefore, will review the growing uncertainty, concern, and angst with which Beijing has viewed the United States over the past couple of years. He will attempt to view the world through Chinese eyes. He will attempt to convey the Chinese analytic framework vis-à-vis the United States—an analytic frame of mind, if you will—as well as specific policy concerns.

The best way to do so is to review for readers the serious national security debates that have taken place in China in the very recent past that, in many ways, have been driven by Chinese angst about the United States. The author will present an overview of the very significant national security debate that took place in China in 1999 in the aftermath of NATO's Kosovo intervention.[7] He will touch briefly on the April 2001 EP-3 incident, and address the "America debate" that was unfolding in Beijing as of the summer of 2001, just prior to September 11. Finally, the author will speculate about the concerns Chinese analysts might have as they view the security implications of the American campaign in Afghanistan, and, presumably, the war against terrorism beyond.

A caveat at the outset is in order. It is important that the Chinese *Weltanschauung* be fully understood and explained, especially as it concerns the United States. However, doing so does not imply agreement.

1999: Kosovo and the "Great Peace and Development Debate."

Overview. From March 1999 through the late fall of 1999, a national security debate took place in China. It was remarkable on two counts.

For the first time since 1985, Deng Xiaoping's basic assessment of the state of the international security environment—that "peace and development" (*Heping Yu Fazhan*) were the trends of the times—was seriously questioned and intensely scrutinized. Of key significance, the efficacy of China's foreign policies and the validity of China's national defense policies were especially subjected to fervid internal debate.

The second reason that this was a remarkable event was that this was likely the first time since 1949 that Chinese foreign policy and defense policy were openly discussed and debated in the government-controlled media as matters of public concern—to include criticisms of government policies by the general populace.

Judging from the Chinese press, during the height of the debate (the summer of 1999) almost every literate sector of the China polity was apparently engaged in a media free-for-all on foreign policy and defense issues. This included intellectuals, middle class entrepreneurs, students, and even Chinese government analysts who took to the op-ed pages, radio call-in shows, and TV roundtables.[8]

Public discourse revolved about the state of the world, China's place in it, the state of Chinese security, as well as what the government in Beijing should do about these issues and about the United States.

The proximate cause of this debate was NATO's military intervention in Kosovo in March 1999. NATO's errant

23

bombing of the PRC Embassy in Belgrade in May added fuel to the debate. However, behind these issues were long-simmering Chinese concerns that the post-Cold War international order was not unfolding as Chinese international relations theorists had predicted. The debate, especially the internal debate, was also driven by increasing Chinese concerns about U.S. strategic intentions and policies in the post-Cold War order in general, and towards China in particular.

At its most fundamental level, the debate that took place in 1999 was about how the Chinese government should assess the state of the unfolding international security environment. But most important, it was about the implications of that assessment for China's external security.

The overarching question was simple: had China's external security situation fundamentally deteriorated as a result of NATO's intervention in Kosovo? This question brought others to the surface: What did other global and regional security developments portend? And should China adjust its domestic priorities, its foreign policies, or its defense policies?

On the diplomatic front, for example, questions were raised as to whether the Chinese government had been placing too much emphasis on cultivating the "developed world"—especially the United States—instead of the "developing world," which it had traditionally emphasized? Others asked whether the government was becoming involved in international affairs that were too far removed from China's traditional, more narrowly defined national interests. In effect, this question asked whether the central leadership was walking away from Deng Xiaoping's oft-quoted dictum that in foreign affairs "China should keep a low profile and never take the lead."

On the issue of national defense modernization, some voiced concerns that the "U.S.-led" Kosovo intervention was evidence that China could no longer afford to continue to subjugate defense modernization to economic development. Indeed, some argued that it was now time to place equal emphasis on the two.

As we shall see, it was not just the Kosovo intervention that made this an issue. Other issues simmering in the background were at work, and it is important to point out that those who saw a need for enhanced military defense were not just in the People's Liberation Army (PLA): they were as likely to be found in civilian ministries and their affiliated institutes.

But at the heart of the debate in official circles were questions about the United States as a world actor in general, Washington's specific intentions toward China, and the future of U.S.-China relations. Indeed, almost all Chinese on every side of the debate were able to agree that any deleterious changes in the international security environment and any degradation of China's own security were a function of the actions and intentions, real or perceived, of the United States.

By most accounts, the "U.S. question" in particular was the most contentious issue debated internally by Chinese government analysts and other officials. As one Chinese put it, "The Chinese reaction to Kosovo created the political atmosphere that unleashed a debate by those unsatisfied with PRC policy toward the U.S." At a certain point in the discourse, the question of whether confrontation with the United States was inevitable became the centerpiece of discourse. Other questions revolved about how to deal with the United States and the tradeoffs between cooperation and confrontation with Washington.

In the lexicology of Chinese analyses, all of these issues and others were captured by asking whether "peace and development" was still "the keynote of the times."

To grasp the significance of the question, one must understand the implications of questioning the validity of "peace and development" as the "keynote of the times" (*shidai zhuti*). Doing so requires a step back to recall Mao Zedong's assessment and Deng Xiaoping's reversal of that assessment. In China these assessments are not mere exercises in theoretical discourse: they are the starting point for justifying or rationalizing specific national policy decisions.[9] Therefore, a review of the differences in domestic, foreign, and military policies justified by the very different assessments made by Mao and Deng provides a historical context with which to view the debate of 1999.

The Maoist Line: "War and Revolution." In the 1960s and 1970s, the Maoist assessment of the international security environment was commonly stated as "war and revolution" (*zhanzheng yu geming*). This was a result of the perceived military threats to China from the United States and especially the Soviet Union after the break between Moscow and Beijing. It was also a function of the ideological lens through which Mao viewed the world.

As a result of this assessment, China's security posture and its domestic policies were characterized by keeping the Chinese nation and the PLA on a war footing, perpetuating "class struggle" within China, and pursuing a foreign policy focused on the "socialist camp" and the revolutionary "Third World." For the most part, China remained "closed" to the capitalist world.

As we know, this assessment had a profound impact on the economy and society. The combined requirements of being on a war footing and Mao's ideological imperatives resulted in an autarkic economy; an emphasis on heavy industries moved inland; the perpetuation of the policies of the communization of agriculture and industry; and the near-destruction of the national bourgeoisie.

For its part, the PLA was told to expect "early war, major war, and nuclear war." This meant maintaining a massive defense establishment, relying on "People's War" as a military strategy, and a belief that "superior" political will could overcome the advanced technologies of potential

26

opponents. It also perpetuated the highly elevated status of the PLA in the Chinese polity.

The Dengist Line: "Peace and Development." In the late 1970s and early 1980s, Deng Xiaoping began taking China down a path of bold change. Deng's reassessment of the "keynote of the times" provided a critical ideological basis for the myriad of sea-change reforms that would ensue. It also was the justification for a change in national priorities. By 1985 Deng had reversed the Maoist assessment completely.

Where Mao saw "war and revolution" as the context for international security, Deng acknowledged the changes in superpower relations and China's own prospects. Deng's reassessment held that "peace and development" *(heping yu fazhan)* more correctly described the trends in the world. The Dengist view held that, in spite of the continuing dangers to China posed by wars and conflicts, the possibility of a world war was remote, the chance of a nuclear war between the superpowers was slight, China did not face the prospect of imminent invasion, *and China would enjoy at least 2 decades of a peaceful international environment.*

The policy changes derived from this assessment are well known. Domestically, "economics as the central task" replaced "class struggle as the key link." In foreign relations, China began to seek contact and good relations with the capitalist world as well as the socialist camp, and with developed countries as well as developing countries. "Reform and opening up" (*gaige yu kaifeng*) became the major thrust.

In the area of defense policy, the PLA was taken off a war footing and shifted onto a prolonged period of "peacetime army-building," thus initiating the reforms of the Chinese military that persist today: namely moving toward a (relatively) leaner, but more technologically advanced PLA. Just as importantly, Deng placed military modernization as the last priority in his "Four Modernizations."

27

At an enlarged meeting of the Central Military Commission in June 1985, Deng explained his reassessment to his generals. While recognizing the dangers that persisted, he asserted that "the world forces for peace are growing faster than the forces for war." Deng told his military leaders to be patient, to place economic construction above all else, and to wait for at least 20 years. At that time China's economic strength would permit a greater emphasis on military modernization.

Fast forward to 1999. Clearly then, the critique of the Dengist assessment during the Kosovo debate engendered major implications for the broad sweep of Chinese domestic, foreign, and defense policies. If "peace and development" were no longer the trend, what was? Did Kosovo signify the triumph of the "forces for war" over the "forces for peace"? Should China raise defense modernization at the expense of economic reform? Should Beijing turn its back on the developed and capitalist world and focus its foreign policies on the developing world exclusively? Is conflict with the United States inevitable?

Draconian as these questions may seem, the highly charged atmosphere in Beijing in the aftermath of the Kosovo intervention (and especially after the errant bombing of the PRC Embassy in Belgrade) provided a backdrop against which these types of questions could be asked and debated for the first time in many years as Chinese analysts attempted to make sense out of a post-Cold War international order that, from the perspective of some, now seemed to be moving against Chinese national interests.

The degree of angst in Beijing during this period is partially explained by comparing China's successes in the preceding 3 years, 1996-99, with events in late 1998 and in early 1999.

Prior to 1999: Riding the Waves of Self-Confidence. Between 1996 and late 1998, Beijing had every reason to feel newly confident in its place in the world order, especially in foreign affairs.

- In the wake of the 1995-96 Taiwan Strait crises, U.S.-China relations seemed to be back on track after the two presidential summits in 1997 and 1998. An agreement to seek a "Constructive Strategic Partnership" was announced, and President William Clinton publicly stated the "Three No's" in Shanghai.[10]

- Nearly 10 years after Tiananmen, almost all foreign economic sanctions against China had been lifted.

- Between 1996 and 1998, a very proactive foreign policy spearheaded by Jiang resulted in the establishment of a series of "partnerships" around the globe with key developed countries.[11]

- Hong Kong's retrocession to China was accomplished, and Macao's was to be next.

- Human rights issues no longer appeared to be a major impediment to China's foreign economic relations. Not only had Europe seemingly lost interest in this issue but also, for the first time in many years, the United States in 1998 did not sponsor a resolution condemning China at the annual meeting of the United Nations (U.N.) Human Rights Commission in Geneva.

- Beijing was making excellent progress in resolving border disputes with neighbors, notably Russia and even Vietnam. Moreover, the "Shanghai Five" arrangement between China, Russia, Kazakhstan, Tajikistan, and Kyrgyzstan was well under way.[12]

- China had received accolades from around the world for "responsible" behavior during the Asian financial crisis, and for the moment the focus of regional concern in Asia was on financial recovery, not China's rise as a regional power.

- On the Taiwan front, the PRC seemed to be on the move, and Taipei appeared to be on the defensive. In addition to obtaining the "Three No's" from the U.S. President, China was pressuring Taiwan for political talks and waging an active diplomatic offensive to woo those countries that still recognized Taipei. The loss of diplomatic relations with South Africa in 1998 was a serious blow to Taiwan in this regard.

Domestically, the situation was tolerable. China was able to weather the Asian financial crisis without devaluating its currency. Growth was acceptable, if not as great as desired. The social dislocations attendant to economic reform seemed manageable, although concerns about labor unrest persisted.

1999: A Year of Disasters. Juxtaposed against 3 years of relatively smooth sailing, the close of 1998 and the first months of 1999 brought, from a Chinese perspective, ominous developments in key areas of concern: Japan, Taiwan, and relations with the United States. Some of these events took place before the Kosovo intervention or the Embassy bombing, others afterwards. The net effect, however, was to raise fears among many Chinese officials and analysts that security trends were now turning against China's interests. These events provided both a context for the debate of 1999 and, in some cases, new impetus during the debate.

Japan. Throughout this period (1998, 1999) developments in Japan begin to be viewed with increasing apprehension by the Chinese analytic *xitong.*

- In December 1998 the Government of Japan announced its decision to join the United States in co-research of the upper-tier Theater Ballistic Missile Defense program.

- In March 1999 the Japan Maritime Self-Defense Force fired upon North Korean vessels—the first shots fired in anger by the Japanese armed forces since the end of World War II.

- The Japanese Diet ratified the Revised Guidelines for Defense Cooperation with the United States in May 1999, refusing to specify for Beijing whether Taiwan was included in the ambiguous phrase "areas surrounding Japan."

- All of this added to concerns about Japan in the wake of Jiang's less than successful visit to that country in late November 1998.

Taiwan. In early July 1999 then-President Lee Teng-hui issued his "Two-State Theory," which resulted in another "mini-crisis" in cross-Strait relations. Enough said.

United States. To one degree or another, the United States, during the debate, began to be viewed by many analysts in Beijing as the root cause of the negative trends in Japanese and Taiwan affairs in addition to becoming a problem in its own right. What did Chinese analysts focus on?

- In January 1999 the Clinton administration announced its decision to move forward on National Missile Defense.

- In April 1999 Zhu Rongji's visit to Washington for the expressed purpose of negotiating Chinese permanent normal trading relations (PNTR) and WTO membership ended in failure. Indeed, in late March there had been a "mini-debate" in China as to whether Zhu should have gone at all, given the inauguration of the NATO air campaign against Serbia and a lack of consensus within the Chinese bureaucracy about the types of concessions Beijing could afford to make in those negotiations.

- Throughout this period, Chinese analysts began to assess that the so-called "anti-China" voices in the United States were gaining the upper hand over China policy. Some of the more prominent "data points" they cited included the "Cox Committee Report" (May) and the Los Alamos espionage case; the tabling of the Taiwan Security Enhancement Act (April-May); the requirement levied on the Department of Defense to publish its study on hypothetical theater ballistic missile defense (TBMD) architectures in Asia including Taiwan; the possibility of the sale of TBMD-related radars to Taipei (June); and the concern over China's alleged future influence over the Panama Canal (July).

NATO and Kosovo. Then, of course, there was the issue of Kosovo itself. Some Chinese security analysts believed it established precedents for military interventions in the "internal affairs" of sovereign states and demonstrated the "will" of the United States (as viewed from Beijing) to use force "to maintain its world dominance." Kosovo shocked many Chinese into questioning whether the global trends were in fact away from war and toward China's much-touted multipolar world order—the previous analysis.

The air campaign began in March while Jiang Zemin was in Italy, a NATO member, as part of a three-nation European visit. In deciding to intervene with military force, NATO sidestepped the U.N. and marginalized Security Council members China and Russia. Then, in early May, the PRC Embassy was inadvertently attacked.

Just as disconcerting to the Chinese were other NATO-related events. In April, NATO accepted Poland, Hungary, and the Czech Republic as new members. During NATO's 50th anniversary celebrations in Washington, a new "Strategic Concept" was declared that included out-of-area missions. Also around that time (June) was the coining of the "Clinton Doctrine," which was interpreted in

China as espousing the legitimacy of military interventions in sovereign nations for humanitarian purposes. Beijing immediately thought of the implications for Taiwan, Xinjiang, and Tibet, and carefully watched developments in Chechnya.[13]

Domestic Concerns. Even on the domestic front, the first half of 1999 presented issues for concern within *Zhongnanhai*. High-profile corruption cases continued to embarrass the Party; reforms of the state-owned enterprises were becoming difficult to carry out; and consumer demand at home was slowing. If the Hong Kong press is to be believed, large-scale and often-violent incidents of labor unrest continued to plague local governments on the mainland. Even more unsettling were the rise in the profile of the China Democracy Party following the Clinton visit to China (1998) and the "shock" of the *Falun Gong* phenomenon beginning in April 1999 and continuing today.

Overall then, in just a few months the confidence of Chinese leaders and their analysts was significantly shaken. They were no longer so certain of their place in the world order or of their assessment of world trends as favoring China's continued rise both at home and abroad.

The Results of the Debate. At the end of the day, after reams of analysis and incessant rounds of meetings, the debate re-looked many of these key issues. And by the time the Beidaihe meetings took place in August 1999 there was closure on many of them: at least on an official level (if not intellectually).

That closure came in the form of a new shorthand for the state of the international security situation referred to as "The Three No Changes and the Three New Changes."

The "Three No Changes" assert the following:

- Peace and development remain the trend in international relations and the movement toward a multipolar world continues;

- Economic globalization continues to increase; and,

- The major trend is toward the relaxation of international tensions.

But these three points were modified by the "Three New Changes":

- Hegemonism and power politics are on the rise;

- The trend toward military interventionism is increasing; and,

- The gap between developed and developing countries is increasing.

Clearly, these two sets of seemingly contradictory assessments represented a compromise position between those who were relatively optimistic about long-term trends and those who were very much focused on and concerned about near-term negative developments.

The "Three No Changes" reaffirmed the basic thrust of Deng's earlier analysis. China did not now face "early war, major war, and nuclear war." It reaffirmed the analyses by Chinese international relations theorists since the late 1980s that the world would *eventually* move toward a multipolar international order and that China would become one of the key poles. It also recognized the growing importance of economics in international relations. So, to a great degree, it accounted for the views of those who did *not* see Kosovo and other security-related events of concern as requiring a major readjustment of the Dengist assessment.

This formulation had direct and immediate implications for Chinese domestic policies. It reaffirmed the correctness of "economics as the central task" and provided the continued ideological justification for the leadership in Beijing to press forward with the next phases of economic and structural reform, to include the pursuit of WTO membership. So when Chinese interlocutors say that "nothing changed" as a result of Kosovo, they are not being disingenuous. There was, in fact, no decision to reverse the Dengist line and the direction of domestic reforms.

However, something *did* change after Kosovo. The "Three New Changes" added serious caveats to the generally positive long-term trends cited in the first part of the construct.

For one thing, the "Three New Changes" was an admission that previous Chinese government analyses of the near-term trends in the international security had been much too optimistic about the *pace* of global multipolarization and much too quick to dismiss the potentially destabilizing effects that local wars and worldwide military interventions might have on China's interests.

Clearly, Beijing's much-hoped-for multipolar world order was *not* around the corner. In addition, the new assessment certainly undercut the assertion in the 1998 Defense White Paper that "the influence of armed conflicts and local wars had been remarkably weakened." In fact, the "Three New Changes" undercut the entire tenor of the first section of the 1998 Defense White Paper.

The second change implicit in the "Three New Changes" is the Chinese assessment of the root cause of the problems facing world security and stability.

Previously, Beijing had seen the United States as one source of some of the problems plaguing world security, both economic and military. But there were plenty of other nations and non-national actors viewed as problematic. In the wake of Kosovo and a host of other events since 1998, the mix of problems remained the same. But the United States and its policies were now starting to be viewed as a *principal* source of these problems, especially for China. And by most accounts the "Three New Changes" is about the United States almost exclusively.

Of equal significance, the new assessment, and a reinforced view of the United States as a superpower "hegemon," seemed to have put to rest previous *de rigueur* internal and academic assessments that the "comprehensive national power" of the United States was in a slow decline—an analytic "line" that had been commonplace for at least a decade.[14] The new line seems to be accompanied by an assessment that the United States will maintain its status as "sole superpower" for the next 20 years, if not longer.

At the end of the day, then, the degree to which the post-debate analysis of the international and regional security environment, and the assessment of the US, became an official "line" was reflected in the formulations in the first section of the October 2000 Defense White Paper.

The October 2000 Defense White Paper, *China's National Defense 2000*, provided a much more sober assessment of the trends in international and regional security than had been articulated in the July 1998 version. Some of the assessments from the important first section of the October 2000 Defense White Paper are worth reviewing.[15]

- "In today's world factors that may cause instability and uncertainty *have markedly increased.*"

- "Hegemonism and power politics still exist *and are further developing.*"

- "Certain big powers are pursuing neo-interventionism, neo-gunboat diplomacy, and neo-economic colonialism . . . *which are seriously damaging the sovereignty, independence, and development interests of many countries, and threatening world peace and security."*

- "The United Nations' authority and role in handling international and regional security affairs . . . *are being seriously challenged."*

- "Local wars and armed conflicts . . . *have increased again."*

- "There are . . . *new negative developments... in the security of the Asia-Pacific region."*

- "The Taiwan Straits situation . . . *is complicated and grim."*

Finally, to underscore increasing concern over Chinese security, the Defense White Paper of 2000 announced the following:

> . . . in view of the fact that hegemonism and power politics still exist and are further developing, and in particular, the basis for the country's peaceful reunification is seriously imperiled, China will have to enhance its capability to defend its sovereignty and security by military means.

The Unique Interests of the PLA. If there was any institution in China that had a significant corporate stake in the events surrounding Kosovo, it was the PLA. Needless to say, closely watching and studying NATO's campaign against Serbia as it unfolded was a matter of intense professional interest. But the PLA had an equally large bureaucratic interest in the internal and public debate triggered by Kosovo. The debate provided a window of opportunity for China's military establishment to argue publicly, and likely behind closed doors as well, that national defense and military modernization deserved a greater priority in overall national development than had been accorded hitherto.

The arguments surrounding the need for a greater emphasis on defense modernization by the PLA (and others) gained momentum as a result of two events: the May 1999 bombing of the PRC Embassy in Belgrade (in which a Chinese military attaché was wounded), and Lee Teng-hui's espousal of the "Two-State Theory" in July 1999. In the past, such arguments by the top PLA leadership in public fora had been somewhat politically incorrect, although once in a while a senior PLA leader would make his case. For example, in 1996 Defense Minister General Chi Haotian wrote a long article in CCP's official journal, *Seeking Truth (Qiushi)*, in which he stated, "The building of national defense . . . cannot exceed the limitation of tolerance of economic construction, *nor can it be laid aside until the economy has totally prospered.*"[16] For the most part, however, in public, the top PLA leadership had for years dutifully recited the Dengist mantra that "defense modernization must remain subordinate to economic construction." Here was a chance to press the case for more funding.

It should be pointed out, however, that *publicly* the top PLA leadership did *not* challenge this line during the debate. As mentioned above, having the leadership of the Central Military Commission, for example, make the case in the press during such a period of emotionalism and sensationalism was likely still too sensitive from a domestic political standpoint.[17] Nevertheless, there seemed to be plenty of senior colonels and other field grade officers who were quite willing to make the arguments. Consequently, during the period of the debate the PLA's official newspaper, *Liberation Army Daily (Jiefangjun Bao)*, carried an unending stream of "opinion pieces" from individual officers that warned the nation of the consequences of ignoring national defense, hyped the threat posed by the United States to international peace and stability, and, in some cases, argued that military modernization should at least be equal to national economic construction.

In these regards, the timing of Kosovo could not have been better. For one thing, work on the 10th Five-Year Plan (2001-2005) was already under way but not yet complete. There was still a chance to press for an increase in funding. Moreover, just 8 months earlier, in July 1998, Jiang had ordered the PLA to divest itself of its commercial enterprises—the large corporate empire that it had run for many years which provided the military with a source of (1) extra-budgetary funds for soldier "quality of life," (2) employment for PLA spouses and demobilized officers, (3) supplemental operations and maintenance (O&M) funds, and (4) funds for equipment procurement. Not only did the PLA lose many of its corporate entities, but it did so under a cloud. The decision to have the military divest was tied to evidence brought to the attention of Jiang of large-scale smuggling and corruption by some military commercial entities in the south. Consequently, the Kosovo intervention, and especially the bombing of the PRC Embassy in Belgrade, gave the PLA an opportunity to burnish its image among the general public by riding the crest of nationalist sentiment as the defenders of Chinese sovereignty.

These particularistic interests aside, NATO's Kosovo intervention also drove home to many in the PLA once again just how large a capabilities gap still existed between their own armed forces and those of the advanced Western nations, especially the United States, even after nearly a decade of post-Gulf War reform and modernization. The frustration of some military officers at the relatively low priority of military modernization in the greater scheme of national development was articulated by a general line of argument that goes like this: "We were told that we would have to be patient, that military modernization would have to await economic modernization. We have been patient for 20 years. How long must we wait?"

But the PLA rhetoric surrounding Kosovo served another important purpose. It was used to highlight to the Chinese armed forces the importance of following through with the wide-ranging programs of reform that had been underway for the last decade. Many of these reforms—especially in the areas of force structure downsizing and personnel administration—had been meeting some resistance below. As Chief of the General Staff Fu Quanyou had pointed out a year earlier, grassroots units had to overcome "selfish departmentalism and overemphasis of local interests" and move forward with change for the greater good of the PLA.[18] Especially in light of the situation on Taiwan, the PLA leadership used the Kosovo intervention and the debate to lecture its own people that reform and modernization of the military was a serious undertaking and not merely a bureaucratic exercise.

While it is clear that military modernization was not going to supplant economic construction as the national priority, or even be equal to it in emphasis, some of these arguments by the PLA, or by others on behalf of the PLA, probably had an impact on the top Chinese leadership. Clearly, for various internal political reasons, the concerns of the PLA could not be totally ignored. Consequently, not long after the PRC Embassy bombing, rumors abounded that the central government had provided the military with a large, supplemental lump-sum infusion of funds.[19]

Given the call for enhanced national defense by the PLA and others in the post-Kosovo debate, the demise of many PLA business interests, the security assessment articulated in the October 2000 Defense White Paper, and the politics of succession, it was not too much of a surprise when in December 2000 the Chinese Finance Minister announced an increase of 17.7 percent for defense spending for 2001.

Overall then, the debate of 1999 was an occasion for Beijing to vent, anguish, and wonder about China's national security and the future of U.S.-China relations.

Interregnum: December 1999 Through April 2001.

At an official level, "the great debate" came to a close in late August 1999 when the Beidaihe leadership meetings promulgated the "Three No Changes and Three New Changes." It was not until December, however, that the public debate in the Chinese media finally came to a close. At this point in time, the central authorities apparently decided that enough public debate on the issues of national defense, national security, and Chinese foreign policy had taken place among the masses. By the end of 1999, editors of the major newspapers were reportedly no longer accepting op-eds from their readerships or writing editorials on these issues. There were other pressing issues with which to grapple: WTO accession, the inception in February 2000 of the "Go West" campaign, the continuing "Three Represents Campaign," and a host of other domestic and foreign policy issues; not the least of which was the work needed to be done on the 10th Five-Year Plan, the beginning of the succession process, and the preparatory work for the 16th Party Congress.

By the summer of 2000, however, Chinese foreign policy analysts were once again running fast to keep up with events in the United States. Attention was now focused on two issues: the ongoing presidential election campaign and the perception that American military strategy was shifting to Asia—a Chinese concern that surfaced even before the Bush election victory and the subsequently published *Quadrennial Defense Review* (QDR) issued by the Pentagon in September 2001.

The catalyzing event for Chinese analysts wondering about a U.S. "strategic focus shift" (*zhanlue zhongdian zhuanyi*) to Asia were news reports that the U.S. Air Force desired to forward-deploy stockpiles of cruise missiles to Guam in the summer of 2000. Chinese concerns about a "strategic shift" linger today, especially given some of the language in the recent QDR document.

41

For the most part, however, the Chinese community of America experts was fully engaged following election politics in the United States and wondering and speculating about what would be "better for China"—a Bush or a Gore election victory. The only people likely more frustrated than the American public at the time it took to decide finally the election winner was the corps of Chinese America experts who were probably under tremendous pressure to explain what was going on, and what the implications of a Bush or Gore victory or defeat meant for China. And many a Chinese institute wasted its funds in having delegations go to the United States in late November 2000 for post-election fact-finding, only to arrive without an election decision made.

After the Bush election was confirmed, arguments went back and forth in China as to the implications. Cautious optimists pointed to Bush's father, "Lao Bushe," as a probable force for ameliorating the Republican Party campaign rhetoric. Especially disconcerting to Beijing was the excoriation of the Clinton-Jiang "Constructive Strategic Partnership" construct and the substitution of the "Strategic Competitor" label. They pointed out as well that, sooner rather than later, economic realities would triumph, and the U.S. business community would eventually weigh in. After all, Bush and some of his principal deputies were from corporate America. They argued as well that all administrations start out "tough" on China, and they recalled the Clinton campaign slogan about "coddling dictators." Those on the other side of the argument dismissed these lines of analysis as delusion. The trend, they argued, was already clear: the United States is bent on confronting China on all fronts and the Bush victory means the ascendance of the "anti-China" elements. At the end of the day, they argued, the United States was still determined to pursue a strategic objective of "westernizing and splitting" China.

When the EP-3 incident occurred on April 1, 2001, these arguments were far from resolved, but for the moment they were held in check as the PRC Government tried to decide what to do about a situation that could quickly deteriorate. It is far too early to even attempt to understand (if we ever can) the calculus by which Beijing acted vis-à-vis the United States during the 11 days the American aircrew was detained on Hainan Island. But for this student, at least, it was clear at the time and remains clear today that domestic politics in China were paramount.

Jiang and the senior party leadership had learned some important lessons as a result of the errant NATO attack on the PRC Embassy in Belgrade in May 1999. Most of these lessons had to do with the domestic scene, not international relations or U.S.-China relations. It was clear at the time of the EP-3 incident in April 2001, that Jiang would not countenance a repetition of the situation that took place after the bombing almost 2 years earlier.

There were three very clear indicators of this. First, Jiang and the central leadership came out "tough" on the United States from the start. There would be no room allowed for accusations from any quarter in China that the Party and government was unwilling or incapable of defending Chinese sovereignty and dignity as was the case, some had argued, after the Belgrade bombing.

Second, there would be no students marching through the streets or gathering at or besieging the U.S. Embassy as in May 1999. This, one suspects, was not so much out of concern for the Americans as out of concern about stability on the streets of Beijing and beyond. The sensitive "May 4th" period was much too close at hand, as was the anniversary of the death of Hu Yaobang (April 15, 1989), a significant event for the student movement in the spring of 1989. And, of course, the Falun Gong problem had yet to be completely resolved.

Third, unlike the immediate period after the bombing in May 1999, there would be no media "free for all," no great and public debates about national security policy, no criticisms of the government, and no re-opening of the "peace and development" question. All things considered, during the EP-3 incident, the PRC Government demonstrated once again how capably it is able to reign-in the media when it chooses to do so.[20] Relatively speaking, there was no radical editorializing that could undercut PRC government positions or serve to reopen debates that had already been resolved "officially."[21] Any bile that needed to be vented in the press could be done at the expense of the United States this time around.

In other words, and overall, in the wake of the EP-3 incident, the Party this time stayed ahead of Chinese nationalism and popular indignation and was not chasing after it, as was the case after the embassy bombing in 1999.

Post EP-3 and the Summer of 2001: Is China the U.S.'s New Enemy?

The EP-3 incident did not reopen debate on the prospects for "peace and development" or the state of the international security situation. But it did reopen the portion of the "Great Debate of 1999" that was the most contentious and upon which there was the least consensus at the time: the future of U.S.-China relations.

Before the U.S. EP-3 was returned, and before Secretary of State Colin Powell even confirmed his visit to Beijing, a new debate was underway among the Chinese America-watching community. Since at least May 2001 they had apparently been engaged in another round of intense debates, seminars, meetings, and conferences at which the issue of U.S. policy toward China was being discussed.

The EP-3 incident was the proximate cause of the new round of meetings and discussions. But it was not the sole cause. Like the unprecedented debate in 1999, the debate that began after the April 2001 incident dredged up a growing list of concerns that were awaiting evaluation.

But there was one aspect of the EP-3 incident that clearly had a very profound impact upon analysts and the general public in China (and, incidentally, upon the American public as well). Specifically, the intense news coverage of the event in the West and in China made very public for probably the first time just how much "cat and mouse" activity was going on between the U.S. and Chinese militaries.

So as of the summer of 2001 the following questions were being explored in Chinese analytic circles once again:

- How should China assess the current state of U.S.-China relations?

- What "China policy" will the Bush administration adopt? and,

- What are the prospects for future relations?

Central to these other questions was "Had the United States decided that China is *the* enemy and that this will drive U.S. policy toward China and the U.S. larger security strategy in Asia?"

As was the case during the debate in 1999, a wide range of views among Chinese security analysts on these questions was allegedly held. Moreover, as was also the case in 1999, analysts of like-minded opinion could be found crossing institutional and bureaucratic boundaries. Some observers offered that the PRC government "learned its lesson" from the debate of 1999: although the debate was "active and intense," it was conducted in a "cool-headed and analytic fashion" and mostly kept out of the media.

No conclusions are known to have been reached. Many Chinese analysts believed that it was still too early to make any conclusions about U.S. policies or intentions toward China. At the same time, many Chinese analysts were said to agree with a general assessment that the trends in U.S. policies and actions toward China in the last few months had been "negative." There was a long list of data points that many Chinese cited as indicating a negative trend in "Bush administration" China policy. (Again, listing these points does not indicate concurrence.) These included:

- The Bush campaign rhetoric portraying China as a "strategic competitor," not a "strategic partner";

- Bush administration plans to move ahead with BMD (perceived to be directed partially at China);

- The strengthening of U.S.-Japan military relations (also perceived to be directed at China);

- The "loud anti-China voices" that openly point to Beijing as the next enemy, and research monographs by some U.S. think tanks (wrongly perceived to represent U.S. Government policy) that propose a U.S. China policy option termed "congagement";

- The perception that the focus of the new U.S. military strategy is shifting from Europe to Asia and that this shift is directed against China;

- The U.S. desire to move closer to India;

- Bush's April 2001 remarks about the defense of Taiwan;

- Increasing arms sales to Taiwan and especially expanding military contacts with Taiwan (some Chinese analysts argue the United States is moving toward a *de facto* military alliance with Taipei);

- The recent U.S. visit by Lee Teng-hui;

- The belief of some Chinese analysts that the United States "pressured" Tokyo to allow Lee Teng-hui to visit Japan;

- The U.S. transit of Chen Shui-bian;

- The "attitude" of the Pentagon toward military relations with China since the EP-3 episode;

- The U.S. "attack" on human rights in China in Geneva;

- The appointment of a State Department coordinator for Tibetan affairs and the Dalai Lama visit; and,

- The general "anti-China" attitudes of some officials appointed to the new administration.

Clearly, there were some Chinese analysts who were already convinced that the United States had designated China as its next enemy. Others believed that the United States had already decided upon a "two-track" China policy that combines "economic engagement and military containment." Still others argued that Bush's China policy had yet to be decided.

Not all were convinced that the future of relations was as dire as recent events would suggest. These individuals tended to argue that Beijing's and Washington's mutual interest in stable relations for reasons of strictly selfish national interests were so strong that the "negative trend" would be arrested "at some point," that pragmatism in Washington "would eventually prevail," and that relations would eventually improve.

For example, in late May 2001 the China Institute of Contemporary International Relations (CICIR) held a forum on U.S.-China relations to which various experts were invited to present their views. In summarizing the results of the conference in their journal, CICIR editors pointed out many of the challenges from Washington. But the conference summary in the journal ended on a relatively optimistic note:

> Most of the participants to the forum traced the current state of affairs to policy guidelines of President Bush in designating Beijing a "strategic competitor" and its tilt to the Taiwan

authorities in support of elements advocating "Taiwan independence." China has clearly been the target of Washington's current endeavor at strengthening ties with its allies and pushing ahead with its NMD program. But all this does not signify the last word in the Bush team's China policy because external and internal restraints would make the Bush administration return to a relatively rational course after a period of reassessments. Based on the above analysis, most participants believe that there is no need for pessimism about the future of China-US relationship. Unavoidable contradictions and frictions do not necessarily spell loss of control because the prices for conflicts would be prohibitively high for both parties.[22]

It is difficult to say with any certainty that the above "optimistic" assessment ("hopeful" might be a better word) was representative of a majority of PRC security analysts or that it represented a commonly held viewpoint. Some of the actual papers that were presented at the CICIR conference seemed, on the whole, less optimistic than reported above.[23]

Operation "Enduring Freedom"—Speculating About PRC Security Concerns.

Obviously, the events of September 11 changed the entire context of the Bush-Jiang Summit. Although the Bush visit to China was much curtailed, the fact that the American President went to Shanghai to attend APEC and meet with Jiang under the circumstances was clearly a decision with positive impact both in China and throughout the region. The meeting clearly provided both leaders the ability to move back on a track toward more stable relations. And to the degree that both men have been constrained somewhat by domestic politics in their approach to bilateral ties, their professed common cause in the war against terrorism enhanced the arguments for engagement on a strategic level.

At the same time, how the United States and the coalition campaign against the Taliban—and the greater war against terrorism—unfolds will be watched with great care by the corps of Chinese security analysts. One can speculate that the Chinese will be very wary of the potential negative collateral impact of the post-September 11 world order for Chinese security concerns in general and specific key Chinese national security interests in particular. In this final section, permit a bit of *speculation* about the negative impact Chinese security analysts *might* see in what has transpired since September 11.

Impact on Pakistan: A Key Security Partner. China claims that it has no military alliances, and in the technical sense that is quite true. But for many years Pakistan and China have been very close security partners. Their common cause is based on shared distrust of an enduring mutual antagonist—India. But China's interests in Pakistan transcend that shared animosity.

For Beijing, Pakistan is one of many key Islamic states that it cultivates in order achieve some leverage in the Moslem world, owing to concerns about its own restive northwest province of Xinjiang. Pakistan's importance to China has been on the rise since January 2001. China has nervously watched as the Bush administration has re-looked previous U.S. allegations that China continues to transfer missile technologies to Islamabad, and Beijing analysts have evinced concerns watching the new impetus in the United States for *rapprochement* with India.

In the blink of an eye the events of September 11 have witnessed an amazingly quick U.S. return to engagement with Pakistan. Forced to "choose" between the United States and the Taliban regime it had hitherto supported, Islamabad made its choice, and Chinese security analysts cannot but wonder about the long-term implications of the reemergence of U.S.-Pakistani security relations for its own equities there. Moreover, should the government in Pakistan undergo its own internal dislocations as a result of its support for Washington, Chinese interests will be open to question. Having moved from proliferating pariah to active partner in the U.S. war in Afghanistan, a long-time and very close Chinese security partner now has a foot in both camps.

Impact on Sino-Russian Relations. Rapprochement with Russia is likely the greatest Chinese foreign policy success of the post-Cold War (1991) period. Geostrategically, the end of Sino-Russian animosity has resulted in China having today the most secure land borders it has ever enjoyed. In July 2001, capping 10 years of steadily improved relations, Presidents Jiang and Vladimir Putin signed a major treaty aimed at institutionalizing their "Cooperative Strategic Partnership."

While Beijing and Moscow have their own historical reasons to look askance at each other, events of the last few years have drawn them closer together politically. Both nations are fundamentally dissatisfied with how the post-Cold War world order has unfolded. In short, the global political, economic, and military prowess of the United States has been an unhappy state of affairs for each. Both nations want global power diffused—with at least some power accruing to them—in a much-theorized multi-polar world order.

The convergence of political views between Beijing and Moscow has been manifold: opposition to the expansion of NATO and Partnership for Peace; common cause against the strengthening of military alliances in the Pacific (read U.S.-Japan, U.S.-Australia, U.S.-ROK); opposition to the U.S. National Missile Defense program; mutual support for their respective claims to sovereignty in Chechnya and Taiwan; conjoined opposition to external military interventions under the "pretext" of humanitarianism; a new-found belief in the sanctity of the U.N.; mutual concerns about instability in Central Asia, and a security arrangement of convenience in which Beijing procures military weapons and technologies unavailable to it elsewhere in return for propping up Russia's failing defense industrial complex with those purchases.

In October 2001, less than 3 months after inking the much-heralded treaty, Russia seemed to be throwing its tacit support behind the U.S. military operations against Afghanistan by not standing in the way of American forces staging in former Soviet clients in Central Asia, and, reportedly, Moscow began to step up its arms shipments to the opposition Northern Alliance forces.

But probably much more disconcerting from a Chinese perspective, Putin began transmitting what appeared to be serious "feelers" about actually joining NATO under certain conditions of change in that organization. Russia seemed to realize that the tragic events of September 11 might actually be an opportunity finally to align itself in a serious way, with dignity, as an equal partner with the West after almost 10 years of Russian foreign policy limbo. It may just be that Putin realized this was Moscow's opportune moment to do so in a way that could ultimately resuscitate Russia's faltering economy and at the same time enhance its international prestige. Indeed, the Bush-Putin meeting on the fringes of APEC in October 2001 seemed to be reported in the western press as much more robust than the meetings with Jiang in the latter's own country. The prospects of Russia "leaning to the West" cannot be a comfortable thought in Beijing, even though revived Russian relations with the West would certainly not be at the expense of China in the sense that such alignments were played out during the Cold War.

Impact on the Shanghai Cooperation Organization. If *rapprochement* with Russia is likely the greatest Chinese foreign policy success of the post-Cold War period, then Beijing's second is achieving membership in the WTO. Beijing's third major foreign policy success, although less well known, was serving as the motive force behind the creation of the Shanghai Cooperation Organization (SCO) in June 2001.

Originally known as the "Shanghai Five," China, Russia, Kazakhstan, Tajikistan, and Kyrgizstan had been working together since 1996 to resolve their border disputes, enhance military confidence-building measures among their armed forces, and coordinate security work against the so-called "three evils" of "terrorism, separatism, and fanaticism" in Central Asia. In short, the SCO represents one of the post-Cold War world's first new regional security architectures. And to the degree that China has been the motive force behind it, it is claimed as a success.

In June 2001 the "Shanghai Five" transformed itself into the "Shanghai Cooperation Organization," added Uzbekistan as a sixth member, and formalized its intentions to pursue military security in the border regions in a multilateral fashion, to include establishing a counterterrorism center in Bishkek and even holding out the prospects for combined military exercises in the future. The importance of these initiatives to China's security interests in Central Asia is underscored by the fact that this is the first time ever that the PRC has been a formal signatory to a multinational security architecture. Moreover, should combined military exercises ever take place, it will be the first time ever that the PLA has trained or exercised with any foreign military in anything other than the role of "advisors" or trainers—this is simply unprecedented for China.

Enter the events pursuant to September 11. Where China and Russia enjoyed dominance of presence in this critical region, there is now the obvious presence of the U.S. military—not merely as trainers or as participants in combined exercises such as CENTRAZBAT-97—but in force and prosecuting a joint, and likely combined, military offensive. To the degree that the SCO served the collateral Chinese interest of keeping U.S. military forces from achieving a foothold in Central Asia, that objective has been undermined in a clear, significant, and profound way. To what degree the *de facto* presence of U.S. military forces in the region, and the obvious political and economic presence in the region that will persist post-combat, will change the viability or nature of the SCO as an organization is a question that must be getting asked in Chinese analytic circles. At a minimum, a U.S. presence in Uzebekistan in a post-Taliban Afghanistan is a real possibility, given the security assurances Tashkent has reportedly asked of Washington in return for its very active support.

Impact on Japan. Tokyo's decision to be proactive in offering the United States logistic support by the Japan Maritime Self Defense Forces in the vicinity of the Indian Ocean is not going to assuage Beijing's concerns about Japan's "real security aspirations" in the region—in spite of Prime Minister Junichiro Koizumi's assertion that Jiang expressed his "understanding" of the rationale behind it during their meeting in Beijing in early October 2001.

Always on the alert for any indication of Japan's potential for an expanded military presence in Asia, Chinese analysts will likely view Tokyo's support of Operation ENDURING FREEDOM as a codicil under which the Japanese will continue what the Chinese believe is the inexorable march away from Article 9 of the "Peace Constitution." (And it may just be that Beijing's concerns on this account will be buttressed by like-minded thinking emanating from Seoul.) Japan's actions in support of the United States will be seen through the lens of a continuum that includes perceived Japanese support for Taiwan independence, concerns about the *Revised U.S.-Japan Guidelines for Defense Cooperation*—especially the nebulous phrase "areas surrounding Japan," and Tokyo's co-research with Washington on upper-tier sea-based TBMD.

Impact on Border Security. Clearly, the most obvious deleterious effect of Operation ENDURING FREEDOM for China is the very fact that it is taking place in a country with which China shares a border. Stability and security in the 14 nations with which China shares common borders—not to mention maintaining good relations with those countries—is a priority-one security issue for Beijing.

Controlling events on its periphery, stability on its periphery, and ensuring there is no spill over from instability on its periphery are ongoing and historical Chinese concerns. One might point out that since 1949, China has consistently viewed instability on its periphery as a serious threat, and most of its military interventions, overt or otherwise, have been the result of the perceived need to shape wars along its border, preempt possible aggression, or assert sovereignty along those borders.[24]

The immediate Chinese concern will be the potential for refugees to stream across the small border it shares with Afghanistan. China's second concern will be the potential for "blowback" in Xinjiang Province by non-Han Turkic Uighurs who oppose Chinese rule. The third tier of Chinese concerns will be longer term—how long will the U.S. campaign last, what type of government will replace the Taliban, and how long will U.S. military forces remain in the region after the collapse of the Taliban? And, of course, as mentioned already, the impact of all of the above on the viability of the Musharaf regime in Islamabad. Overall, from a Chinese point of view, it is unlikely the current U.S. campaign will be viewed as a "good thing."

Impact on National Missile Defense. China's objections to the U.S. National Missile Defense Program are well known by now and need no explanation. Suffice it to say that Beijing will be concerned that the attack on the United States will accelerate the nuclear missile defense (NMD) program, not inhibit it. The best indicator of Chinese concerns along these lines is the analytic argument one could read in the PRC press post-September 11 declaring that the terrorist attack on the United States "proved" that the greatest threat to the United States is not a so-called "rogue state" with a missile, but low-tech weapons used by nonstate actors.

The efficacy of this argument aside, there will be concern that in the wake of September 11 previous disagreements over NMD with certain European allies will fall by the wayside in an ongoing show of support for Washington. Also, there will be Chinese concern that the voices in the United States citing the September 11 events as "proof positive" of the need for NMD will prevail—especially now that the specter of biological weapons is no longer hypothetical. But most disconcerting, from a Chinese perspective, will be the possibility that Russian resolve on the issue of the Anti-Ballistic Missile (ABM) Treaty will start to weaken.

Overall then, while the events of September 11 and the Bush-Jiang summit have served a critical Chinese (and U.S.) security objective—namely stabilizing bilateral relations—it is not entirely clear, based quite admittedly on my own speculation, that the overarching prosecution of the war against terrorism waged by the United States and the potential collateral changes in the international security *milieu* will be seen as positive for China across the board. By the time this volume is published, the international security environment may well have changed and turned over once again, and the Chinese calculus might be quite different in ways that at time of writing are impossible to speculate about.

Concluding Comments.

One constant in the U.S.-China relationship that will persist and that will transcend current events, is simply this: there is ample reason in both Washington and Beijing to seek and secure mutually beneficial bilateral relations—especially security relations.

However, there is a deep-seated mutual distrust between the respective security establishments on both sides of the Pacific that will not go away very soon, regardless of the pragmatic steps each nation takes on the road to better relations. This chapter, by assignment, has focused on Chinese concerns. The United States has its own set of misgivings.

If the trend in Chinese security analyses presented in this chapter is even close to being on the mark, then it will be very difficult to change attitudes in Beijing. Chinese concerns about U.S. intentions are beginning to transcend specific policies in contention, transcending perhaps even the issue of Taiwan. In China, analytic momentum has been building over the past few years that argues that the United States is inherently hostile to China and that the strategic objective of the United States toward China is nothing less than the obstruction of China's rise as a more rich and powerful nation—despite statements by Bush and Powell to the contrary. Consequently, U.S. policies in the region or toward China itself will be increasingly filtered through a set of lenses that are already calibrated to ensure some distortion. The phrase, "Seeing the acorn but imagining the oak tree" comes to mind.[25]

Relations with the United States more and more present the Chinese leadership with a growing dilemma. On one hand, a stable relationship with the United States is increasingly viewed by Beijing as one prerequisite for the success of the all-important reform agenda that faces *Zhongnanhai* at home. And to the degree that successful continuing reform at home is the key to the longevity of the CCP, the "U.S. factor" plays as well, even if indirectly.[26]

At the same time, perceived challenges by the United States to Chinese national interests—especially those viewed as challenges to sovereignty—cannot be ignored by the Chinese leadership. One hears and reads more and more in the Chinese press about the need to uphold "the dignity" of the Chinese people, not just the sanctity of Chinese sovereignty.

The summit of October 2001 augurs a hopeful beginning for the two nations to renew serious strategic dialogue on the spectrum of issues that have been addressed in this chapter. But amid the pledges by the two presidents to establish new mechanisms for strategic dialogue, amid the rededication to continue mutually beneficial economic cooperation, in the midst of presenting a united stand in dealing with global terrorism, there was one summit "basket" that was conspicuous by its absence—a statement about future military-to-military relations.

Since at least 1989 the military dimension of bilateral relations has become one of the most contentious and difficult aspects of U.S.-China ties. It has become a domestic political issue in both Beijing and Washington. Even in the best of times, finding a mutually satisfying military dimension to bilateral ties has been a frustrating endeavor for both parties due to growing mutual suspicion, institutional asymmetries, and competing objectives. In times of bilateral duress, military relations are the first links to be suspended. In the best of times, they are the last to be put into place.

Some in the United States have argued that, with the demise of the Soviet Union, there is no longer a "strategic rationale" for the United States to engage the PLA. In Beijing, some Chinese have also argued that the "rise of American hegemonism" has likewise undermined a Chinese rationale for engagement with the U.S. Department of Defense. Detractors of military relations in the United States have complained that the PLA does not "reciprocate" U.S. openness and that "the PLA gets more out of the relationship than does the United States." For their part, some Chinese argue that the objectives of U.S. military ties and U.S. "openness" are inherently "hostile." The United States wants "to change China," to "deter (scare) China," and "collect intelligence" on China by using the military relationship.[27]

All of these arguments may very well be true of the past. But it is not correct for either side to argue that there is no longer a strategic rationale for a military relationship. The fact of the matter may be that at long last, for the first time since the end of the Cold War, there finally *is* a strategic rationale for military-to-military contacts. And it is simply this: conflict avoidance.

It is clear that the military forces of the United States and of China will increasingly be operating in proximity to each other. This was shown most graphically on April 1, 2001, and the subsequent EP-3 incident. It is also clear that there is a growing distrust between the two military establishments. It is clear as well that both sides acknowledge (sometimes quietly, sometimes publicly) the possibility of an unwanted confrontation over Taiwan. These points alone are the most pressing arguments for the resumption of military contacts, the enhancement of venues in which discussion of differences can take place, and new venues aimed at dispelling misperceptions.

Hopefully, as the months go on, as political dialogue increases and the benefits of stable relations are seen to outweigh mutual suspicions, then wise men and sober thinkers on both sides will start searching for new and realistic ways to manage differences, and conclude that both the U.S. Armed Forces and the PLA will have a constructive role to play.

ENDNOTES - CHAPTER 2

1. Cancelled altogether were the President's planned stopovers in Tokyo and Seoul prior to arriving in Shanghai.

2. Tang Hongwei, *Zhongguo Xinwen She*, *Foreign Broadcast Information Service* (hereafter *FBIS*), October 19, 2001.

3. "U.S., China Stand Against Terrorism: Remarks by President Bush and President Jiang Zemin in Press Availability, Western Suburb Guest House (Shanghai, PRC)," October 19, 2001, *www.whitehouse. gov / news / releases* (hereafter, White House).

4. White House.

5. This is a concern that has become somewhat heightened since February 2000 when Beijing issued its "Taiwan White Paper" that articulated the "third if." Since that time a common question debated in Washington's analytic circles is whether Beijing has a "timetable" for reunification.

6. For an excellent review of the actions and policies of Beijing that will continue to give pause to U.S. Government officials, see Bates Gill, "Powell In China: Modest Progress Will Be better Than None," *International Herald Tribune*, July 27, 2001.

7. For a very detailed account and analysis of the post-Kosovo debate in China, see David M. Finkelstein, *China Reconsiders Its National Security: The "Great Peace & Development Debate" of 1999*, Alexandria VA: The CNA Corporation, Country Assessment, December 2000.

8. The construction of the narrative account of the debate that follows was possible due to the highly public nature of the debate. The Chinese press was an invaluable source for following the debate. Most of the key Chinese newspapers devoted space to reader comments on the key questions under contention after the bombing of the PRC Embassy. Examples are the PLA's *Liberation Army Daily* (*Jiefangjun Bao*), *China Youth Daily* (*Zhongguo Qingnian Bao*), *Brightness Daily* (*Guangming Ribao*), and *People's Daily* (*Renmin Ribao*). By most accounts, the periodical that ran the column most read and most contributed to by government specialists (and most contentious in that analysts took each other on) was the *Global Times* (*Huanqiu Shibao*), a subsidiary newspaper of *People's Daily*. The column in question was entitled "China's Countermeasures and Choices" ("Zhongguo Duice Yu Xuanze"). I am grateful to Dr. Alastair Iain Johnston of Harvard University for bringing this column to my attention. This account of the debate was also informed by a good number of interviews as well.

9. For a superb primer on the necessity in China for having theoretical assessments of the international security environment and their evolution since 1949, see Ren Xiao, "The International Relations Theoretical Discourse in China: A Preliminary Analysis," Sigur Center Asia Papers Number 9, Washington, DC: Elliott School of International Affairs, The George Washington University, 2000.

10. The United States affirmed its policy of: (1) No independence for Taiwan, (2) No "One China, One Taiwan" formula, and (3) No membership for Taiwan in international organizations that require statehood as a prerequisite for membership.

11. "Cooperative Strategic Partnership with Russia" (April 1996); "Comprehensive Cooperative Partnership" with France (May 1997); "Constructive Strategic Partnership" with the U.S. (October 1997); "Good-neighborly Partnership of Mutual Trust" with ASEAN (December 1997); "Long-term and Stable Constructive Partnership"

with the European Union (April 1998); "Enhanced Comprehensive Partnership" with Great Britain (October 1998).

12. In June 2001 the "Shanghai Five" was transformed into the "Shanghai Cooperation Organization" and a sixth member, Uzbekistan, was added.

13. As remarkable as it may seem from a U.S. perspective, there was a good deal of discussion in some Chinese analytic circles as to whether the United States would intervene in Chechnya.

14. In his excellent volume, China *Debates the Future Security Environment*, Washington, DC: National Defense University Press, 2000, Michael Pillsbury argues that previous Chinese political constraints precluded analysts from asserting that the "comprehensive national power" of the United States would do anything but eventually decline. While that may have been the case prior to 1999, the post-Kosovo debate in China clearly removed all taboos along this line.

15. Emphases added by author.

16. Chi Haotian, "Taking The Road of National Defense Modernization Which Conforms to China's National Conditions and Reflects the Characteristics of the Times—-My Understanding Acquired From the Study of Comrade Jiang Zemin's Expositions on the Relationship Between Building the National Defense and Economic Development," *Qiushi*, No. 8, *FBIS*, April 16, 1996. Emphasis added.

17. Of interest, however, was a reprint of a December 1986 speech by former Defense Minister General Zhang Aiping in which the venerated general warned that, even though the international security situation did not portend world war, the nation needed to remain vigilant, move forward with defense modernization, and recognize the potential threats to China's security. In retrospect, the speech, given to an expanded meeting of the Central Military Commission in 1986, can be viewed as having caveated Deng's reassessment of China's security as espoused in June 1985. It was reprinted in the journal *Zhanlue Yu Guanli (Strategy and Management)*, published by the Chinese Society for Strategy and Management, with the permission of the retired General Zhang. See Zhang Aiping, "National Defense Development in Peacetime," *Zhanlue Yu Guanli, FBIS*, August 1, 1999.

18 Fu Quanyou, "Make Active Explorations, Deepen Reform, Advance Military Work in an All-Round Way," *Qiushi*, No. 6, *FBIS*, March 1998. For an overview of the PLA's programs of reform, see Finkelstein, *China's National Military Strategy*.

19. For example, see John Pomfret, "Chinese Military Uses Anniversary to Polish Its Image," *The Washington Post*, October 2, 1999. According to Pomfret, "In March (1999) and again over the summer, the army is said to have received billions of dollars in additional funding . . ." Pomfret's use of the term "billions" is likely an overstatement. Knowledgeable observers do agree that there was a one-time infusion in the summer of 1999 and that it was about 1.2 billion U.S. dollars (USD). This figure is separate and distinct from the lump-sum payment the PLA received in December 1998 as a result of the order to divest itself of its commercial holdings. The latter payment, according to David Shambaugh, was about 400 million USD. See David Shambaugh, *Reforming China's Military*, Berkeley: University of California Press, forthcoming.

20. Clearly a scientific sampling of the Chinese press during this period was not made by this student, and I am open to counter arguments on the issue of the Chinese press during the April through May 2001 period. But having just completed a very detailed study of the post-Kosovo debate, I fully expected the EP-3 incident to reopen the entire issue. It did not occur.

21. There were a few interesting, but rare exceptions. At least one paper tried to reopen the "peace and development debate." But it did so not by criticizing the PRC Government, but by criticizing those Chinese analysts who still "cherished illusions" about the United States. See "Cherishing Illusions About China-U.S. Relations Will Bring Harm To Both the Country and the People," Commentary article in *Guangzhou Ribao*, FBIS, May 16, 2001.

22. "Free Discussion on China-U.S. Relations," in *Contemporary International Relations*, Beijing: China Institute of Contemporary International Relations, June 2001, pp. 7-30.

23. *FBIS* has posted some of the conference papers in translation.

24. We recall Korea (1950), the French-Indochina War (early 1950s), the Sino-Indian War (1962), the U.S.-Indochina War (1960s), the northern clashes with the Soviets (especially 1969), the Sino-Vietnamese War (1979), Chinese concerns about Cambodia, and, in a "back to the future mode," Chinese concerns about the Soviets in Afghanistan (late 1970s), not to mention ongoing Chinese concern about Indo-Pakistani clashes over Kashmir. While the Chinese likely hold no brief for the Taliban, the prosecution of a major campaign in Afghanistan—especially one waged by the United States—is not going to be a reassuring event from a Chinese point of view.

25. This is not just a Chinese phenomenon. It occurs in the United States as well.

26. This is not to suggest that the United States is the "sole" foreign factor in Beijing's domestic reform agenda. China has hedged against the possibility of a prolonged period of tension with the United States. Over the past few years, it has worked to diversify and strengthen its foreign ties across the developed world, one suspects, because it realizes the "danger" of having all of its eggs in the U.S. basket when it comes to foreign investment, trade, technology acquisition, etc.

27. For an in depth study of Chinese views of the military relationship, see David M. Finkelstein, "Engaging DoD: Chinese Perspectives on Military Relations with the United States, Alexandria, VA: The CNA Corporation, CRM 99-0046.90, October 1999.

CHAPTER 3

A VIEW FROM TOKYO:
CHINA'S GROWING MILITARY POWER
AND ITS SIGNIFICANCE FOR JAPAN'S
NATIONAL SECURITY

Hideaki Kaneda

CHINA'S AMBITION

China's Maritime Advance.

China has pursued a national strategy of consistent and active advancement toward peripheral waters. China's activity patterns, as they did in the 1970s to the South China Sea and in the 1980s to the East China Sea, have been to advance to such areas using force, while ignoring the sovereign rights and jurisdiction rights of neighboring nations. Finding little or weak resistance from these countries, China strengthened presence there by creating a fait accompli, ultimately leading to the practical control of these areas. What is the objective of China's maritime advance? The answer is the key to designing Japan's deterrent strategy against China.

First is the economic aspect involved. China aims to develop and utilize biological and nonbiological resources in its peripheral waters, especially seabed oil resources. In addition, China's food and energy supply situation is rapidly deteriorating as a result of its remarkable economic growth since the adaptation of policies for economic revolution and the opening of China's market to the world, combined with its drastic population growth. In particular, China's energy situation is so severe that the world's seventh largest oil producing nation can hardly keep up with the growing demand, and today China the oil producer has become an oil-importing consumer.

For further economic development, China must continue to secure food and energy supplies. Therefore, it becomes extremely important for China to procure fishing grounds in the peripheral waters and adjacent seas, to acquire good quality seabed oil resources, and to secure sea lines of communication (SLOCs) for oil imports from the Middle East. Dependence on the seas is a logical consequence for China in order to maintain continuous economic growth.

Second is the issue of national security. In China, naval and air forces have been built and operated as supporting forces to assist the army. However, they learned from the historical experience of the Qing Dynasty when, because of China's lack of awareness of the importance of seapower and maritime rights, foreign powers usurped their sovereign and territorial rights. Based on these experiences, China adopted a clear military strategy of "near water defense," with the so-called "First Island Chain Defense Line" being China's sea defense line, connecting the Aleutian Islands, Kuril Islands, Japanese Islands, Ryukyu Islands, Taiwan, Philippine Islands, and Borneo. The Senkaku Islands, claimed by Japan, and the Spratly and Paracel Islands, over which several South-East Asian countries claim territorial rights, are included in this First Island Chain Defense Line. Taiwan also has claims on some of these islands, an issue which China calls a domestic matter. In other words, China's near water defense strategy includes military force deployments to attack Taiwan and prevent counterattacks. One must not forget that the military forces that are capable of crossing the water to attack Taiwan and preventing counterattacks can certainly be used against the Senkaku, Spratly, and Paracel Islands.

With the end of the Cold War, China's negotiations on national border issues and military withdrawal from borders with Russia and former Soviet Union countries in

Central Asia have progressed smoothly and the opportunity for negotiation with India to solve border issues has arisen. China can feel secure for the moment regarding its land borders to the north and west and can reduce its army forces drastically, thereby generating enough reserves to shift their interests and redistribute resources to focus on their east and southern "oceans."

Third is the shift of China's military strategy. By 1985, the People's Liberation Army (PLA) had already attempted the strategic shift from a "global war" to a "local war" orientation, and after the end of the Cold War, shifted from a mere "general local war" to a "local war under hi-tech conditions" based on what they learned from the Gulf War. Through such strategic shifts, then General Secretary Jiang Zemin started to emphasize the "defense of maritime interests" along with the defense of sovereign rights of territorial lands, air space, and seas.

By October 2000, China had conducted large-scale exercises of "all army exchange activities to demonstrate the result of scientific-technological training" incorporating the "new three attacks and three defenses" (attacks by stealth aircraft, ballistic missiles, and armed helicopters, and defense by precision weapons, electronic interference, and reconnaissance surveillance), which involved learning from the Kosovo air-raids as well as from "scientific-technological military training." At that time, it was noted that the exercises were "attack" oriented with the oceans as the main stage, rather than conventional "defense" oriented maneuvers.

Fourth is an intention to improve China's position in the international community. China's view toward international relationships is to break away from the situation of "one superpower and several powers" dominated by the United States and to work toward "multi-polarization," with China itself sharing the position of one of the powerful pole leaders. China recognizes that the unstable situation of the international community will persist longer because of tensions between the major countries, China's own conflicts in securing its sphere of interests, and increased incidents of regional conflicts. However, China assumes that such a situation is merely the transition toward the establishment of a new international order, and will eventually lead to the collapse of U.S. single-country dominance and the emergence of a multi-polar world with China, the United States, the European Union, Russia, and Japan as the poles. At any time in history, the China-U.S. relationship has had a mix of stability and instability factors, but in purely military terms, they are basically in a contentious relationship. From China's point of view, the path toward multi-polarization must go through the point of rivalry and contention with American military power.

The tone of logic in China that stands out these days is that the power that controls the ocean is the one that earns the right of survival and development. Moreover, there is much evidence of the importance of comprehensive marine power and that the 21st Century will be the "Century of Oceans." The search to grow from "near water" to "open ocean" operations is already underway in the PLA. In a situation of increased confidence in the economy and limited elements of instability in national security, China's ultimate ambition appears to be preparing to step beyond the basic strategy of near water defense to secure domination over the Pacific Ocean, which is adjacent to its peripheral waters.

Japan's "Defense White Paper" of 2001 reported the recent striking build-up of China's military preparedness in the quality and quantity of both its navy and air force. What is their ultimate objective? To speak in extremes, is it not possible to put forth a hypothesis that China uses the excuse of capturing Taiwan to hide China's true and ultimate objective of winning a war against the United States? We, the Japanese people, must ascertain China's future intentions.

China Takes a Serious Step toward "Multi-Polarization"—Establishment of the "Shanghai Cooperation Organization."

On June 14 and 15, 2001, the "Shanghai Five" countries of China, Russia, Kazakhstan, Kyrgistan, and Tajikistan, with the newly-added Uzbekistan, established the "Shanghai Cooperation Organization." A "Shanghai Five" summit has been held yearly since 1996, originally for the purpose of resolving border tensions between China and the Central Asian countries that had newly arisen after the collapse of the Soviet Union, with China leading the discussion. Since they successfully agreed upon the reduction of military forces deployed to border areas, the focus has shifted toward cooperation in the control of Islamic extremists, which has been the major problem of the Central Asian countries. Moreover, in recent years, China has used the Shanghai Five forum as a means to check the United States, as demonstrated in its appeal for ties between Russia and China, especially on international security and disarmament issues, and against the U.S. monopolistic control of global political, economic, and military affairs.

The significance of this organization for China is, on the surface, multi-national regional cooperation to control expanding Islam extremists. In reality, it is a way to deal with the threat of Xinjiang separatism, which is like a snake in China's bosom, the stability of Xinjiang being essential for the realization of China's national project of the Great West Development. Reading even deeper into China's intentions, however, one can find the possibility of China's desire to transform this organization into an alliance against the United States and its set of bilateral alliances with regional countries, which will have a greater significance for China in the future.

Originally, China was eager to improve bilateral relationships with their continental neighboring countries. In June 2001, China concluded the Treaty of Good and

67

Friendly Relationship with Russia. They also concluded bilateral agreements with each Central Asian country as the fruit of the Shanghai Five process. Among major continental neighboring countries, only India has not entered into a bilateral agreement with China. However, China is attempting to improve its relationship with India, as evidenced by the re-opening of a Sino-Indian dialogue that had been halted since India's nuclear test in 1998, probably in response to the recent U.S. approach toward India.

The "Shanghai Cooperation Organization" is the first multilateral organization begun under China's initiative. Some moderates believe this organization will develop into a moderate Association of Southeast Asian Nations (ASEAN)-type regional forum. Others consider that the current member countries of this organization aim to "promote multipolarism of the world" and other countries such as Pakistan, Mongolia, and Iran will seek the opportunity to join the organization, while North Korea and Vietnam are said to show interest in it. Through this organization or its advanced form in the future, China possibly will attempt to extend its influence over a vast land and water area extending from the Asia-Pacific region to Southwest Asia and the Middle East, with continental China and Central Asia as the central force.

In addition, China is likely to use this forum to counter perceived U.S. containment against China, and in the future to confront the existing web of alliances centered on the United States, while hiding the potential to develop it into an organization similar to the Warsaw Pact at the time of the Cold War. For the moment China will use it as a platform to eliminate U.S. influence by expressing opposition to the missile defense initiative and international and regional talks led by the United States, as well as to express China's persistent claim that Taiwan, which is under the influence of the United States, is an inseparable part of Chinese territory. In this sense, how

China will react to the U.S. response against the September 11, 2001, terrorist attacks may be significant.

China Aims to Become a Regional Superpower—Preparedness on the Continent and Advancement Toward the Oceans.

What is the meaning of China's advancement toward the oceans, and improved relationships with its continental neighbors? Originally described as "ships in the South and horses up North," China is a country that has two faces: "Continental China" and "Oceanic China."

Despite having some domestic problems, China seems to realize that it has successfully created an unprecedented stable situation in diplomatic and military relationships with neighboring countries. Moreover, China has grown from being a regional political power to becoming a regional superpower, both in name and actuality, in all political, military, economic, and industrial aspects, and is about to secure a position as one of the world superpowers (and the strongest in Asia), capable of threatening the U.S. monopoly. To achieve such an objective, China cannot afford to limit its interests to the continent and must have the strong maritime capability of an "Oceanic China."

In view of the Chinese Communist Party's position in a one-party-ruled country, it is impossible for China to allow the United States to remain the "one ultra-superpower" indefinitely. At least, China wishes to gain the power of "not losing," if not winning over the United States in every spectrum. Thus, China, starting with stability on the continent, steadily will promote a drive for the attainment of its secret ambition to fulfill the supreme proposition of "confrontation in the ocean" with the United States and its allied countries, within China's unique time scale, regardless of their targeted year.

Certainly, China never makes the mistake of mentioning the possibility of direct confrontation at sea with U.S. military power. There is no need, for it has an appropriate and convenient excuse called Taiwan. At every opportunity, China sends out a strong warning to U.S. forces against intervention in relation to the Taiwan issue. Moreover, China stresses that it will not hesitate to confront U.S. forces if anything happens in Taiwan. However, this is not likely to be China's true intention. Though I used the word "hypothesis" earlier, China's real intention is confrontation beyond Taiwan, not with Japan, Korea, the ASEAN countries, or Australia, but with the United States.

To find proof of this, one only needs to look into the nature of Chinese military forces. If China seriously considers taking over Taiwan at present, what is the significance of the limited capability of the Chinese navy to transport troops across oceans? Undoubtedly, they have troops and equipment with a certain capability, so China might venture attacks on Taiwan, should the political necessity arise. Yet in view of Taiwan's defense capability, it would be difficult for China to send troops to Taiwan's main island. The natural interpretation is that China's capability is only sufficient for a very limited attack, such as ballistic missile attacks against part of the main island for intimidation purposes, or the attacks on Quemoy Island and Matsu Island, which China could complete before the United States could intervene.

On the other hand, viewing the recent direction of naval and air force modernization of the Chinese armed forces, one can easily notice that these efforts cannot be described in terms of quality, let alone quantity, as the rational development of equipment and systems purely to capture Taiwan or defend the neighboring seas. Wouldn't aircraft carriers, fleet ballistic missile submarines (SSBNs) with sea-launched ballistic missiles (SLBMs), and nuclear attack submarines (SSNs) with ship-launched cruise missiles (SLCMs) under development by the armed forces be better suited for confrontation with U.S. forces? Also, what does China's oceanic advancement into the Pacific Ocean, including Japan's exclusive economic zone (EEZ), mean? Isn't it logical to interpret these moves as China's efforts to steadily prepare to confront the United States by building up a maritime operational capability and assuming the United States and its allies are potential enemies?

Chinese Way of War—"Beyond Limited War" (Irregular and Asymmetric Tactics).

We can also see China's future prospects for the direct confrontation with the United States in its concrete military strategy and tactics. The book, *Beyond Limited War— Concept of War and Tactics for the Times of Globalization* written in 1999 by two Air Force colonels in active service of the PLA, is drawing attention in China and the United States. "Beyond limited war" means "a war that transcends any limitation" or a "war without any norms and regulations." In other words, it can be called a "forbidden strategy." The authors recommended that China implement such a strategy to confront the United States. They say "modern war is a hi-tech war, and China cannot win over the United States, which has overwhelming power, unless it confronts with them through this beyond-limited-war."

The book recommends seeking "irregular" war tactics that go beyond the nation, territories, methods, and war scales, including so-called "illegal" tactics. The authors themselves claim, "For the weaker to confront the stronger, the weaker does not need to follow the rules set by the stronger." Among the items of consideration in *Beyond Limited War,* we need to note "asymmetric tactics." U.S. military forces are troubled with the Chinese forces' inclination to regard asymmetric tactics as important. A former U.S. Ambassador to China indicated, "China regularly adopts a unique strategy to make up for its own weakness and to display its strength." This concept has a common thread with the September 11, 2001, terrorist attacks on America.

This book is said to have been written without any instruction from the Chinese leadership. Some observe, however, that the book has won strong support from Chinese political and military leaders.

As stated above, China has learned numerous lessons from the large-scale conflicts involving the United States in the post-Cold War era: the Gulf War and Kosovo conflicts, and China has proceeded with a great strategic conversion to "improvement of defensive combat capability under the high-tech conditions," while exerting efforts to eliminate functional shortcomings and avoiding any significant technological and operational gap. In other words, China is exerting efforts to avoid showing any decisive weakness of its own, while consistently being conscious of the possibility of war against the United States.

However, such a strategy does not provide any opportunity to win against overwhelming U.S. military power. Therefore, China pursues its own areas of superiority over U.S. weaknesses and will try to strike the weak spots of the United States. Such strategies are "irregular tactics" and "asymmetric tactics." China's recent emphasis on cyber wars, for which it has made little effort to hide its intentions, is an example. By taking such dual stances, China seems to be looking for an opportunity to ensure future victory over the United States.

JAPAN'S DETERRENT STRATEGY AGAINST CHINA

China's Strategy against Japan.

Now, how must Japan build its deterrent power against China? First, let the United States investigate China's strategy against Japan based on an analysis of China's political and military ambitions discussed in the previous section.

In China, there is a group that perceives the Japan-China relationship merely as a part of the power balance in the Asia-Pacific region. Also, it wishes to let Japan remain an economic giant only. To have Japan as a political superpower or military giant is hardly acceptable for China, as its greatest wish is to be the only superpower in Asia.

China's ultimate objective is to become the "unitary superpower" in the region. In Northeast Asia, four political poles consist of Russia, China, Japan and the United States. The Soviet Union used to be the threatening power during the Cold War but it collapsed, and its successor, Russia, maintains friendly relations with China as they share the basic policy of taking a hard-line against the United States. Concerning Japan, China anticipates Japan's contribution to China's economic growth as a economic and technology superpower, yet tries to prevent Japan from becoming a political and military superpower. For the United States, China is likely to maintain a friendly "engagement" relationship as long as the United States approves of China's economic development, which is key for China's promotion of its national power while recognizing potential rivalries in every political, economic, and military aspect.

For China's ambition, to become the only superpower in the region, the greatest barrier will be the stable and strong alliance between the United States, the world's unitary superpower, and Japan, a strong regional pole. Considering a future confrontation with the United States, it will be preferable for China to minimize the number of powerful countries allied with the United States. China is likely to take every opportunity to break up any Japan-U.S. alliance and to attempt the alienation of these two countries. China can use several methods for this purpose, and the one with the highest probability of success is China's special tactic of "to win without fighting," that is "beyond limited war." First, China will try to weaken or lessen U.S. sentiment and consciousness to support and cooperate with Japan, then to undermine Japan's capability and intention to support the United States. Next, China will campaign in Japan and the United States for the alienation of the Japan-U.S. relationship. In addition, China can make "beyond limited war" more effective by building a capability to fight an information technology (IT) war, such as cyber war, toward which China is directing its efforts. This is not the talk of something to come. Such a fight has already begun.

Even if Japan and the United States successfully maintain their alliance, it is most convenient for China when Japan has as many restrictions on defense cooperation with the United States as possible, like those imposed in Japan today. The greater the number of restrictive measures in Japan's defense cooperation with the United States, the higher the appreciation in China. What China would like to see is for Japan to maintain its exclusively defense framework, not to change its constitution including collective self-defense rights, not to proceed with wartime or national emergency legislation, and not to loosen the actual restrictions under "the law concerning measures to ensure peace and security of Japan in situations in areas surrounding Japan."

Basic Strategy against China.

Then what strategy should Japan take against China? The best approach is a strategy of building a very practical and mutually beneficial economic relationship, while avoiding political aspects as much as possible. China is a country that can maintain close economic ties even with Taiwan. It cannot ignore Japan's economic and technological strengths, which far exceed those of Taiwan. In turn, Japan finds sufficient appeal in the enormous scope of China's ever-growing market. In other words, for Japan as well as for China, a mutual close economic relationship is essential.

From the military viewpoint, China does not actually seem to consider Japan's defense power as a true threat, contrary to its political propaganda claims, which at every opportunity refer to "Japan's tendency of militarization." It is feasible to assume that China has already factored into its strategy all the shortcomings in Japan's defense functions: imperfection in defense-related legislation; independent defense policies; defects in equipment; restrictions on various operations defects from such policies; less awareness of the Japanese people and government in defense matters; and the lack of fundamental strength to sustain wars, such as a basically weak defense industry and defense logistics system. Therefore, one must not ignore the possibility that China may maneuver Japan into some conflicts over, for example, the Senkaku Islands and other territorial and EEZ conflicts if a situation can be generated in which the United States will not (or cannot) intervene. Japan must deter such possibilities by itself and establish a system that can respond to crises effectively. It must stop being a nation without any sense or preparation for emergencies as described above, and establish its own national security system to respond against China. Otherwise, such a time will come some day.

Securing U.S. and Japan Alliance as an Axle.

For Japan, the best possible option in national security adaptable to the various future prospects is a secure Japan-U.S. alliance. No other option is conceivable. In the environment of the geo-political situation of Northeast Asia, Japan is certainly free to consider other options such as nonalliance, bilateral alliance with a country (even China) other than the United States, or a multilateral alliance including Russia, China and the United States. Some debates and propositions about such options have taken place in and out of Japan. However, these options are either implausible, or lack future prospects. Certainly after the end of the Cold War, the aspect of a peace dividend was emphasized, and some even questioned whether a Japan-U.S. alliance would be needed any longer. The joint declaration of Japan and the United States in 1997 redefined the alliance and identified a clear direction toward an even stronger relationship.

For the United States, the significance of a Japan-U.S. alliance is, first of all, providing regional deterrent effect through the presence of U.S. forces in Japan, mainly Navy, Air Force, and Marines. The second significance is developing acceptable support mechanisms that can satisfy the U.S. standard in terms of everything from supply and repair to medical services. From a different viewpoint, the United States is well aware that its military withdrawal from Japan would provide Japan with a good motive to fortify its military power. Moreover, the United States realizes that the alliance serves to deter any possible conflicts between a unified Korea, China, and Japan in the future.

Whether such U.S. aims are involved or not, it is preferable for the region for the United States and Japan to maintain a solid alliance and to retain a mutually complementary relationship, while the alliance remains as a linchpin for regional security, including Japan's security. China and North Korea do not welcome such an alliance. Russia is no longer like the Soviet Union of the old days. North Korea does not have sufficient power to confront the United States. Only China occasionally has shown a willingness to confront the United States in military power, and it is the only country that has the potential to do so. Thus the only option for Japan is to maintain and solidify the Japan-U.S. alliance, which not only provides the stability necessary for favorable regional development, but also is important for the safety and security of Japan. At the same time the alliance is anticipated to function as a deterrent against China.

The Bush administration considers Japan as the most important U.S. ally in Asia. An Institute for National Strategic Studies (INSS) Special Report,[1] which is said to be the fundamental statement of the administration's Japan policy, expresses, with carefully selected phrasing to avoid the impression of pressuring Japan, the strong wish to secure and further solidify the Japan-U.S. alliance through Japan's efforts to solve the problem of the right of collective self-defense.

China will take every opportunity to disrupt the relationship between Japan and the United States. Japan must not be influenced by such a move, and must exert every effort to solidify the Japan-U.S. alliance, while perseveringly eliminating any elements that might alienate Japan and the United States.

Creation and Maintenance of Defense Power without Functional Deficiencies.

What will happen if Japan develops effective military deterrents against China? Because of its national policy, at least, Japan will not become a military superpower. Its basic strategy is to rely on the deterrent effect of U.S. support based on the Japan-U.S. alliance. However, some future argument may develop as to whether the role sharing in the Japan-U.S. alliance must be limited to Japan providing the shield and the United States providing the sword.

The United States is currently studying a new defense strategy incorporating the missile defense initiative. Preceding this, a new Quadrennial Defense Review (QDR) was announced on October 1, 2001. The new QDR, strongly reflecting the shocks of the September 11 terrorist attacks on America, abandoned the conventional two major theater war (2MTW) strategy and identified a policy of securing new U.S. bases, stations, and facilities for temporary uses, while reconfirming the importance of forward deployed forces. Inevitably it will become more difficult to operate U.S. armed forces abroad, and, in some cases, the situation of reduced military capability may continue semipermanently or temporarily.

Under such a situation, Japan needs to create defense forces that are fully functional qualitatively, if not quantitatively, to sustain the deterrent power against China that previously has been maintained through the Japan-U.S. alliance. Such a move will inevitably bring changes in role-sharing in the Japan-U.S. alliance, but at the same time will enable Japan to take on the role of a deterrent against China independently. Assuming the case of U.S. hesitation to exercise the articles of the Japan-U.S. Security Arrangement, for example, in the case of intimidation attacks related to the Japan-China territorial dispute area over the Senkaku Islands or mid-range ballistic missile attacks on nearby U.S. bases in Japan using conventional warheads, Japan must effectively and independently deter or defend against such intimidation or actual attacks by China and thwart China's intention. For this, it is necessary for Japan to build sufficient defense forces in every spectrum, including capabilities for ballistic missile defense, swift amphibious operations against islands by marines, paratroop landings, and assault landings by heliborne troops. Furthermore, possessing the capability to attack enemy strategic centers by anti-surface cruising missiles will become the next issue. To develop such defense forces, Japan needs not only to have domestic discussions, but also to make adjustments with the United States concerning its share of military functions.

Developing Political and Military Diplomacy against China, with Both Hard-line and Moderate Stances.

Japan must take a stance that is both hard-line and moderate against China's political and military diplomacy, which is based on China's unique view of nations and values.

First, Japan needs to ask China to be "an open country" in military aspects as well as in others. China recently stressed that its military forces are purely defensive. China published its "White Paper on National Defense," but China's transparency is still far below that of neighboring countries. In Europe, there is rapid and significant promotion of confidence-building measures embracing former West and East countries, with developments to ensure transparency. Recognition of China as a country that complies with the world's standards is wide-spread in economic and cultural aspects, as exemplified by China's World Trade Organization (WTO) membership and winning the bid for the 2008 Olympics in Beijing, despite domestic human rights problems which have not been fully corrected. Japan must take every opportunity to ask China to act as a more open country in the aspect of confidence-building, and to try to improve military transparency.

Second, Japan must ask China to take a more positive stance toward regional dialogue. China used to be inactive in regional councils, but today there is a striking change in China's posture. China has begun to participate actively in regional councils, especially on political and economic issues. However, China's participation is extremely limited in security-related matters, probably because China finds it disadvantageous in many cases, or it has less awareness of the need for transparency.

In terms of maritime issues, regional-wide SLOCs are the property not only of Japan or China but are also common to the region, and to secure their safety is a common task shared by regional countries. For regional development, it is important that SLOC safety be ensured through the joint efforts of regional countries and not be left under the control of any particular country. We need to let China realize that the region as a whole must share such recognition.

In recent days, the focus of attention has been piracy at the converging points of international sea routes such as the Malacca Strait. It may be important for Japan to take the initiative to create an environment in which China can participate, starting from the easy-to-address issues of safety, environment, and human rights cooperation, and as a part of regional efforts to deal with common issues like piracy, drug sales, the slave trade, and environmental pollution, ultimately and gradually stepping up to national security issues.

Regarding such pending problems between Japan and China as the mid-line between them in the East China Sea, an issue related to EEZs, Japan must abandon its obscure attitude and initiate a serious discussion to establish a temporary border for the true Japan-China mid-line. Moreover, where both countries claim territorial rights, the two countries need to agree to temporary joint control of these regions and to establish a council to control them while immediately establishing guidelines for Japan-China joint control over the regions.

Simultaneous to such negotiations, Japan must prevent any illegal activities performed by naval vessels and survey ships that clearly infringe upon Japan's jurisdiction in its territories and EEZ. Japan must declare that it will take necessary and decisive actions against any illegal activities and adopt effective measures. As long as Japan leaves such territorial issues pending, China will undoubtedly proceed with one act after another to promote its effective control over the East China Sea, as it did in the South China Sea.

The Japanese government needs to implement these actions methodically, meticulously, and vigorously based on a grand strategy. For this, we must remember how U.S. diplomatic strength in international negotiation has been supported by "brains" consisting of and organized by international law researchers, think-tanks and relevant authorities and experts in various fields represented by the Department of State or the Department of Defense.

China's oceanic expansion is somehow reminiscent of U.S. actions. For Japan to win over international competition, it must aggregate the wisdom of not only the bureaucrats, but also of the private sector, and develop a strong spirit to launch a national strategy. Thus, it is strongly anticipated that Japan will pursue its national interests jointly by public and private sectors under the strong leadership of Prime Minister Junichiro Koizumi.

ENDNOTES - CHAPTER 3

1. *The United States and Japan: Advancing Toward a Mature Partnership*, Richard L. Armitage, ed., Washington, DC: National Defense University, October 2000.

CHAPTER 4

A VIEW FROM MOSCOW: CHINA'S GROWING MILITARY POWER

Anatoly V. Bolyatko

China's military doctrine is an outgrowth of Beijing's strategic concept of national security, their perception of external threats, and their estimation of the likelihood of war. This military doctrine includes positions not only on the training of the armed forces, but their composition and role. The leadership of the Peoples Republic of China (PRC) sees national security as a process of eliminating internal and external threats, and as a way to achieve regional and global objectives by escalating what China's strategists call "the comprehensive power of a state." A well-developed economy, a high level of science and engineering achievement, internal political stability, and a strong defense are considered as main components of the comprehensive power of a state.

In China, military threats are seen in connection with potential challenges in the economic and socio-political spheres. Judging from Chinese publications, Beijing still sees economic growth as its main priority. Another significant domestic concern is the maintenance of the social-political order and "national unity." This includes opposing what Beijing sees as the tendencies of minorities, and Taiwan, to separate from the Chinese state. Based on Beijing's assessment of the contemporary international situation at the regional and global levels, the maintenance of military security ranks third among the major national priorities of China.

The PRC leadership, meaning the Chinese Communist Party (CCP), Central Military Commission (CMC), and the Politburo Standing Committee, believes that the prospects for an outbreak of a world war are low. Therefore, the process of building the Chinese military can be carried out methodically under conditions that depend on long-term peace matched with the nation's economic development. Thus, the requirement for the People's Liberation Army (PLA) is to increase strength acording to military and civil developments.[1]

In the international sphere, Chinese leaders foresee a return to a multi-polar world because of several regional conflicts, albeit with different duration and varying intensity, and the increasing occurrence of civil wars.

In China's view, the security situation in the Asia-Pacific region is stable, although there are some negative developments:

- The increased military presence of the U.S. in areas close to China's borders;

- The scheduled deployment of the theater missile defense (TMD) system in East Asia;

- The development of a base of support in Japan for a relaxation of restrictions on military action in a zone surrounding Japan;

- Increase in the scope of joint military exercises, especially between the United States and its allies; and,

- Instability on the Korean Peninsula and in South Asia and territorial disputes in the South China Sea.[2]

Taiwan is a special concern of the Chinese leadership. Weakened by a bitterly divided political leadership, Taiwan is further subject to the influence of external forces, easing the way for eventual reunification with the motherland. In

China's opinion, certain factors are inimical to their interests in Taiwan:

- Activities of those who harbor separatist aspirations among Taiwan's leaders;

- Military aid from the United States, which includes weapon sales, with the likelihood of future increases if the American Congress passes the Taiwan Security Enhancement Act;

- The possible inclusion of Taiwan into the U.S.-led theater missile defense system; and,

- The presence of U.S. troops in Japan, which enables the United States to intervene in a possible military confrontation in the Taiwan Strait.[3]

In resolving the problem of Taiwan, the Chinese government adheres to the principles of peaceful reunification and "one country, two systems." It has put forward some proposals on developing cross-strait relations, with the eventual goal of peaceful reunification. China considers the Taiwan question wholly an internal affair and insists that it will do everything in its power to achieve peaceful reunification. However, if events result in a separation of Taiwan from China under any slogan, China is willing to use force to protect its sovereignty and its territorial integrity.[4]

With this as its impetus, China has upgraded its military capability, retrofitting its armed forces in an effort to transform them into a powerful, modern army. Ideally, the PLA should be able to protect China against external threats, maintain internal stability, and—if necessary—guarantee Taiwan unification with the motherland.

In order to achieve its goals, China seeks to boost its tactical capabilities, including battlefield management, particularly during radical shifts in conditions, as well as usage of modern technology. Thus, China has paid special attention to improving the battle efficiency of its troops, shifting the focus to quality rather than quantity. This recent trend of military improvements came from a operational analysis of Operation DESERT STORM in 1991. This is reflected in the solutions proposed by the CCP's Central Committee in September 1995 and in the directives of the PRC Perspective Development Program until 2010, which the National People's Congress (NPC) Standing Committee approved in March 1996.[5]

At the end of 1998, China's CMC approved a schedule of defense modernization as well as a new military strategy and doctrine. In its new military strategy, the PLA is directed to train for waging battle in peripheral regions of China, small in scale and short in duration, but nonetheless intensive. The preparation for such a war differs radically from its previous strategy which focused on waging wars of attrition, which was the focus during its period of confrontation with the Union of Soviet Socialist Republics (USSR).[6]

China's military strategy foresees five main types of local wars:

- Small scale wars within the territorial boundaries of China;

- War to control adjacent water areas and islands;

- Sudden air attack on strategic resources within Chinese territory;

- Defensive operations against deliberate invasions of restricted areas of China; and,

- Counteroffensive against an opponent's territory in retaliation for aggression and to protect national sovereignty.[7]

Common to all those listed above is the pursuit of limited political ends achievable with the help of a military ready for immediate deployment and capable of routing the opponent. The main prerequisite for achieving such an outcome is the effective use of military force. Thus, Beijing considers the readiness to wage local wars an indispensable tool for achieving limited political ends, and this should include effective intimidation and the ability to escalate to a full-scale war.[8]

The strategic concepts of reassessing the sources of military threats and targeting the political and military leadership to create a new military paradigm was approved in the doctrine of China. China's military reorganization would allow for a sufficiently constrained military during peacetime and the deployment of a large armed force during war. The armed forces of China should correspond to its economic capabilities, ensure socio-political unity, and not violate the integrity of the country. Within the framework of possible military conflicts, the nuclear forces of the PRC are invoked to deter aggression against China and the conventional forces are intended to manage local wars.[9]

The modern Chinese nuclear strategy is characterized by the following two positions. During peacetime, nuclear forces are intended to deter potential adversaries from unleashing nuclear war against China and to guarantee that China is free to exercise an independent foreign policy. The purpose of nuclear forces during wartime is to prevent China's enemies from turning a conventional war into a nuclear war.

China has several hundred warheads, including several intercontinental ballistic missiles, some of which are deployed on tactical aircraft.

Apparently, China has no intention of achieving nuclear parity with the United States and Russia. It has found a philosophy, adopted in the 1980s, of "restricted nuclear counter attack with the purposes of self-defense." This concept not only takes into consideration the limited financial resources of the country, but also recognizes that the United States and Russia plan to retrofit existing systems or deploy new defensive systems that will neutralize any achievable Chinese strategic nuclear buildup. The calculation demonstrates that Chinese delivery vehicles are not capable of overcoming prospective anti-ballistic missile systems and air defense systems; consequently, they will lose the ability to prevent the United States from interfering in China's political affairs. This is one of the main potential threats China faces at the global level.[10]

China's leaders have openly declared that they will not use nuclear weapons first. Furthermore, China's strategic nuclear forces operate on a three-component structure: strategic missile forces, strategic aviation, and nuclear submarines. This compact structure of forces is necessary to deter wars against the China, to execute combat missions in response to various international scenarios, and to intimidate the smaller hegemonists in the Asia-Pacific region.[11]

It is necessary to identify the inconsistency between China's political declarations regarding its no first-use policy and its technological capabilities. Only about a dozen of China's strategic nuclear delivery systems are located in protected silo launchers. Hence, in terms of the theory of mutually assured destruction, China's existing nuclear forces have neither a first strike capability nor is China capable of unleashing a massive retaliatory strike to wipe out an aggressor. This reality is mentioned in the military doctrine of China.

However, it does allow China to avoid participation in nuclear weapons reduction agreements, such as the strategic arms reduction treaties. In 2000, this author asked Mr. Sha Zukang, Director-General of the Department of Arms Control and Disarmament of the Chinese Foreign Ministry, what China's role was in the U.S.-Russian arms reduction initiatives. He believes that China would participate in such treaties when Russia and the United States reduce their existing arsenal to one-fifth of their current levels. It is difficult to imagine Moscow and Washington taking this step.

Chinese battle training and strategic nuclear-missile exercises are contingent on properly maintained rocket systems. The Chinese rockets are technologically similar to the Soviet R-5 and R-7. These rockets were designed in the late 1950s—a period of cooperation between nuclear-missile specialists in the USSR and China. The extent of the Russian-Chinese exchange should not be overestimated. Far from the quoted level of $20 billion, a realistic amount lies in the region of $5-7 billion per year of which only $1 billion consists of military equipment. An amount this small will have little significance in increasing military modernization. At the same time, the relationship between Russia and China should not be underestimated. It takes time and effort to build a partnership in which the sharing of information—especially related to weapons—is done willingly. In addition to Russia, China has received limited military aid from other countries and broad economic assistance from western powers—both types of aid are efficiently incorporated into the Chinese plan for national modernization.

It is unlikely that the Chinese arsenal will perform well in educational and combat-trainer tests, due to the small volume of production and limited early testing. China's technological lag behind the U.S. missile program bolsters doubts of any successful missile firings.

On July 12, 2001, U.S. Deputy Defense Secretary Paul Wolfowitz submitted a statement to the Senate Armed Services Committee describing the unsuccessful test launch of American Thor (4 of 5), Atlas (5 of 8), and Polaris (66 of 123) strategic missiles.[12] Soviet missile testing during the 1960s yielded similar results. Apparently, China's missile experimentation has met with the same outcome. Though government and industry forces want more extensive testing of China's arsenal to eliminate design flaws, the high cost of failure has frustrated further efforts. A missile system must be tested periodically to ensure immediate response in a combat situation. The lack of testing on a large scale poses two major problems for the reliability of China's arsenal: first, the current stock may have flaws, and second, the probability of a flawed launch increases the longer a missile sits idle and unmaintained.

The Chinese rely on lessons from past conflicts to shape their view of building general-purpose forces and deploying them into battle. Of particular importance in this respect has been the Gulf War in which technological superiority was used to quickly defeat the opponent. Thus, China's strategy has evolved from the traditional "grand army" model in favor of concepts like "fast reaction" and "local warfare." These concepts mandate that joint state and military institutions be able to quickly and effectively mobilize in the face of combat situations and that the armed forces be prepared to immediately wage war in one or several theaters.

The new ideal of "fast reaction" has fostered considerable change in battle training, unit organization and unit formation as the modernization of the PLA advances. The creation and content of the PLA battle component structure ("alert forces" and "fast-reacting forces" capable of quick decisions on emerging issues) has been recognized as indispensable.

The PLA military command is well-trained and has equipped battalions and brigades to be used as impact units capable of quick, retaliatory action. These units are trained to execute the following primary objectives:

- Breakthrough,

- Shock missions on the base camps of enemy military,

- Massive retaliations with the purpose of defeating opposition strongholds, and

- Tactics by which PLA troops flank the opponent.[13]

Units intended to execute these mission objectives are currently trained in each military district. The changing international situation, in connection with the end of the Cold War and economic concerns, has induced China to reduce the ranks of the PLA in the short term. The army will drop to 2.5 million members (from more than 4 million) and embark on a vigorous modernization effort. This effort will close a number of bases and reduce the number of military divisions and regiments. However, the problem of updating the army to modern levels has not been addressed. The present condition of the PLA is characterized by a lack of materials used by more developed countries and a great deal of obsolete equipment and weaponry.

The traditional military doctrine of China since Mao Zedong held that people were indispensable to develop a modern army. Currently, though, this view has been tempered with doctrines of expediency and capability— concepts that surfaced after China's civil wars and conflict with Japan. In addition to their own experience, the Chinese also "steadfastly keep track of strategic situations in the world and combine the best tactics from foreign countries with national experience."[14] In the end, the doctrine of "People's War under Modern Conditions" was adopted. This doctrine recognizes the increasing importance of technology in warfare and envisions an army with a balance between weaponry and troops that effectively functions in five dimensions: air, land, sea, space, and technology. In addition, the plan calls for the updating of already existing military-industrial operations.

Special attention is paid to the preparation of armed forces in peace time to allow for immediate response in case of conflict. Additionally, however, plans are made to efficiently transform the national economy, civil air defense, and national transportation defense from a peaceful state to one of wartime operations. Legislation has been passed so that, if the state so decrees, all state bodies, political parties, firms, institutes, and citizens are obligated to mobilize according to enacted guidelines[15].

During the last 2 years, fundamental changes have taken place in the field of defense education. The state has transformed the curriculum to target all citizens by training in broader and more general areas. Defense education now consists of regular, intensive training combined with correspondence and daytime classes.[16]

It will be difficult for the Chinese to combine the traditional military practice of mass infantry and simple tactical operations with the usage of new, high-precision weaponry and aerospace technology. Undoubtedly, the transformation will demand severe modifications to the existing military infrastructure.

The most serious impediments to China's military development are its aging military bases and centers of production. In contrast to the way in which former Cold War period installations were funded, the current administration recognizes the need for a solid national economy and the importance of coordinating economic and military building efforts. Chinese propaganda works to create a unified economic system in which production can serve both civil and military uses—the former during times of peace and the latter during times of conflict. Creating the system, however, will be problematic due to China's current level of technical expertise.

At present, military research and development is largely ineffective due, in part, to poor state financing. China's bureaucracy also has a hand in the slow pace of military R&D. The rigid chain of command often stifles scientific ideas before they can reach decisionmakers. In addition to poor organization, negative public reactions hamper progress when news of military development leaks out to the public. Small gains have been realized by studying Russian military equipment like submarines, destroyers, aircraft and air defense systems; the knowledge gained, however, is minimal.

The modernization of the PLA often proceeds at the whim of officials; even then, it moves at a slow pace due to the limited defense budget and obsolete equipment. The sectors of the military slated to advance most rapidly are nuclear operations and rapid deployment-type land troops. Import purchases are forgone to boost spending on military transport planes as well as air-defense troops. Chinese naval vessels with high performance ratings are entered into service.

In the short term, prospects for military development will rest on China's continued economic growth—currently 8 percent per year. However, the current administration has recently assigned a low probability to future, external military threats; this places military spending near the end of the line for budget increases. At this point, it appears as if the bulk of government spending will focus on retrofitting a research complex, creating new arms with Chinese-produced elements, and laying the financial groundwork for a military technology base.[17]

The process of developing market mechanisms in the country and obtaining the experience of commercial activity led to similar developments in the PLA. Special attention was paid to maintaining scientific and technological development in areas pertaining to defense building and raising the standards of engineering to modern requirements. China has conducted structural reforms to create a new, high-performance science of defense systems, engineering, and industries. Among these was the creation of the Commission of Science, Technology and Industry for National Defense in March 1998. This commission operates as a leading department of the State Council and enacts policies, laws, rules, schedules, and standards in areas of military influence. In July 1999, five military organizations that specialize in nuclear weapons, spacecraft, aircraft, naval vessels, and weapons manufacturing were reorganized into ten corporations.[18]

With the help of the national defense science, engineering, and industry reforms, competition was introduced into the military production sector. The war industry's structure was improved, its ability to transition between peace and war streamlined, and plans were made for the creation of a new open system of military production.[19]

The current style of battle training focuses on making individual soldiers part of a cohesive unit. On the regiment and division scale, officer drilling through computer simulation has largely replaced the expensive, live ammunition training practiced earlier. The combined tactical training base system provides a versatile training ground by providing networked tactical, weapon, and service simulation models. An interactive command and control simulation, new equipment operation simulation, and computer-aided training systems have been widely applied.[20]

Poor military financing, the inability to incorporate technologically advanced equipment with current troops and the evolving model of small-scale operations troops have forced PLA officials to create a number of "elite" brigades and battalions, specially trained for immediate mobilization. These divisions receive the larger part of allotted funds and are thus better equipped with arms and equipment, which enhances their training.

The majority of the PLA, PLA reserve units, the Chinese People's Armed Police Force, and the militia are provided with few resources for training exercises. For example, an ordinary PLAAF pilot typically trains in a Soviet prototype jet designed in the early 1950s. He only spends 80 hours per year in the air—not enough time to master the complex skills of piloting, let alone grasp the handling of high-tech weaponry used in combat planes.

The gap between current military doctrine about modern war and the actual practices of the armed forces has resulted in a deficit of experience among Chinese soldiers.

Though political rhetoric promotes extensive training and increased usage of technology in combat operations, the bulk of the military has no modern equipment with which to train. The situation became so pronounced in 1998 that the PRC CMC decided to train cadres abroad and recruit foreign specialists to train various elements of the PLA. Though many Chinese soldiers trained in the Soviet Union during the 1950s, this is no longer the case. The decreased desire to learn Russian has contributed to the decrease in numbers, while schools that offer English have become more popular. Although the Chinese still hold conferences with the Russian military, they are mostly restricted to the general headquarters and district level. The military leaders feel that the impact of foreigners will raise technological knowledge throughout the PLA. The participants in this new initiative will be officers of high and middle rank, those who received a broad education, or those possessing specialized military knowledge. President Jiang Zemin himself stated that "it is better to let the professionals wait for weapons than for the weapons to wait for professionals."[21]

The practice of training troops for battle looks imposing, even on paper. The quantity of required exercises, maneuvers, and officer drillings testifies to the challenging studies of the PLA. With the advent of military reform, the number of exercises was increased, but the subject content became broader and displayed a deeper understanding of geopolitics and military structure. After 1980 combined arms exercises became more commonplace. Strategies of encirclement, disembarkation from marine and air-vehicles, and usage of weapons of mass destruction were discussed from both offensive and defensive positions. As early as 1984, 27 divisions, 269 regiments and over 200,000 servicemen were trained in the Shenyang and Lanzhou districts alone. Involved in exercises were 3,600 artillery pieces, over 1,000 tanks and other armored vehicles, 13 ships, and 10,000 automobiles. The number of aircraft missions completed was 508. The military districts of

Shenyang, Jinan, and Wuhan saw an increase of battalion scale exercises (1,726), regiment scale exercises (596), and division scale exercises (67). Strategic operations exercises were run with the participation of tens and even hundreds of thousands of servicemen.[22]

Each of the seven military districts of the PLA carries out annual independent staff and field exercises in preparation for local war. Joint operations in retaliation for border skirmishes and other local incidents are regularly carried out. Increased hostilities along border regions fostered the desire that such exercises should create a military zone where independent operations could be carried out during certain times. The commander in chief of a military district becomes the head of an integrated command. Orders to all attached land, air, and, when necessary, naval troops are sent from a central command facility in a seaside zone.[23] Also contributing to peaceful borders is the Friendship and Cooperation Treaty between the Russian Federation and the PRC. Although the treaty contains many military-support sounding references like, "concerning guards of state unity and territorial integrity," the agreement is effectively a statement of mutual support for policy concerns; it falls far short of a military alliance.

Until the end of the 1980s, the majority of large-scale operations were conducted in northern military districts based on the supposition that conflict would arise between China and the Soviet Union. In addition, the Guangzhou region also hosted large-scale exercises with Vietnam as the potential opponent. Special attention was paid to these later exercises, though, for two reasons. First was the need to carry out the defense of coastal territories, especially those along the South China Sea, with as much efficiency as possible. Second was the comprehensive nature—divisions from all branches of the PLA were used—of the training missions. Of special import was the commander of the coastal district, who also had control of naval operations. The skills of this leader could easily be transferred to battle in other countries. PRC Naval Command wants to increase the battle capabilities of the Chinese fleet to a zone of operations of 400 miles and enable independent operations of the fleet.[24]

In the 1990s, specialized exercises commenced with the use of high-tech armament and equipment. The development of electronic warfare, such as implanting viruses into enemy computer systems, is considered the primary goal of these simulations. The military district of Sheyang hosted these specialized exercises, which included Chinese specialists in electronic technology.[25]

During the last few years, the military districts of Lanzhou, Jinan, Nanjing, and Guangzhou hosted training missions incorporating multiple branches of the armed forces.[26]

Chinese military specialists have been able to acquaint themselves with the expertise of other countries. Combining foreign learning with their knowledge of historic conflict, they modify and shape military strategy and doctrine as it relates to tactical operations and troop preparation.

A similar trend was seen in Soviet forces during the 1970s and 1980s. During this time, Russian preparation for nuclear world war was completed, and included the amassing of thousands of rockets and tens of thousands of nuclear warheads. The central research base of the country provided a huge variety of Russian and foreign designed armaments. In the advent of another world war, a massive nuclear strike against the opponent could be guaranteed.

The situation became more complicated when the United States and NATO—followed by the USSR and countries of the Warsaw Pact—began preparations for conventional warfare in addition to nuclear war. This preparation resulted from the change in perspective called the "antinuclear revolution in military affairs." It appeared, though, as if the mindset had changed without a result in actual practice. New ideas became widespread, such as the use of missiles, artillery and air forces to guarantee success; multi-point observation of opponents; and usage of a division—or even an army—to flank an adversary. In view of the great advances in military engineering, all of these things seemed possible. In training simulations, the speed of an offensive was established at 50 or even 100 kilometers per day. When questioned on how the necessary ammunition, fuels, lubricant oils, means of operation, and battle maintenance would come to be, the common answer was that in a short time these "necessaries" would be invented. Samples of arms had already been created, and there were promises of spreading them throughout the armed forces. On paper, the revolution had already encompassed all aspects of military art. The reality of the situation, however, was quite different. The Soviet army simply did not have the proper formations and number of troops to carry out the tactical plans they had.

The problem of possible transition to the use of nuclear weapons was solved by diagramming hundreds of potential nuclear strikes on cards. Each drew the appropriate impact zone and estimated the consequences of using nuclear weaponry. Included in the plans were 2-3 days to allow the effects of a nuclear attack to clear. This period, however, was not included in field training exercises. There is also a decided lack of skill, even in the elite units, relating to material support, logistics, and even the use of some forms of weaponry.

It is believed that the gap between PLA ideals like "high-tech local warfare" and "revolution in military affairs" and the actual practices of military units is even more pronounced than in the Soviet Army. Although the PLA is linked to the concept of "people's war" through weapons and equipment designed in the 1950-60s, its target of territorial defense creates a foundation of reliable security for China. The 1960-70s were a difficult time for the PLA as the administration did not allow military spending on updating weapons and engineering. They waited while other countries went through 2-3 generations of armaments.

Even now, there is not enough support in the Chinese leadership to fund a full scale modernization of the PLA. I believe that the Chinese will continue applying existing weapons to their military theories for quite some time.

One area in which the PLA has attained a high degree of success is in the creation of a courageous officer and executive soldier class. These servicemen are willing to wage war in the name of their country despite the army's aging equipment and untrained troops.

The author's above representation of Chinese military doctrine was only in brief. The question then arises as to whether China's military policy has recently changed due to warming relations with the United States. The answer is, of course, negative. The doctrine and practice of battle training are staples of the Chinese military structure and require tremendous impetus before alteration.

The U.S. hardening policy towards China is expressed first in intentions, second in political steps, and finally in military action. It will be interesting to discover how the George W. Bush administration's new foreign policy initiatives will be met by the PRC—both politically and militarily.

In China, as in other countries of the world, the latest steps of the United States in the international arena are perceived as America's attempt to assert itself as the last superpower and disrupt the present world order in the field of international security.

The developments of such a policy include:

- A power *diktat* and the use of force without international approval;

- The departure from the 1972 Anti-Ballistic Missile (ABM) Treaty and the organization of a national ABM and theater missile defense (TMD) system which upset the strategic balance and fractured the system of agreements regarding the limitation and reduction of offensive forces and nuclear arms; and,

- The expansion to the East.

The developments in U.S. foreign policy have little direct impact on the Asia Pacific region in which China is situated. There has been, however, a buildup of smaller incidents like the bombing of the PRC embassy in Belgrade and the collision of the Chinese fighter with the American EP-3 off the island of Hainan. Furthermore, the Bush administration's support of Taiwan could substantially complicate the political and military situation in the region.

This is, of course, not a full list of the events instigated by the United States to overtly restrain the concerns of the PRC. If continued, these events may lead to complex operating measures in both political and military spheres between the two countries.

The PRC leadership strongly reacted to the events in Yugoslavia—to the extension of NATO and the creation of an anti-missile defense system. Its reactions are of a political and diplomatic nature: statement, demonstration, consulting and coordination with like-minded countries. There are also, however, cases of military reaction as evidenced by the illegal airspace infringement of the EP-3.

The PRC has put forth a schedule of transformation that lasts into the middle of the 21st Century. This plan consists of 3 parts: first, economic growth and an increased living standard for the Chinese people; second, the socio-political stability of the country; and third, the guarantee of military security and the territorial integrity of the country.

The first part of China's strategy allows little room to decisively act in the international arena. Moreover, any Chinese plans of military expansion will severely damage its foreign economic relations and slow its national economic growth.

The second part of the Chinese plan is connected to the active extraction of government forces from the economy. One of the functions of China's armed forces has traditionally been to assist in natural disaster relief projects and to rebuild damaged houses. Natural disasters seem to plague the country and so distract the PLA from training objectives. Furthermore, with the significant reduction in the army (from 4 to 2.5 million) and the continuing call for disaster relief, China may hasten the removal of the PLA from the economy.

The third part of the Chinese plan relies on its military potential and the modernization of the PLA. The pattern has been the gradual destruction of obsolete items (including tanks, artillery systems, aircraft, etc.) and the purchase and dissemination of new equipment throughout the army. This process is not threatening to other countries and does not change the balance of power on regional or strategic levels.

It should be noted that, when laying out its national goals, the Chinese leadership traditionally thinks in large categories, in large time periods, and exhibits significant patience. China never entered an arms race by massing its field troops or by buying expensive modern weapons systems. Since the 1950-60s, the PRC has based its strength on ground troops, although it has received and created samples of nuclear weapons, missiles, aircraft and marine vessels. Subsequently, China did not conduct broad retrofits of its existing weaponry, though it was considerably outdated. It has only done the minimum to ensure military security during the difficult times of the 1960-80s during which minor confrontations occurred with the Soviet Union and the United States.

Currently, the international situation is more favorable for Chinese security. Using the concept of "people's war," the PLA reliably guards the country's borders. China's nuclear arms serve only as a deterrent to potential aggressors.

China is not prepared for major conflicts outside of its own territory, and there have been no rumors of plans in this direction. Even the statements of Chinese leaders regarding the possibility of forcing Taiwan to rejoin the country should be dismissed as no more than a political show. Now, and in the near future, an assault on Taiwan is outside of China's capability.

This situation can be changed by large international political and military events such as:

- Obstacles on the path of reunification with Taiwan, international support of the Taiwanese government, or careless political and military maneuvers in the Taiwan strait;

- Allowing the PRC to build a nuclear arsenal unrestrained; and,

- Dramatic changes in the political or military situation in the Asia Pacific Region or in the world as a whole.

Developments of this nature may force the leadership of the PRC to revise its military strategy and pursue an accelerated modernization of the armed forces. The rapid economic growth of China and its increasing military potential—combined with its active and firm military policy towards its opponents, including the United States—may result in an unexpectedly large threat, should China be forced to think outside of its borders.

Should these events occur, China will have to overcome considerable difficulties, including:

- A weak technical and technological base;

- A vulnerable economy if a drastic increase in military consumption and research and development (R&D) demands occurs; and,

- Decreasing economic relations with other nations.

The path to war is fraught with economic and socio-political difficulties for China, thus there is slight chance the country will pursue it. It has as an example the Soviet Union, which could not balance the arms race with its overstrained economy. At the same time, however, foreign powers should not expect China to take a passive stand in military operations. At a minimum, the PRC can engage in military action within its borders.

If the Chinese tendencies manifested over the last 15-20 years persist, the PLA will only have the potential to defend the PRC. It is difficult to imagine a scenario in which China would pose a real threat to the continental United States or even to American military bases in East Asia.

For this reason, the international situation over the next 15-20 years will be determined largely by U.S. policy. If America shows restraint, does not excessively increase its military, does not promote unilateral expansion plans in foreign regions, does not destroy the present system of strategic stability, does not engage in an arms race (under the pretext of deployment of ABM systems, for example) and does not proliferate nuclear and conventional armaments, then China will have no incentive to increase its own military capacity. Rivalry between China and the United States will then originate only from economic and political sources.

If the United States and its allies dictate politically or militarily to other countries, it may place the United States and China on the road to a new Cold War. We are now witnessing the destruction of a series of international agreements regarding the reduction and limitation of nuclear armaments. The United States has terminated its participation in the ABM Treaty of 1972. U.S. National Security Adviser Condoleezza Rice recently compared the present system of agreements to the geocentric concept of the universe; the future system of the world to the heliocentric system. Copernicus, though, had to formulate his concept of the cosmos and demonstrate its consistency with fact before he received the recognition of the world.[27]

Russia is often charged with giving China the modern air, anti-aircraft, and marine arms that helped increase the military potential of the country. Making this statement, however, requires the following suppositions:

1. Russian arms shipments to China were meant as defensive tools to protect the nation's borders.

2. China does not itself possess the capacity to manufacture its entire spectrum of military equipment. It also testifies to the reluctance of the Chinese leadership to enter an arms race and, in so doing, to become dependent on the military-industrial complex.

Former President Dwight Eisenhower spoke of the relationship between a country's leadership and its arms producers in his farewell address. He warned of a military-industrial complex that dictates both defense and economic policies.

Neither the United States nor the USSR could avoid such a situation, however. The United States has not experienced the consequences, though, for two reasons: (1) high general economic potential, and (2) military-industrial corporations producing diversified commodities, selling both to the military and to civilians. In the Soviet Union, though, a diktat of the producers of military equipment resulted in the economic weakness of the country's private sector, a redundancy of production, and that production's low quality.

It is plausible to view the national ABM system proposed by the Bush administration as a concession to the military-industrial complex of America, which stands to profit substantially from the undertaking. They prefer not to speak about the battle effectiveness of the system, but rather to point at the nonexistent threat of North Korean nuclear weapons. China, though, perceives the creation of the American national anti-missile shield very differently.

The military policy of the United States will shape that of China. If momentum is given to the missile shield, it will provoke the Chinese to institute a full-scale military-industrial complex capable of producing thousands of rockets, aircraft, and tanks. Should this occur, it will heavily stress China's economic base, yet the transformation is possible.

In the early 1980s, the author studied at the Military Academy of General Staff of the Soviet Armed Forces. Here he learned the three major strategic zones of the globe: the West, the South, and the East. The Soviet Armed Forces had the resources and capabilities necessary for such operations. The PLA, on the other hand, does not have the capability to think of theaters outside of the Asia Pacific Region. I do not think that the United States and its allies should view the PLA as having such capabilities—a fact that should be taken into account before hardening foreign policy against China.

The transformation of Chinese military doctrine and the combat training of their armed forces characterize a country trying to reach a higher level of conventional military capabilities. It is obviously necessary for China to react against aggressors, but not always through military operations. The fundamentals of strategy and deception are with good reason the bases of "people's war" at the strategic level.

CHAPTER 4 - ENDNOTES

1. *Renmin Ribao*, October 9, 1995.

2. *China National Defense in 2000*, Beijing, October 2000, p. 6.

3. *Ibid.*, pp. 6-7.

4. *Ibid.*, pp. 12.

5. *Renmin Ribao*.

6. *ITAR-TASS*, Beijing, December 9, 1998.

7. *Ibid.*

8. *Ibid.*

9. *ITAR-TASS*, Beijing, May 23, 1996.

10. *Krasnaya Zvezda*, July 11, 1995.

11. *Zarubezhnoe voennoe obozrenie*, 9, 1994.

12. Paul Wolfowitz, Prepared testimony on Ballistic Missile Defense, July 12, 2001.

13. *ITAR-TASS*. Beijing, December 9, 1998.

14. P. Kamennov, *Military-Technological Aspects of China's Defense Modernization*, Moldova: International Foundation for Election Services, 2001, p. 19.

15. *China's National Defense in 2000*, p. 18.

16. *Ibid.*, p. 19.

17. P. Kamennov, "PRC Military Construction in 1990s," *Problemy Dalnego Vostoka*, Vol. 3, 1997.

18. *China's National Defense in 2000*, p. 24.

19. *Ibid.*, pp. 24-25.

20. *Ibid.*, pp.37-38.

21. *ITAR-TASS*, Beijing, December 10, 1998.

22. *Military activities of contemporary Chinese Army, Part 2*, Beijing, 1989, p. 362.

23. *The China Quarterly*, No. 146, June 1996.

24. *Ibid.*

25. *ITAR-TASS*, Beijing, December 10, 1998.

26. *China's National Defense in 2000*, p. 38.

27. Remarks by Condoleezza Rice at the National Press Club, July 12, 2001.

PART II: CHINA'S BALLISTIC MISSILES AND EAST ASIAN REACTION TO U.S. MISSILE DEFENSE INITIATIVES

CHAPTER 5

CHINESE BALLISTIC MISSILE FORCES IN THE AGE OF GLOBAL MISSILE DEFENSE: CHALLENGES AND RESPONSES

Mark A. Stokes

INTRODUCTION

Since the days of Sunzi and beyond, nations have pursued defenses against offensive weapons. Naturally, sparked by the advent of the first ballistic missiles in World War II, interest in defending against ballistic missiles over the past several decades has increased significantly. Today, strategic and conventional ballistic missiles pose challenges to the United States and to its national interests around the world. Weapons of mass destruction (WMD) and their means of delivery place significant portions of the U.S. population at risk. These systems, in the hands of governments that are hostile to U.S. national interests, challenge the security of allies and friends. No system exists today that is capable of defending U.S. territory and only a limited capability exists to protect allies and friends, as well as U.S. forces deployed overseas.

To address the growing proliferation of ballistic missiles and WMD, President George W. Bush has set out on a path to field ballistic missile defenses to protect the United States, its forces overseas, and allies and friends. At the same time, the United States seeks to reduce its nuclear arsenal to the "lowest possible number of nuclear weapons." U.S. missile defense programs are designed to counter the existing and growing short, medium, and intermediate range missile threats to our allies and friends and deployed forces; as well as the long-range threat to American cities that is just over the horizon.

The People's Republic of China (PRC) is concerned about U.S. plans to deploy a global missile defense architecture. From Beijing's perspective, even a modest missile defense system could have serious implications for the viability of its nuclear deterrent and for its expanding inventory of conventional short and medium range ballistic missiles (SRBMs and MRBMs). Beijing's anxiety over maintaining its nuclear deterrent is not new. Development of missile defense countermeasures dates back at least to the mid-1980s, when a series of responses to the U.S. Strategic Defense Initiative (SDI) were contemplated. These responses included plans for a significant expansion of China's nuclear intercontinental ballistic missile force.

The author of this chapter examines the PRC's strategic and theater ballistic missile development and the growing role of ballistic missiles as an integral component of PRC coercive strategy. U.S. missile defense programs are outlined in order to provide the necessary context for subsequent discussion of the wide range of PRC technical responses that are underway. These countermeasures are intended to undercut the political and military utility of U.S. missile defense programs.

In addressing PRC technical responses to U.S. missile defenses, three caveats are in order. First, this discussion does not necessarily imply that U.S. missile defense programs are motivated by a perceived Chinese threat to the U.S. homeland. U.S. missile defense programs are driven by rogue nations equipped with limited numbers of relatively unsophisticated ballistic missiles, as well the prospects of an accidental Russian or Chinese launch. While missile defenses are not necessarily driven by a perceived PRC threat, Beijing's track record of proliferating ballistic missile-related technology to rogue states—to include countermeasures—is a legitimate concern.

Secondly, defense against ballistic missiles, particularly the shorter-range threats, requires an integrated approach consisting of survivable command, control, communications, and battle management systems; passive defense such as hardening and rapid recovery measures; active ballistic missile defenses that destroy missiles in the boost, mid-course, and terminal phases of flight; and attack operations intended to suppress the use of ballistic missile forces at their source. This chapter focuses only on the active component of missile defense.

Finally, China's opposition to missile defenses often is viewed through the cognitive prism of Taiwan. Therefore, special attention is placed on the relationship between the development of missile defenses and their potential use in a Taiwan Strait conflict, since it is within this context that Beijing perceives U.S. development of missile defense. The PRC's growing arsenal of strategic ballistic missiles and increasingly accurate and lethal theater ballistic missiles threatens to disrupt the security situation in the Taiwan Strait and limit U.S. freedom of action should the PRC resort to the use of force to resolve differences with Taiwan. The People's Liberation Army (PLA) of China has an expanding inventory of conventional ballistic missiles, linked with other forms of coercive airpower, which could give Beijing a decisive edge in any future conflict with Taiwan. From a political and military perspective, missile defenses threaten to undermine the PRC's ballistic missile "trump card."

PRC BALLISTIC MISSILE DEVELOPMENT

The PRC relies heavily upon its ballistic missile forces—the PLA Second Artillery Corps—for deterrence, coercion, and warfighting. With some foreign assistance, Beijing is expanding and modernizing its limited inventory of nuclear ballistic missiles and is continuing to deploy increasingly accurate and lethal conventional ballistic missiles opposite Taiwan. Its small intercontinental ballistic missile (ICBM) force provides a modicum of assured retaliation should China suffer nuclear attack. The Second Artillery's conventional ballistic missile force is becoming not only an important instrument of psychological intimidation, but also a potentially devastating force of military utility. The nuclear and conventional missile buildup is taking place regardless of the scale of any future U.S. missile defense architecture or the provision of missile defenses to Taiwan. A 1998 U.S. Department of Defense report asserted that China's space and missile industry probably will have the capacity to produce as many as 1,000 ballistic missiles in the next decade.[1]

The PRC's strategic nuclear doctrine is based on the concept of limited deterrence—the ability to inflict unacceptable damage on an enemy in a retaliatory strike. China's nuclear forces generally are believed to follow a countervalue strategy that targets population centers. China has sufficient nuclear weapons to hold approximately 15-20 million U.S. citizens at risk, or about 5-10 percent of the total U.S. population.[2]

China's primary organization for ballistic missile research, development, and production is the China Aerospace Corporation's First Academy. The First Academy, also known as the China Academy of Launch Technology (CALT), consists of an overall design and systems integration department, 13 research institutes, and 7 factories which are responsible for engines, control technology, inertial systems, warheads, materials, testing, and launchers. With more than 27,000 personnel, the First Academy is the largest research and development (R&D) organization within the China Aerospace Corporation (CASC). In its work on solid systems, the First Academy is dependent upon the Fourth Academy in Hohhot, Inner Mongolia, for its solid motors. CALT is also supported by institutes and factories subordinated to various bases deep inside China. One of these bases, the Sanjiang Space Group (066 Base) in Hubei province, has developed its own complete ballistic missile system, the 300-kilometer DF-11 and its 600 kilometer variant, the DF-11A.

Today, the First Academy's research and development resources are devoted to ensuring its nuclear ballistic missile force remains a viable deterrent in the face of missile defenses. CALT and the 066 Base in Hubei province are leveraging foreign technology in order to achieve tremendous advances in accuracy. At the same time, they are diversifying the payloads of their ballistic missiles to increase their lethality. CALT and the PLA are also examining a wide range of countermeasures to ensure their ballistic missile force remains effective as missile defenses are introduced into the Asia-Pacific region. Key organizations responsible for technical countermeasures include CALT's 4th Planning Department (systems design); the 14th Research Institute (warhead/payload development); and the 703rd Research Institute (materials). CALT and the 066 Base are working on no less than six research and development programs that will increase the range, size, mobility, accuracy, and survivability of the Second Artillery's inventory of ballistic missiles. Many of these programs have been placed on an accelerated R&D schedule since May 1999.[3]

Intercontinental Ballistic Missiles

The PRC's existing ICBM force consists of liquid-fueled DF-5 (CSS-4) and DF-4 (CSS-3) systems. Mobile, solid fueled ICBMs will augment these older systems over the next 5 years. The Second Artillery currently possesses approximately 20 DF-5 ICBMs that are capable of targeting any location in the United States. This figure is expected to grow to 24 over the next few years. CALT is working on an improved version of the DF-5 that could incorporate multiple independent reentry vehicle (MIRV) technology. Deployment of at least twelve 6,000-kilometer range DF-4 (CSS-3) ICBMs began in the mid-1970s. Western sources indicate that these two stage, liquid fueled missiles are distributed among three brigades under the 54 Base in Henan province, 55 Base in western Hunan province, and 56 Base in Qinghai province.[4]

China's liquid fueled ICBM force will be augmented by mobile, solid fueled systems within the next 5 years. At least one source alleges that China could deploy up to 100 new land or sea-launched ICBMs over the next 15 years. These new systems include the DF-31, an extended range DF-31, and a sea-based version of the DF-31, the JL-2.[5] The DF-31 is a solid-fueled, three stage nuclear missile with an 8,000-kilometer range, sufficient to strike targets in Hawaii, Guam, Alaska, and some portions of northwestern United States. Two successful DF-31 flight tests were conducted in 1999 and 2000. Slated for deployment before 2005, the DF-31 eventually will replace the DF-4 intermediate range ballistic missile (IRBMs). The DF-31 is estimated to carry a single warhead and could incorporate penetration aids, including decoys and chaff. At least 10-20 DF-31 missiles can be expected to enter the force over the next 5 years, sufficient to outfit one brigade with a notional structure of 9-16 launchers assigned to three or four battalions.[6]

Two variants of the DF-31 also are under development. First is an extended range version of the DF-31 with a range of at least 12,000 kilometers. This longer range missile, known as the DF-31A, likely will be tested within the next several years and will be targeted primarily against the United States. Japanese observers note that the DF-31A is in some respects more advanced than some Russian systems, such as the Topol-M. As many as 10 DF-31A ICBMs could be fielded by 2010. Another variant of the DF-31—the JL-2—will be launched from submarines. The JL-2 missile was successfully tested in early 2001. A modified Type 94 submarine that will be equipped with 16 tubes allegedly will carry the JL-2. Projected for deployment by 2005, the 8,000-kilometer range missile would be able to strike targets in Alaska, Hawaii, and the western part of the United States when operating in

Chinese coastal waters.[7] Indications exist that the timeline to field the DF-31, its longer range variant, and the JL-2 was accelerated in May 1999.[8]

DF-21 MRBM System.

The PRC's principal MRBM is the solid fueled DF-21 (CSS-5). Research and development on the DF-21 began in 1967 and the missile was first tested in 1985. Assembled at the 307 Factory in Nanjing, the initial introduction of the missile into an experimental regiment took place as early as 1991. With a 600-kilogram warhead and an estimated CEP of 700 meters, the 2,100 kilometer range DF-21 is currently equipped for nuclear missions only. A longer range version of the DF-21, the 2,500 kilometer range DF-21 Mod 2, is reportedly under development. Both the DF-21 Mod 1 and Mod 2 likely have missile defense countermeasures, including endo-atmospheric decoys that were tested in 1995 and 1996.[9]

There are indications that a conventionally armed variant of the DF-21—the DF-21C—has been underway since at least 1995. This system may adopt a terminal guidance package that uses on-board computers to correlate stored images with landmarks and that theoretically could achieve a circular error probability (CEP) of 50 meters or better.[10] Such a capability naturally would require a maneuverable reentry vehicle. The reentry speed of the DF-21C is likely to be fast enough to preclude engagement by lower-tier missile defense systems, such as the PAC-3. Equipped with a conventional warhead as large as 1,500 kilograms, the DF-21C could force defenders on Taiwan to move toward mid-course or upper terminal phase missile defenses, such as the Theater High Altitude Area Defense (THAAD) system and sea-based mid-course interceptors. As many as two conventional DF-21 brigades could be in operation before 2010.[11]

Because of the its warhead size and the limited ability of lower tier missile defense systems to engage longer-range

MRBMs, incorporation of a terminal guidance system could have significant military implications. The high reentry speed significantly reduces the footprint of the area that is defended by terminal interceptors, such the PAC-3. A high reentry speed, combined with a penetrator warhead, also could be effective against hardened targets, such as intelligence facilities and strategic/operational command centers. The DF-21C could also range U.S. bases in the region. In addition, a terminally guided system with a maneuvering payload could complicate the U.S. carrier operations in the Western Pacific.[12]

SRBMs.

The deployment of the first conventional SRBM brigade opposite Taiwan in 1994 marked a significant departure from the traditional role and mission of the Second Artillery. Conventionally armed SRBMs have become a key tool of PRC statecraft. The PRC's expanding SRBM inventory is intended to deter or coerce neighbors such as Taiwan. Should Beijing resort to the use of force, conventionally armed ballistic missiles, operating jointly with the PLA Air Force and other armed services, could serve as critical enablers in gaining information dominance and air and naval superiority. Second Artillery conventional doctrine stresses surprise and disarming first strikes to gain the initiative in the opening phase of a conflict.[13]

The Second Artillery is said to be currently equipped with 350 conventional SRBMs distributed among three brigades opposite Taiwan. One source indicates that during annual meetings at Beidaihe in August 1999, China's senior leadership decided to accelerate the production and deployment of enough ballistic missiles to outfit four SRBM brigades by 2002.[14] Western sources believe the PLA may deploy as many as 650 SRBMs opposite Taiwan over the next several years, while Taiwan's Ministry of National Defense statements indicate that as many as 800 SRBMs could be deployed by 2006.[15] These missiles would be distributed into as many as seven brigades in the 2005-2010 timeframe.[16] Chinese writings indicate that after an initial salvo, launchers would move to new pre-surveyed launch sites within that brigade's assigned area of operations.[17] Should the PRC decide to use force, the PLA intends to carry out synchronized launches from a wide range of azimuths in order to stress active missile defenses and associated battle management systems.[18]

To be politically and militarily effective, the PLA's conventionally armed ballistic missiles must survive any attempt to intercept the missile in flight; and impact within a set radius that will damage the intended target. The PLA is seeking to maximize the lethal radius with more effective warheads and minimize its CEP with improved guidance systems. Such a development strategy is intended to reduce the number of ballistic missiles required per target and perhaps minimize collateral damage. Until CEPs reach 50-100 meters, it is difficult to hit a single point. Therefore, the PLA would require expending a considerable number of missiles per each target. As a general rule, two ballistic missiles would be required for a 50 percent probability of hit if they have a 50 meter CEP; three with a 100 meter CEP; and nine with a 300 meter CEP.

In a future contingency in the Asia-Pacific region, PLA writings indicate intent to use highly accurate SRBMs, MRBMs, and land attack cruise missiles against U.S. assets, to include key bases in Japan and aircraft carriers operating in the Western Pacific. Chinese researchers have conducted extensive feasibility studies of the use of theater ballistic missiles against aircraft carriers. Analysts have noted how such a capability would require four components: ocean surveillance; mid-course guidance; terminal guidance; and applicable control systems to maneuver the reentry vehicle to the target. Proponents advocate use of a global positioning system (GPS) for mid-course inertial corrections and the use of a millimeter wave seeker for terminal guidance.[19] Aware of the vulnerability of millimeter wave seekers to jamming, PLA engineers are surveying electronic counter-countermeasure (ECCM) techniques to ensure effectiveness of terminally guided ballistic missiles.[20] In addition to aircraft carriers, Chinese writings indicate other targets would include regional airbases, naval facilities, and key C4I and logistical nodes.[21]

DF-15 (CSS-6).

The DF-15 is a solid-fueled, 600 kilometer SRBM. Manufactured by CALT, the DF-15's payload reportedly has an attitude control mechanism that permits steering corrections from separation to impact.[22] The detachable warhead offers a much smaller target than a surface-to-surface missile system (SCUD), and its potential maneuverability would complicate missile defense radar tracking, computations, and interception. Assuming a nominal trajectory at a range of 500 kilometers, the DF-15 would reach an altitude of about 120 kilometers, achieve a reentry speed of about two kilometers per second, and have a flight time of only 6 or 7 minutes.[23] Some reporting indicates the DF-15 currently has a 100-meter CEP.[24] However, there are indications that the DF-15 has been flight tested to an accuracy of better than 50 meters.[25]

To diversify its theater ballistic missile inventory, the PRC is said to be developing a 1,000 to 1,200 kilometer range version of the DF-15.[26] Strong incentives likely exist to develop an extended range version of the DF-15. An extended range DF-15 would significantly reduce the defended area or "footprint" of land- and sea-based lower tier missile defense systems due to its reentry speed. Deployment of a longer range DF-15 in Southeast China would eliminate the requirement to transport missile assets nearer Taiwan, permit the targeting of Okinawa from sites along the East China Sea, and, if mated with a terminally guided payload, potentially force carrier battle groups (CVBGs) operating east of Taiwan to move further away from the area of operations.

DF-11 (CSS-7).

The DF-11—better known by its export designator, the M-11 (CSS-7)—is a solid propellant, road-mobile SRBM with an estimated range of 300 km. The main advantage of the DF-11 over the DF-15 is its ability to carry a larger payload. Some sources credit the 300-kilometer version with an 800-kilogram warhead and a 150-meter CEP.[27] The DF-11 is manufactured by the CASC's 066 Base, also known as the Sanjiang Space Corporation, based in Hubei province. The DF-11's 300-kilometer range presents challenges for active missile defenses due to its brief flight time of 3 minutes. Because its flight would remain within the atmosphere, upper tier systems would be unable to engage the 300-kilometer DF-11.[28] Deployment of a 600 kilometer extended range version of the DF-11, the DF-11A (CSS-7 Mod 2), is reportedly underway as well.[29]

U.S. MISSILE DEFENSE PROGRAMS

Beijing views U.S. plans for a limited missile defense capability as a threat to the viability of its growing inventory of increasingly accurate and lethal ballistic missiles. While U.S. missile defense programs are not necessarily driven by a perceived PRC threat, Beijing's ballistic missile development and export of technologies to rogue states has increased regional interest in missile defenses. The key driver for U.S. investments in missile defenses is a potential missile attack by rogue nations, such as North Korea, Iraq, or Iran. A limited national defense is also needed to defend against an accidental or unauthorized Russian or Chinese missile launch, which might involve only one or a few warheads. Ballistic missile defense requires layered, active defenses that can intercept ballistic missiles in all phases of their flight: (1) the boost phase, (2) mid-course phase, and (3) the terminal phase.

Boost Phase.

Boost phase begins at launch and lasts up to 5 minutes for a primitive liquid-fuel ICBM or 3 minutes for solid fueled systems. Intercept during the boost phase engages the missile when it is at its most vulnerable stage of flight. Boost phase intercept enables destruction of the missile before it is able to deploy countermeasures and can reduce the number of targets that mid-course and terminal systems must engage. The key boost phase system under development is the Airborne Laser (ABL). Experimental space-based systems are under development as well. Chinese sources note that the ABL system, slated for initial demonstration as early as 2003 and initial fielding in 2008, could be deployed to the theater of operations in a matter of hours. The PRC believes that at least one operational concept is for a pair of Boeing 747-400F ABL aircraft to orbit over friendly territory above the clouds at 40,000 feet, 90 kilometers off the enemy coast, scanning the horizon for the plume of missiles rising above enemy territory. With a maximum laser range of several hundred kilometers and mission time of 12-18 hours, each aircraft carries enough fuel for 200 laser shots against missiles in the boost phase when the missile offers a bright, slow target under high aerodynamic stress.[30]

The Space Based Laser (SBL) flight experiment is a demonstration effort to explore the feasibility of destroying ballistic targets with a high powered laser. According to Chinese sources, at least one architecture under consideration includes 30 satellites, a constellation of five rings with six satellites each at 40 degree inclinations, and an altitude of 1,300 kilometers. The 30 satellite constellation can counter more than a 100 SRBMs in a 2-minute period. Such a system provides a 24-hour intercept capability and would neutralize ballistic missile strikes before implementation of countermeasures, to include early release submunitions and decoys. The Chinese note that the SBL also is highly effective against direct ascent anti-satellite systems. An experimental SBL could be tested early next decade.[31] In addition, there are experiments underway that examine the feasibility of space based kinetic interceptors.[32]

Mid-Course.

During the midcourse phase of flight, the warhead travels freely through space outside the atmosphere. For an ICBM, this stage lasts about 20 minutes, making the mid-course the longest phase of missile flight. Engaging ballistic missiles in the mid-course phase offers several advantages for the defense. Mid-course intercept solutions offer greater time for higher level decision making to be integrated in the command and control system. Multiple shoot-look-shoot opportunities become possible. Midcourse defenses may be based farther away from the country launching the missile, possibly reducing system vulnerability. There are at least two systems under development that will be able to engage missiles during the mid-course phase of flight: (1) land-based exoatmospheric kill vehicles to counter longer range ICBMs; and (2) a sea-based mid-course system to counter medium- and short-range ballistic missiles.

Land Based Mid-Course. The Land Band Mid-Course system is the principal mid-course intercept system for defense of the United States. Its mission is to intercept incoming ballistic missile warheads outside the earth's atmosphere (exoatmospheric) and destroy them by force of the impact. During flight, the interceptor receives information from a battle management, command, control, and communications (BMC3) system to update the location of the incoming ballistic missile, enabling the kill vehicle's onboard sensor system to identify and home in on the target. The land based interceptor would consist of a multi-stage solid propellant booster and an exoatmospheric kill vehicle (EKV). Three options are being examined for the booster: the Minuteman III ICBM; a combination of other existing solid-rocket systems; and an entirely new booster. Until booster development is complete, EKV flight tests will be flown on the Payload Launch Vehicle (PLV), which is a booster consisting of a Minuteman II second and third stage.[33]

The EKV would use a highly capable infrared seeker to acquire and track targets, and to discriminate between the intended target (i.e., the reentry vehicle) and other objects, such as tank fragments or decoys. This enables the interceptor to be launched against a cluster of objects and subsequently identify and intercept the targeted reentry vehicle. The seeker will be able to discriminate penetration aids and warheads, though it would require assistance from ground-based radar systems or space-based sensors to address more complex and sophisticated targets. The EKV would receive one or more in-flight target updates from other ground and space-based sensors in order to enhance the probability of intercepting the target. Based on this data and its own sensors, the kill vehicle uses small on-board rockets to maneuver so as to collide with the target.[34]

In a previous concept, an initial architecture for defense of all 50 United States, known as "Capability 1" (C1), would have included deployment of 20 interceptors in the middle of Alaska.[35] An additional 80 interceptors could be added (100 interceptors total) to form a "Capability 2" (C-2) architecture.[36] An even more advanced architecture (C-3) would have added and spread interceptors between two or more sites.[37] Today, however, this growth plan is under review. The ultimate scope or architecture of a U.S. missile defense system has yet to be determined and will be based on the existing or projected threat at the time a decision is made.

Sea-Based Mid-Course. The Sea-Based Mid-Course missile defense system builds upon the Navy Theater Wide (NTW) program and the cancelled Navy Area Defense program. Sea-Based Mid-Course will use a hit-to-kill interceptor—the SM-3 Light Exo-Atmospheric Projectile—

instead of the proximity fused SM-2 Block IVA that was developed for the Navy Area Defense system until that program was cancelled in December 2001. The Sea-Based Mid-Course missile defense program is unique in that Aegis destroyers equipped with the SM-3 missile can patrol a large area to intercept ballistic missiles without the need to be collocated with the defended asset. The ships can be positioned forward of the defended area allowing for exoatmospheric mid-course or even ascent phase engagements after the missile departs the atmosphere. In doing so, a single Sea-Based Mid-Course platform can defend an area or footprint that is tens of thousands of square kilometers. Like the THAAD system and the GBI, the SM-3 interceptor is a hit-to-kill system that uses an infrared seeker and miniature thrusters. Due to speed limitations (4-5 km/sec), the SM-3 is intended to counter primarily medium range ballistic missiles. An initial NTW capability should be available by the 2005-2010 timeframe.[38]

Lower Tier.

Lower tier missile defense systems intercept ballistic missiles in the terminal phase of flight, within the atmosphere at an altitude below 100 kilometers, during the last 1 or 2 minutes of flight, depending upon the range of the missile. The warhead, along with any decoys or chaff, reenters the atmosphere. Aerodynamic drag then produces different behavior for light as opposed to heavy objects. Decoys decelerate significantly and may burn up, but the warhead does neither. Thus at reentry the defense can discriminate the warhead. At least two lower tier systems are intended to counter short range threats during the terminal stage of flight: 1) THAAD; and 2) the PAC-3 missile.[39]

THAAD. The THAAD system will be able to engage longer range theater ballistic missile threats (i.e., less than 3,500 kilometers) during the upper terminal phases of flight. As an essential component of a family of systems, THAAD can reduce the number of missiles that other terminal defense systems must engage. Using hit-to-kill technology to destroy its target, THAAD can operate autonomously, but is required to be interoperable with other lower tier defenses and external sensors. An important feature of the THAAD weapon system is its shoot-look-shoot capability. Kill assessment will determine if a warhead is destroyed, and, if necessary, a second interceptor should be launched. The THAAD system uses a mobile X-band ground based radar with a detection range of up to 1,000 kilometers. The interceptor uses a staring infrared seeker assembly, including an indium-antimonide focal plane array; cryogenic cooler assembly; signal processing electronics; and an electro-optical telescope. THAAD will operate in the upper tier to 150 km and in the intermediate tier down to around 40 km.[40] Chinese sources estimate the THAAD probability of kill against a 3,500-kilometer ballistic missile using a single interceptor at 85 percent, and 97.7 percent if two interceptors are used.[41]

The ultimate plan is to equip two THAAD battalions to support two major regional conflicts. Each THAAD battalion includes four subordinate fire units each with a Battle Management Command, Control, Communications, and Intelligence (BMC3I) element, one radar, nine launchers and 144 missiles. Design parameters call for each THAAD system to be transportable by land, rail or road, sea and air (by C-141 or larger aircraft).[42] The May 1999 *DoD Report to Congress on TMD Architecture Options in the Asia-Pacific Region* notes that only one THAAD fire unit would be needed to provide complete coverage of Taiwan.

PATRIOT Advanced Capability 3 (PAC-3). The missile defense system slated for nearest term deployment is the PAC-3 missile. Scheduled for introduction before the end of 2001, many in the Asia-Pacific region, including Taiwan, are expected to procure the PAC-3 missile over the next several years.[43] Taiwan currently is equipped with PAC-3 ground systems (radar, trucks, command and control) and the Guidance Enhanced Missile (GEM), which has some missile defense capability.[44] Procurement of the PAC-3 missile will complete the PAC-3 Growth Plan that began with the initial deployment of PAC-3 ground equipment in 1997. One prominent Taiwan journal, *Defense Technology*, posits that Taiwan eventually may procure enough PAC-3 missiles and additional PAC-3 ground equipment to outfit between nine to 12 fire units.[45] The PAC-3 is a much more capable derivative of the GEM system in terms of both coverage and lethality. The PAC-3 has a new interceptor missile with a different kill mechanism—rather than having an exploding warhead, it is a hit-to-kill system. The PAC-3 missile is an evolutionary outgrowth of the Extended Range Interceptor (ERINT). The canister is the same size as a GEM canister, but contains four missiles and tubes instead of a single round. Selected Patriot launching stations will be modified to accept PAC-3 canisters. Each launcher may be loaded with four GEM rounds or 16 PAC-3 missile rounds if the launchers are modified to accommodate the PAC-3 missile.[46]

PLA affiliated sources assert the PATRIOT GEM (PAC-2+) will only be able to intercept 10-20 percent of incoming missiles. Taiwan sources claim that two GEM interceptors will have an 80 percent success rate against PLA short range ballistic missiles.[47] With the PATRIOTs only deployed around Taipei, other critical targets around the island are unprotected. There are indications, however, that the military intends to provide some coverage for Taichung and Kaohsiung.[48]

Command, Control, Communications and Intelligence.

Missile defense systems are reliant upon a steady stream of space- and ground-based command, control, communications, and intelligence systems. Current and future sensors include: (1) Defense Support Program satellites; (2) Space-Based Infrared System-High; (3) Space-Based Infrared System-Low; (4) Upgraded Early Warning Radars; and (5) X-Band Radars.

Defense Support Program Satellites. The U.S. existing missile defenses rely on Defense Support Program (DSP) satellites and 1970s vintage radar systems for early warning purposes. The U.S. DSP satellites can detect a launch 50-60 seconds after launch and then relay warning information about 90 seconds after launch. In clear weather, these satellites can detect a missile launch within 10 seconds of launch. Cueing a ground based radar from space based sensor data can greatly reduce the airspace that must be searched to find the theater missiles. Such data can cue ballistic missile defense assets to search a specific area, allowing radar acquisition at the maximum range.[49]

Space Based Infrared System-High (SBIRS-High). The SBIRS-High satellites will begin to augment the DSP satellites as early as 2002. The first SBIRS-High will be placed into a highly elliptical orbit for coverage of polar regions. Of the seven satellites being procured, four will be placed into geosynchronous orbit above the equator and the other two will be in the highly elliptical orbits. SBIRS-High offers numerous advantages over the DSP system. It will have a revisit rate of once every few seconds thus enabling establishment of a track on the missile flight based on more numerous plots of the missile's location. The SBIRS system will have a larger focal plane array, providing a launch point prediction of less than one kilometer. The system also will provide continuous coverage of the polar regions. SBIRS-High will have a "stare" capability that will allow them to continuously observe a designated sector of the earth. This technology can be particularly useful in countering fast burn boosters that limit the time available to determine the missile's flight path.[50]

Space-Based Infrared System-Low (SBIRS-Low). An outgrowth of the SDI, SBIRS-Low will provide precise mid-course missile tracking and target discrimination. The

124

SBIRS-Low program is a low earth orbit satellite constellation that could observe the deployment of reentry vehicles and penetration aids immediately following burnout of the booster. Projected for initial deployment during the latter part of the decade, 24 SBIRS-Low satellites, operating in a low earth orbit of about 1000 kilometers, will be equipped with two independent sensors. First is an optical system that can track the booster and reentry vehicle throughout all phases of flight. The second are infrared sensors that can detect heat signatures in various portions of the frequency spectrum—shortwave infrared that can detect targets in the boost phase; and medium and long wave infrared that are able to detect reentry vehicles in the mid-course phase of flight. Once a target is acquired, information on the target will be forwarded to a telescope that would be able to track the missile after booster burnout.[51]

Because penetration aids deploy differently than reentry vehicles, it is easier to identify those objects that must be attacked if the deployment is observed. SBIRS-Low will also be able to provide missile defense operators with sufficient tracking data to enable interceptors to be launched soon after booster burn-out and well before the early warning radar detects the incoming reentry vehicles. SBIRS-Low offers first generation processing capabilities to interpret a target object map that was derived from another infrared sensor rather than a radar.[52]

SBIRS-Low is considered to be a critical factor in any future decision to adapt the AEGIS-based mid-course interceptors for use against longer range ICBMs. AEGIS radar—the SPY-1D—has limitations that prohibit it from being used in an autonomous mode. For example, its range is limited to approximately 500 kilometers, depending on the size of the target and the frequency at which it operates (S-Band: 2-4 GHZ). The SPY-1D does not provide as much resolution as the X-Band radar system. AEGIS requires some type of external cueing to engage an ICBM in mid-course.[53]

Upgraded Early Warning Radars. The current U.S. early warning network relies on ultra-high frequency (UHF) radars (430 MHz range), as well as one L-Band radar based in Shemya, Alaska. These systems were designed to provide warning of an incoming attack, permitting sufficient time to launch our bomber force and facilitate movement of key government officials. They were not designed to supply fire control quality data of sufficient precision to guide interceptors and discriminate individual objects within an incoming target array.[54] However, the United States intends to upgrade existing radars in order to provide more precise and timely data that can be used to anticipate a future intercept area. This will allow an interceptor to be launched and begin its flight—the earlier the fly out, the larger the defended area or footprint. These Upgraded Early Warning Radars (UEWRs) would be able to discriminate between dozens or hundreds of objects that could be in a target cluster and eliminate objects that do not fit the characteristics of a reentry vehicle.[55]

X-Band Radars. While UEWR systems will provide a greater degree of accuracy, they still will not be able to provide the detailed data needed to discriminate the right objects in a target array that must be destroyed in flight. The degree of precision requires a radar that operates in the X-Band (8-12 GHz). X-Band radar systems provide a detailed "picture" of the target array, including calculating the amount of nose wobble motion that would be characteristic of a reentry vehicle, measuring the diameter and length of objects within the target array, as well as the spin rate, velocity, and position of objects.[56] Because X-Band radar systems will operate within a fairly broad bandwidth, they are considered difficult to jam.[57]

One concept is for one X-Band radar to be deployed to Alaska. However, a single radar based at this location likely will not be able to provide radar coverage of all potential threats to the United States. Additional radar systems would be needed. X-Band radar systems should be able to detect an incoming target array at a range of about 4,000 kilometers, although discrimination will not be possible until the target array is at a distance of around 2000 kilometers.

CHINESE RESPONSES

From Beijing's perspective, U.S. ballistic missile defense programs threaten to undercut the political and military utility of the PRC's growing inventory of strategic and conventional ballistic missiles. The PRC places a premium on ensuring its ballistic missile force would be able to penetrate any future missile defense architecture. Defense industry analysts are examining a range of sophisticated missile defense countermeasures in order to reduce the effectiveness of active missile defense systems. PRC collection of information that would support development of effective missile defense countermeasures has a relatively high priority. With a limited force consisting of only a couple dozen ICBMs, Chinese analysts believe that even a limited American missile defense system with 20 interceptors (i.e., the previous "C1" architecture) could reduce or negate China's minimal nuclear deterrent. PRC military planners have been contemplating a worst-case scenario in which the U.S. could launch a first-strike destroying most of the Chinese ICBMs on the ground because these missiles require several hours to fuel, arm, and launch. In the aftermath, a limited U.S. missile defense system could engage the remnants of China's second-strike missile force.[58]

Background

Beijing's interest in countering ballistic missile defenses dates back to the 1960s. In response to U.S. missile defense programs in the 1960s, Beijing began to examine means to ensure the viability of its incipient missile force, and, at the same time, develop the basic technologies that would be needed to field an indigenous strategic missile defense system. This effort, known as the 640 Program, was cancelled in the 1970s.[59]

Interest in missile defense countermeasures reemerged in the wake of President Ronald Reagan's March 1983 SDI. The Chinese Ministry of Foreign Affairs drafted an initial study to assess the implications of SDI in 1984. In late 1984 or early 1985, the central leadership tasked several ministries and research institutes to develop a detailed examination of the SDI and its implications for China. During 1985, the defense industrial complex sponsored a series of conferences on SDI, and a consensus was developed that Soviet and U.S. development of ballistic missile defense systems had significant implications for China's nuclear deterrent. By 1986, Chinese experts generally agreed there were three potential responses: expansion of offensive forces; development of technical countermeasures, such as hardening and spinning of ballistic missiles, to penetrate missile defense systems; and deployment of anti-satellite (ASAT) weapons to destroy space-based systems.[60]

The Commission of Science, Technology, and Industry for National Defense (COSTIND) played a key role in formulating Beijing's response to the "global technical revolution" prompted by the U.S. missile defense initiative. In September 1984, COSTIND delivered a proposal to the Central Military Commission (CMC) suggesting that relevant PLA branches develop defense science and technology gameplans out to the year 2000. Working in conjunction with the State Council, COSTIND formulated a defense technology strategy that focused on key technologies and presented it at a November 1985 meeting with the CMC leadership. Afterwards, in February 1986, COSTIND, with CMC support, commissioned a long term development program that included the formation of 18 study groups to focus on designated critical technologies.[61]

However, some within the defense S&T community believed COSTIND's plan was not sufficient to meet the technical challenges posed by U.S. missile defense programs. In March 1986, four of China's most prominent defense engineers presented a petition to the Central Committee calling for establishment of a "High Technology Research and Development Plan Outline." The plan, referred to as the 863 Program, was implemented in parallel to COSTIND's Long Range Plan to Year 2000 and was jointly managed by COSTIND and the State Science and Technology Commission. The 863 program, still a guide and funding source for numerous preliminary R&D projects, focuses on some of the same technologies included in the SDI and Europe's answer to SDI, the Eureka program, including space systems, high powered lasers, microelectronics, and automated control systems.[62]

Technical.

With studies and research conducted in the 1980s providing the foundation, Beijing has embarked upon a far-reaching and multi-faceted program to ensure the viability of its ballistic missile force. These programs include technical countermeasures, an expansion of its missile force, as well as asymmetrical measures, such as anti-satellite operations. The PRC is investing significant resources into countering missile defense through the development of technical penetration aids. Contemporary Chinese literature on technical countermeasures is focused on "two categories and eight major penetration technologies" (*liang dalei, ba datufang jishu*): These include countersurveillance (electronic countermeasures, stealth, decoys, and fast burn motors) and counterintercept (multiple warheads, maneuvering reentry vehicles, hardening, and saturation).

Countersurveillance. One technical strategy is focused on denying U.S. sensors the ability to properly detect and discriminate ballistic missiles and their payloads. Chinese research and development into countersurveillance (*fanzhencha*) systems is centered on four areas: 1) electronic countermeasures; 2) stealth; 3) decoys; and 4) fast burn motors.

1. Electronic Countermeasures. From China's perspective, passive and active electronic countermeasures are a fundamental yet effective means of ensuring ballistic missiles are able to reach their targets. Chinese literature cites use of passive electronic countermeasures, such as chaff, to confuse enemy radar systems, such as the X-Band and UEWR systems. Chinese testing has demonstrated that ballistic missiles can carry a significant amount of chaff that can affect a large volume of space. Development is focused in part on production of metallic strips that are 1.5 centimeters in length that can target radar systems that operate at 10 GHz (i.e., X-band radars).[63]

Research also is underway on radio frequency and infrared countermeasures. CASC has conducted tests on active jammers that can broadcast a signal designed to interfere with a radar's ability to detect the target object or corrupt the signal in such a way as to cause the radar to receive a false echo.[64] National University of Defense Technology analysts have examined electronic countermeasure packages on board theater ballistic missiles as a means to counter millimeter wave amplifiers used on the PAC-3 missile and infrared seekers on GBI, THAAD, and Sea-Based Mid-Course interceptors.[65] The PRC also is investing significantly into ground and air based jammers that could effect radar systems supporting missile defenses deployed around its periphery.[66]

2. Stealth. In addition to active and passive electronic countermeasures, PRC engineers are working to reduce the ability of early warning and tracking radar systems to detect ballistic missiles in the mid-course and terminal phase of their flight. The intent is to decrease available reaction time and thus reduce the probability of kill and footprint of missile defense systems. One of the most effective and readily implemented countermeasures is to reduce the radar cross section (RCS) of the reentry vehicle.

CASC designers already have taken simple steps, such as shaping their reentry vehicles by bringing the nose to a sharp point and rounding the back edges. The DF-11 and the DF-15 have shaped warheads that separate from the remainder of the missile body. Chinese researchers also have experimented with complex reentry vehicle surfaces that use radar absorbent materials that can counter X-band radar systems used by THAAD and the GBI. Engineers have taken note of an advanced Russian stealth technology, a plasma (*denglizi*) coating that does not affect flight dynamics and can significantly reduce the ability of radar systems to detect the reentry vehicle.[67]

PRC missile engineers also are lowering the infrared signature of their reentry vehicles. Engineers have analyzed in detail the types of infrared focal plane arrays that are intended for use on the land- and sea-based mid-course systems and THAAD.[68] Experiments have been conducted using "cold screen" (*lengpeng*) technology that thermally shrouds the reentry vehicle. An aluminum alloy is used to encase the warhead and liquid nitrogen is placed in between the aluminum shell and the warhead. In one experiment, engineers noted that systems, such as the Land- and Sea-Based Mid-Course and THAAD, normally could acquire a reentry vehicle with a five micron infrared signature at a range of 3,000 kilometers. Equipped with the cold screen, detection range of the reentry vehicle would be reduced to three meters.[69]

3. Decoys. Chinese engineers note two basic decoy (*you'er*) measures: 1) saturation; and 2) deception. Saturation (*baohe*) measures include the use of metallic balloons or other objects that simulate the reentry vehicle in the mid-course or terminal phase of flight. Engineers highlight the relative ease of this technology as well as its low cost. In 1995 and 1996, the Chinese allegedly tested DF-21 endo-atmospheric decoys.[70] Deception measures under evaluation include electronic decoys or transponder jammers that transmit a radar return similar to that of the true reentry vehicle.[71]

4. Fast-Burn Motors. Chinese engineers have demonstrated concern over potential deployment of U.S. airborne and space-based lasers. Another method under consideration as an explicit countermeasure to boost phase interceptors is a fast burn booster (*suran zhutui*) for China's next generation of solid fueled strategic ballistic missiles. Chinese engineers caution designers about potential quality control problems related to stage separation and accuracy, and suggest this technology should be divided into three stages based on the pace of foreign missile defense developments.[72]

Boost Phase Maneuvering. One other countermeasure that Chinese observers have noted is a boost phase maneuver designed to fool U.S. DSP satellites. By changing directions during the ascent phase of flight, the ballistic missile can complicate the defense's efforts to predict its flight trajectory. While no hard evidence exists that the Chinese have an active program to develop a boost phase maneuver, there is potential for cooperation between Russia and PRC missile engineers on technology used on the Russian Topol-M program (SS-27).[73]

Counterintercept (fanlanzai).

The second major category of countermeasures seeks to deny missile defense interceptors the ability to properly engage their targets. These include: (1) multiple warheads, (2) maneuvering reentry vehicles, and (3) hardening/spinning of ballistic missiles.

1. Multiple Warheads. China has had the capability to develop and deploy a multiple reentry vehicle system for many years, including a MIRV system. As of January 1996, CALT was in the midst of developing multiple warhead payloads, each with its own guidance system and maneuvering capability.[74] Research and development on multiple independent reentry vehicles (MIRVs) was initiated as early as 1970. Technical difficulties, however, stalled the program. CALT renewed research and

development in 1983, shortly after the SDI announcement in March 1983. The DF-5A, able to strike targets throughout the United States, was the designated recipient of the MIRVs, although there is no evidence to date that they have been deployed. The U.S. intelligence community assesses that China could develop a multiple RV system for the DF-5 ICBM in a few years. Chinese pursuit of a multiple RV capability for its *mobile* ICBMs and SLBMs would encounter significant technical hurdles and would be costly.[75]

Critical to this effort is the miniaturization of warheads, a possible objective of tests at Lop Nur over the last few years.[76] According to Chinese missile designers, real and decoy warheads can be mixed using multiple warhead technology. Real warheads can be coated with radar absorbing materials in order to weaken radar returns and reduce the ability of interceptors to discriminate real from decoy warheads.[77]

2. Maneuvering Reentry Vehicles. CALT also is developing maneuverable reentry vehicles in order to complicate missile defense tracking. Missile designers believe maneuvering is not only a means to complicate ballistic missile defenses, but is essential for terminal guidance packages. While vehicles can maneuver at any time during flight, Chinese engineers see most utility in programming a reentry vehicle to maneuver in its terminal phase, 20-30 seconds before striking its target. A reentry vehicle traveling a notional range of 10,000 kilometers has the ability to maneuver within a lateral range of 556-900 kilometers. Another maneuvering option discussed is to send the warhead up to a higher altitude after separation from the missile, slowly descending in a glide for a very long distance, and then finally dive toward the target. Missile designers have demonstrated a special interest in the speed control maneuver used in the 1,800-kilometer range Pershing-II.[78] Chinese engineers are addressing problems associated with maintaining accuracy after exoatmospheric maneuvering.[79] Through modeling and simulation, CASC

has determined that maneuvering is a viable means to reduce land-based lower tier missile defense systems' probability of kill.[80] China allegedly acquired PATRIOT technology to calibrate an auxiliary propulsion system on the DF-15 reentry vehicle to enable the payload to outmaneuver a PATRIOT system as it reenters the atmosphere.[81] After computer simulations and modeling exercises, CALT is confident that its maneuverable theater ballistic missile reentry vehicles can defeat opposing PATRIOT systems.[82]

3. Hardening. Looking ahead to the potential deployment of boost phase intercept systems, such as the airborne laser (ABL), CASC analysts are examining ballistic missile spinning and hardening. Spinning their ballistic missiles is intended to prevent concentration of a high powered laser on a single spot.[83] Chinese engineers are developing a coating for ballistic missiles that could complicate use of high power lasers. Using their own indigenously developed high powered lasers, Chinese institutes have tested various coating materials to protect the outer shell of ballistic missiles, a process known as laser cladding (*jiguang rongfu*). Laser cladding, together with the spinning of theater ballistic missiles, may not make ballistic missiles immune to boost phase missile defense systems but could increase required lasing time, thus reducing the number of laser shots available per ABL mission.[84]

OTHER.

In addition to the techniques described above, a range of other technical and operational countermeasures also are under consideration. These include: (1) trajectory techniques, (2) longer range development of non-nuclear electromagnetic pulse warheads, (3) indigenous missile defense development, (4) anti-satellite (ASAT) development, and (5) multi-axis strikes.

1. Trajectory Techniques. The type of trajectory Second Artillery engineers select can affect the ability to penetrate

missile defense systems. Types of trajectories include: (1) fractional orbital bombardment system, (2) depressed trajectories, and (3) lofted trajectories. China conducted a feasibility study on a fractional orbital bombardment system (FOBS) in 1966. This system launches a missile into very low orbit, approximately 160 kilometers above earth. Before completion of the first orbit, a retro-rocket reduces the speed of the warhead, which hits the target with only a few minutes warning. Chinese engineers explored the potential of launching a missile to a predesignated point over Antarctica as a means to penetrate the weakest point in the U.S. warning network.[85] Still viewing a FOBS as an alternative, Chinese designers continue feasibility studies on fractional orbiting missiles (*bufen guidao daodan*).[86]

Chinese analysts view depressed trajectories (*yadi guidao*) as another option to counter space-based and mid-course missile defense systems. Chinese engineers note that ICBMs often reach altitudes of 2,000 kilometers on a normal trajectory. However, launching a missile at a depressed trajectory could allow the missile to achieve only a 100 kilometer altitude, complicating the ability of some space-based systems to engage the ballistic missile. Testing and modeling has been done on the DF-3, which normally has a range of 2,780km and an altitude of 550km when flying a nominal trajectory. With depressed trajectory, the DF-3 travels 1,550km at 100km altitude.[87]

Lofted trajectories (*tagao dandao*) are another option that Chinese missileers may consider. A longer range ballistic missile does not necessarily mean the missile will be used at its maximum effective range. A longer range system, fired on a lofted trajectory, can also serve as a technical countermeasure to missile defenses. Lofted trajectories can increase reentry speed, thereby complicating intercept solutions for terminal defense systems or reducing the footprint or defended area.[88]

2. EMP warheads. PRC engineers also are conducting feasibility studies on electromagnetic pulse weapons (EMP)

to overcome defenses. EMP systems, such as a high powered microwave (HPM) warhead, could negate space or ground-based sensors that support a missile defense architecture. PLA writings indicate that fielding of an EMP warhead is a relatively high priority. HPM devices in particular are viewed as a "natural enemy" of more technologically advanced militaries and an "electronic trump card" (*dianzi shashou*).[89] Due to challenges related to weaponizing a device with enough power, a first generation Chinese HPM warhead likely would only be effective against radiating targets within the immediate area of impact. Radar systems and communications centers would be the prime candidates. As the technology progresses, however, HPM warheads could achieve wider effects.[90] The developers of the DF-11 SRBM—the 066 Base—have demonstrated the most interest in HPM warheads.[91]

In addition to non-nuclear EMP weapons, Taiwan observers are concerned about the potential use of high altitude EMP (HEMP) bursts that use an actual nuclear device. Such a device, detonated at an altitude of 40 kilometers, would avoid casualties on the ground, yet would have significant effects on the island's electronic systems. The solution, according to Taiwan analysts, are missile defenses, such as the Sea-Based Mid-Course, that can engage the ballistic missile in its ascent phase and before detonation.[92]

3. Missile Defense. Beijing has an indigenous missile defense development program intended to ensure that at least a portion of its inventory could survive a first strike. China's research on missile defenses dates back to the 1960s. Under the 640 Program, the space and missile industry's Second Academy, traditionally responsible for SAM development, set out to field a missile defense system, consisting of a kinetic kill vehicle, high powered laser, space early warning, and target discrimination system components. While this program was abandoned in 1980, engineers associated with this effort are still active.

Preliminary research on missile defenses was resumed in the 1980s, at least partly funded under the 863 Program.[93]

The CASC Second Academy and the Shanghai Academy of Spaceflight Technology are playing a leading role in missile defense research. Western reporting and Chinese technical journals indicate that the Central Military Commission has approved funding for a 10-year developmental program for a missile defense system, to include satellites for missile launch warning. The PLA Air Force and CASC advocate a 15-year, three-phase approach to missile defense. The first step is to field a "Patriot-like" system, such as the HQ-9, followed by research and development on an extended range interceptor modeled on the PAC-3 missile; and basic conceptual research on a THAAD-like mid-course intercept system.[94]

Chinese engineers are focused on development of infrared and radio-frequency seekers that could engage both medium and short-range ballistic missiles. Engineers are developing short and medium wave infrared band (3-12 microns) focal plane arrays that would be able to engage reentry vehicles during the mid-course phase of their flight path.[95] In addition to infrared seekers that could be used to counter medium and short range ballistic missiles, the PRC has stepped up research into millimeter wave (Ka-band) amplifiers similar to those used on the PAC-3 missile. In fact, a special state laboratory on millimeter wave research was established in Nanjing to help achieve technological breakthroughs.[96] One conceptual design for a lower tier missile defense interceptor adopts an integrated millimeter wave and infrared seeker assembly.[97]

There also are indications that Chinese aerospace engineers are examining the feasibility of space-based early warning. Technical writings indicate the space industry is working to master specific technologies associated with missile early warning satellites. The Second Artillery has conducted modeling and simulation of alternative early warning architectures.[98] China has a well-established technology base in infrared sensors, which, when placed on satellites, can detect a missile almost immediately after launch by detecting the infrared radiation from its engine or motor plume.[99] In a potentially related program, the China Academy of Space Technology is developing a satellite bus for an infrared telescope, which, according to design outlines, will be placed in a geosychronous orbit shortly after the turn of the century.[100]

4. Counterspace. Negating U.S. space systems is another approach to countering missile defenses. Chinese research and development on anti-satellite technologies has been underway since the 1960s. Technical literature suggests that a direct ascent ASAT program is underway involving an assessment of various design proposals for seekers and propulsion systems. As part of a missile defense countermeasure program, ASAT operations would be directed against satellites in low earth orbit, such as the SBIRS-Low system or against the SBIRS-High satellites in highly elliptical orbits. Technical papers demonstrate some of the greatest obstacles in developing an active counterspace capability are with development of a kill vehicle and associated terminal guidance. Modeling has been carried out on infrared, radar, and impulse radar terminal guidance systems.[101] Harbin Institute of Technology and Beijing University of Astronautics and Aeronautics, for example, have carried out modeling and simulation of various space intercept control and terminal guidance systems. One concept introduces several small solid motors for orbital control stabilization.[102] There also have been unconfirmed reports that the China Academy of Space Technology (CAST) is developing nanometer-sized "parasitic satellites" that could function in an ASAT mode.[103]

Engineers have conducted studies to counter satellite decoys as well.[104] The PRC has stepped up its efforts to distinguish decoys from real satellites. One study, carried out by the National University of Defense Technology, determined that this problem could be solved through use of

138

at least three ground stations using infrared sensors and neural networks.[105] China's existing space tracking network can detect and track most satellites with sufficient accuracy for targeting purposes.[106]

China's desire to field a direct ascent ASAT asset may be affiliated with a program intended to support the launch of small satellite constellations. A small solid fueled launch vehicle, most likely a derivative of the DF-21, will be able to place small payloads in orbit at a time and place of Beijing's choosing. China intends to field these mobile, solid fueled launch vehicles by 2005. Reduced size and complexity allows for faster manufacturing time and production in significant numbers.[107] Chinese engineers are conducting conceptual studies on a space based satellite tracking system that would serve as a potentially important component of any ASAT system.[108]

Beijing also is investing in the development of high powered lasers that, under certain conditions, could affect optical components of satellite systems, such SBIRS-Low. The 1998 Report to Congress on PRC Military Capabilities (pursuant to Section 1226 of the FY98 National Defense Authorization Act) states "China already may possess the capability to damage, under specific conditions, optical sensors on satellites that are very vulnerable to damage by lasers. However, given China's current interest in laser technology, it is reasonable to assume that Beijing would develop a weapon that could destroy satellites in the future."[109]

5. Multi-Axis Strikes. In addition to technical countermeasures, the PLA is examining operational methodologies intended to penetrate U.S., allied, or friendly missile defense systems. The Second Artillery and China's space and missile industry have conducted modeling and simulation to test China's ability to break through the wide range of projected U.S. missile defense deployments. Modeling has been carried out that involves various

combinations of surface-to-surface, air-to-surface, sea-to-surface, air-to-air and naval air defense missile systems.[110]

Among the most important are synchronized, multi-axis strikes as a fundamental principle of Second Artillery conventional doctrine (*duodian, duofangxiang, tongshi tuji*). Associated are deception and timing measures that could ensure penetration of at least a large portion of a salvo. These involve coordinated launches from different launch azimuths and use of infrared "disruption" to confuse DSP satellites and complicate enemy attack operations. Another methodology includes closely spaced salvos that could take advantage of reload time. Launches from different azimuths, combined with use of infrared radiation "disruption," could confuse enemy satellite early warning systems and complicate enemy attack operations. Another concept involves the use of two strike waves, the first "screening" the second exhausting missile defenses, before they have time to reload.[111]

Anti-Radiation Missile Development. An asymmetrical approach to countering missile defenses includes attacking critical nodes within the missile defense system, particularly radar systems. The PRC is acquiring and/or developing an anti-radiation missile (ARM), such as the Russian Kh-31P, that is intended to negate early warning and fire control radar systems that are able to detect and/or track ballistic missiles during various phases of flight.[112] There are persistent rumors of PLA procurement or joint production arrangement on the Kh-31P, which Chinese engineers note was specifically developed to counter the PATRIOT's MPQ-53 radar, and AEGIS SPY-1D phased array radar. China's defense industrial complex, specifically the Third Academy with support from the Harbin Institute of Technology, is aggressively pursuing deployment of a long range anti-radiation missile.[113]

Foreign Cooperation on Missile Defense Countermeasures.

There are indications of Russian Space Agency assistance in Chinese development of ballistic missile defense countermeasures, perhaps dating back to the mid-1990s or earlier. Cooperation between China and Russia in the field of space and missiles was formalized into a series of agreements between CASC and the Russian space agencies when representatives from Chinese and Soviet space industries signed an initial agreement in Moscow in May 1990 on 10 cooperative projects.[114] The relationship was solidified when CASC and the Russian Space Agency signed an official protocol for the sharing of space technology in 1992. This agreement was raised again as a deliverable during President Yeltsin's visit to Beijing, but only after the two countries signed a no-first-use pledge. A follow-on agreement was signed by Chinese and Russian space officials. The agreement included ten areas of cooperation, including satellite navigation, space surveillance, propulsion, satellite communications, joint design efforts, materials, intelligence sharing, scientific personnel exchanges, and space systems testing. Chinese sources indicate cooperation also included countering U.S. missile defense programs.[115]

CONCLUSIONS

The United States has expressed its intent to develop defenses capable of defending against limited missile attacks from a rogue state or from an accidental or unauthorized launch. U.S. missile defense engineers are developing layered defenses, capable of intercepting missiles of any range at every stage of flight: boost, mid-course, and terminal. Layered defenses would permit reductions in nuclear forces, thus contributing to strategic stability. These defenses will be introduced incrementally, deploying capabilities as the technology matures and then adding new capabilities over time.

Since research on missile defenses began in the 1980s, Beijing has been concerned about the potential undermining of their limited nuclear deterrence, and, more recently, their ability to deter and coerce neighbors such as Taiwan. To ensure the viability of its nuclear deterrent and for its expanding inventory of conventional SRBMs and MRBMs, Beijing has implemented numerous measures to counter U.S. missile defense programs. These measures are targeted against sensors that support missile defenses and against missile defense interceptors themselves. Other initiatives include ASAT development as well as an indigenous missile defense program that could ensure some modicum of assured retaliation. A number of conclusions can be drawn from the range of measures underway to undermine U.S. missile defense programs.

China's Countermeasure Challenge.

Chinese research and development of missile defense countermeasures is extensive and appears relatively sophisticated. However, countermeasures introduce an added element of complexity into an already complex system. Despite significant investment, PRC countermeasures on longer-range ballistic missiles are unlikely to keep pace with U.S. technology. With more than 30 years experience, the United States is the world's leader in countermeasure technology. Such expertise naturally is integrated into countering penetration aids. Chinese engineers will face challenges as they attempt to put into practice many of the concepts described above. Countermeasures can be time consuming, and can reduce available space and weight. As a result, penetration aids could lower performance (i.e. range and accuracy) or force a reduction in payload (i.e. a trade off between a decoy or a MIRV).

Simple countermeasures, such as chaff and employment of a limited number of decoys, likely already have been incorporated into some missiles, such as the DF-21 MRBM.

Integration of more sophisticated countermeasures, however, such as balloon decoys, fast burn motors, and boost phase maneuvering are likely to be many years away. Russian technical assistance may hasten their timeline. Regardless, as new countermeasures come on line over the next 10 years, the United States should be able to keep pace, particularly given the general requirement for CALT missile designers to conduct flight tests. The layered defense approach is perhaps the most effective means to reduce the effectiveness of missile defense countermeasures.

Nevertheless, the U.S. should hedge against unforeseen breakthroughs in PRC countermeasure technology. China's technological progress, Russian assistance to PRC programs, and Beijing's propensity to provide technical assistance to rogue state missile development all require careful monitoring. Testing of new penetration aids should be easily observed via national technical means.

It should be noted that among the entire range of U.S. missile defense programs, PRC specialists seem most concerned about the deployment of SBIRS-Low satellites. Slated for initial deployment during the latter part of the decade (about the same time as the PRC's new generation of solid-fueled extended range ICBMs are fielded), SBIRS-Low has the potential to undercut an entire category of Chinese countermeasures. Specialists note that the dual surveillance and tracking capability of SBIRS-Low (infrared and electro-optical) would reduce the effectiveness of counter-surveillance measures, such as electronic countermeasures, radar stealth, and thermal shrouds. Therefore, greater emphasis must be placed on counter-intercept measures, and a combination of decoys and thermal shrouds.[116]

Planned Expansion of PRC Ballistic Missile Forces.

The discussion above focuses on technical and asymmetrical countermeasures that the PRC may adopt. To augment sophisticated penetration aids, limited expansion of China's ballistic missile force is to be expected, depending on the scope of the U.S. missile defense architecture. The Second Artillery's arsenal of strategic and conventional ballistic missiles already is expected to grow substantially through the introduction of more sophisticated silo-based ICBMs, such as the DF-5A; mobile systems, such as the DF-31 and the longer range DF-31A; and the JL-2 SLBM. Further expansion, beyond current plans, is to be anticipated. However, the scope likely would be limited due to Beijing's desire to avoid presenting a threatening image to its neighbors and economic partners around the world.[117] If Beijing chooses to expand its nuclear ballistic missile force, the most likely route would be to increase production, beyond current plans, of the DF-31 and its longer range variant.

As discussed above, by 2005, Beijing is expected to have 24 DF-5 ICBMs; 10-20 DF-31 ICBMs that should replace the Second Artillery's approximately a dozen DF-4 ICBMs; and perhaps the same number of JL-2s, assuming the Type 94 submarine is produced according to schedule. At least one additional DF-31 brigade (10-20 missiles) could be fielded by 2010. Initial deployment of the DF-31A could be expected in the 2005-2010 timeframe, with as many as ten DF-31A ICBMs ostensibly being in operation by the end of the decade. With as many as 100 new ICBMs entering the PLA's inventory over the next 10 years, the PRC is in effect more than doubling its arsenal of nuclear ballistic missiles able to range targets throughout the United States. This expansion appears to be taking place independent of U.S. plans to field limited missile defenses.

Upgrading all or a portion of the PRC's DF-5 force structure with MIRVs is another potential response should a CMC decision be made to do so. The specific number of MIRVs per DF-5 can not be determined at this time.[118] Prospects that a layered missile defense system could include a boost-phase intercept capability could dampen any incentive to deploy MIRV's. Boost-phase defenses would destroy the missiles early in flight, when they are most visible and before they can release their warheads.

Missile Defenses and Beijing's Six Specious Arguments.

Since the early 1990s, Beijing's technical and doctrinal responses have been supported by a coordinated foreign policy and propaganda campaign to influence international opinion and shape the debate within the U.S. regarding missile defenses. As its nuclear and conventional ballistic missile inventory grows, Beijing's political leadership has formulated a number of arguments against missile defenses that are based on half-truths and over-simplifications. First, Beijing argues that missile defenses will cause an arms race. In fact, in the conventional military context, arms races generally are caused by one side's rapid buildup in offensive capabilities.[119] One could argue that an accelerated arms race has been underway in the Taiwan Strait since the early 1990s. Undercutting Beijing's overwhelming offensive advantage through viable defenses would enhance cross-Strait stability by raising the costs of using force. Active missile defenses, combined with other approaches, would reduce the perceived utility of ballistic missiles as Beijing's preferred tool of coercion.

Secondly, Beijing asserts that U.S. missile defense programs will violate the Anti-Ballistic Missile (ABM) Treaty. However, at this time, there is no intention to violate the ABM Treaty, which was a bilateral agreement between Moscow and Washington to help manage and stabilize the strategic bilateral relationship. Because the ABM Treaty is an artifact of the Cold War, the treaty needs to be adjusted or eliminated altogether. A dialogue has been initiated with Moscow to ensure that such a move would be made with the consent of both parties.

Beijing also posits a misleading argument that missile defenses will encourage Taiwanese independence sentiment. There are more important factors besides defenses that fan the flames of Taiwanese independence. PRC policies that alienate Taiwan are most relevant. Besides, active missile defenses would not encourage independence sentiment any more than other weapon systems, such as F-16 fighters, PATRIOT Guidance Enhanced Missiles, or PFG-2 frigates. One also could argue that Taiwan's indigenous capacity for defense is only a minor factor influencing public sentiment regarding greater autonomy since, according to some sources, Taiwan's domestic polity is largely uninterested in defense issues.

PRC spokesmen argue that active missile defenses can be used offensively. Much to the contrary, missile defenses are defensive—they threaten no one. If anything, building effective defenses will reduce the value of ballistic missiles, and thus remove incentives for their development and proliferation. One could argue that converting upper tier interceptors to surface-to-surface missiles could enable strikes against targets at long ranges. However, using interceptors in this way is not cost efficient due to payload limitations. It is cheaper and more effective to develop a dedicated ballistic missile than to use a missile defense interceptor.

A corollary to this argument is that missile defenses can shield offensive assets, such as ballistic missiles or strike aircraft. This supposition blurs the distinction between offensive and defensive action—whether or not a system is offensive or defensive depends upon the user's intent, strategy, and doctrine. Beijing also argues that U.S. provision of missile defenses to Taiwan would transfer technologies useful to ballistic missile development. This assertion assumes that Taiwan does not have the indigenous capacity to develop the necessary technology; would be willing to violate Missile Technology Control Regime-related assurances made to the U.S. government; and would take the trouble to reverse engineer propulsion, guidance, or other associated technologies.

Chinese arguments that missile defenses could lead to a militarization of space have some merit. However, since deployment of the first reconnaissance and military communications satellites, space has long been exploited for military purposes. There is a relationship between missile defense and ASAT interceptors. If supported by a robust search, acquisition, and tracking network, upper tier mid-course systems could be used to strike some satellites in low earth orbit. Chinese observers, such as Du Xiangwan from the China Academy of Engineering Physics, have noted that intercepting satellites is easier than engaging reentry vehicles.

Finally, the PRC has argued that provision of active missile defenses to Taiwan would "violate" the Three Communiqués. The Three Communiqués are parallel statements of policy that have little standing in international law. Provision of missile defenses would not "violate" the 1982 Communiqué any more than other weapon systems. As Assistant Secretary of State John Holdridge pointed out in his August 1982 Congressional testimony, the U.S. agreement to reduce arms sales to Taiwan was contingent upon Beijing's peaceful approach to resolving the Taiwan issue, generally characterized by its military posture directed against Taiwan. As Holdridge noted in his testimony, a rise in the military threat to Taiwan theoretically would be accompanied by a rise in U.S. security assistance, in accordance with U.S. domestic law under the Taiwan Relations Act.

Beijing argues that provision of active missile defenses to Taiwan would revive the U.S.-Taiwan defense alliance, undermining the foundation of U.S.-PRC relations as spelled out in the 1979 Communiqué. Such an argument is based on the faulty assumption that a Taiwan missile defense architecture would require some form of operational connectivity with U.S. space-based early warning and command and control systems. While DSP early warning could enhance the effectiveness of missile defenses, systems such as THAAD can operate autonomously against SRBMs. Early warning radar systems can supplant the need for satellite early warning.

Missile Defense in the Taiwan Strait.

As can be seen from these arguments, China's opposition to missile defenses is viewed largely through the cognitive prism of Taiwan. Ballistic missiles are a political and, increasingly, military trump card intended to stem political movement in Taiwan toward greater autonomy. At the same time, China's strategic nuclear force affects cost-benefit calculations of regional players, such as the United States and Japan, as they contemplate intervention. In theory, Washington policymakers would be less likely to intervene if the risks of escalation were high. Beijing has a no-first-use policy, but regional actors can not be assured that Beijing would not use nuclear weapons to retaliate against foreign intervention, particularly if that intervention involved strikes against military targets on the mainland opposite Taiwan.

SRBMs, combined with certain types of countermeasures, present Taiwan's missile defense planners with significant challenges. The potential for large raid sizes; the short flight time of SRBMs (approximately 7 minutes for the 600 kilometer DF-15); and wide range of attack azimuths would stress any missile defense architecture.

Despite these challenges, Taiwan's interest in ballistic missile defenses can be expected to grow with the threat. A modest missile defense architecture could reduce the effectiveness of limited PRC use of ballistic missiles in a coercive air campaign. In addition to land and sea-based lower tier systems, the deployment of conventional MRBMs and extended range SRBMs in significant numbers likely will drive Taiwan's interest in sea-based mid-course missile defense and THAAD.

However, to defend against large-scale raids, exclusive reliance on active missile defenses will be insufficient to offset the overwhelming advantages Beijing holds with its expanding arsenal of ballistic missiles. As a result, Taiwan can be expected to adopt asymmetrical approaches to augment active missile defenses. These include passive defense measures to complicate targeting and enhancing its ability to sustain or reconstitute operations after a first strike. Even more important, Taiwan force planners can be expected to invest in active defense measures, such as suppression of enemy air defenses and interdiction operations that would target critical nodes with a conventional ballistic missile organization.[120]

The PRC is concerned about U.S. plans to deploy a global missile defense architecture. PRC observers understand that the United States, should it so choose, has the ability over the longer term to develop a robust, layered global missile defense architecture that could challenge the viability of China's deterrent. To ensure the viability of its deterrent, Beijing is in the midst of a long-term program to upgrade its strategic nuclear force, in both qualitative and quantitative terms. MIRVing and success in fielding missile defense countermeasures would be factors in the ultimate size of the force. Beijing has the ability to influence the nature and scope of future U.S. missile defense development, as well as the transfer of those systems to allies and friends such as Taiwan. The scope of a future U.S. missile defense architecture has not been determined yet. Positive steps that Beijing could take to moderate development, deployment, and transfer of U.S. missile defenses include a reduction in PLA missile deployments opposite Taiwan and cooperation in limiting the proliferation of weapons of mass destruction and their means of delivery.

ENDNOTES - CHAPTER 5

1. Department of Defense, *Selected Military Capabilities of the People's Republic of China* (Report to Congress Pursuant to Section

1305 of the FY97 National Defense Authorization Act), Washington, DC: U.S. Government Printing Office, 1997, p. 4. The report states that most of these missiles are likely to be short- or medium-range systems.

2. This figure assumes 15-20 ICBMs (between 75 and 100 percent of the PRC's current ICBM force) are directed against U.S. urban areas and able to liquidate a million people per city.

3. A summary of CASC organization is included in Mark A. Stokes, *China's Strategic Modernization: Implications for U.S. National Security*, Carlisle: Strategic Studies Institute, September 1999.

4. See Federation of American Scientists, WMD Around the World, *www.fas.org*; Bill Gertz, *Betrayal*, Washington DC: Regnery Press, p. 250; and U.S. Congress, House of Representatives, *Report of the Select Committee on U.S. National Security and Military/Commercial Concerns With the People's Republic of China* (Cox Report), Vol. I, Chap. 4, 105th Congress, 2nd Session, Washington, DC: U.S. Government Printing Office, 1999. Also see *Foreign Missile Developments and the Ballistic Missile Threat Through 2015*, Unclassified Summary of a National Intelligence Estimate, Director of Central Intelligence, January 2002.

5. Walter Pincus, "China May Add 100 Missiles Over 15 Years," *Washington Post*, May 26, 1999; and "China: Long Range ICBM Could Reach U.S. Mainland," *Flight International*, August 14, 2001.

6. See Federation of American Scientists webpage, *www.fas.org*; Bill Gertz, "Chinese Missile To Threaten U.S. By 2000," *Washington Times*, May 23, 1997.

7. Department of Defense, Proliferation and Response, January 2001, China Section; "China: Long Range ICBM Could Reach U.S. Mainland," *Flight International*, August 14, 2001; "Kongjun yu haihang zhuangbei fazhan" (Air Force and Naval Modernization) in *Zhonggong junshi xiandaihua* (PRC Military Modernization), Taipei: Ziyou Publishing, June 2000; and Shintaro Ishihara, "An Urgent Threat," *The Shield*, Vol. xviii, No. 2, March/April 2001. The relationship between the DF-31A and the DF-41 is unknown. The number of Type 94 submarines that will be built is unknown; one could surmise that two-four hulls (i.e., 32-64 tubes with a like number of JL-2s) is a safe estimate.

8. A series of meetings were held in the aftermath of the accidental bombing of the Chinese Embassy in Belgrade. A total of 15 programs were designated for acceleration. A CASC committee was formed to plan for the accelerated timeline. See "Beiyue zhaxing: wuqi yanzhi jiasu,"

(NATO Bombing: Accelerate Weapons R&D), *Zhongguo Hangtian Bao*, May 12, 1999, p.1. Attending the meetings were retired aerospace advisors, Xia Guohong (CAMEC Director), Zheng Quanbao (First Academy Deputy Party Chairman), Yin Xingliang (Second Academy Deputy Director), Huang Ruisong (Third Academy Deputy Director), Ye Peijian (Fifth Academy Chief Engineer), and Hua Linsen (066 Base Director).

9. The 700-meter CEP is extracted from *Janes Strategic Weapons Systems*, 1998. See Bill Gertz, "New Chinese Missiles Target All of East Asia," *Washington Times*, July 10, 1997. Also see "Dongfeng-21 zhongcheng daodan (DF-21 MRBM), *Shijie junshi luntan* (World Military Forum), January 2000, in Chinese; and Bill Gertz, *The China Threat*, Washington, DC: Regnery Press, 2000, pp. 234-235; and Bill Gertz, *Betrayal*, p. 254.

10. The conversion of the DF-21 from a strictly nuclear mission to a conventional role was reported as early as 1994 in the Chinese journal, *Guoji Hangkong* (International Aviation). Further indications of a terminally guided DF-21 are from discussions between Richard Fisher and an engineer from CALT's Beijing Research Institute of Telemetry (704th Research Institute) at the 1996 Zhuhai Air Show. Extensive CASC technical writings on terminally guided theater ballistic missiles tend to substantiate the engineer's comments. Other sources indicate that the conventional DF-21C program, referred to as the DF-21 Mod 3 by some sources, is influenced in large part by the Pershing-2, entered the applied R&D (*xinghao yanzhi*) phase in 1995, and that the primary payload will be a penetrator warhead (*zuandi dantou*) for use against semi-hardened facilities such as command centers. See Will Young, "Shenmi de zhongguo daodan budui" (The Development of the Chinese Second Artillery), *Shijie junshi luntan* (World Military Forum), internet edition (*www.wforum.com*), January 2000, in Chinese. It is not clear how far engineers have gone in their preliminary research in this type of ballistic missile terminal guidance. For a discussion of terminally guided ballistic missiles, see Gan Chuxiong and Liu Jixiang, *Daodan yu yunzai huojian zongti sheji* (General Design of Missiles and Launch Vehicles), Beijing: Defense Industry Press, January 1996, pp. 68-69. Also see Wang Honglei (Second Artillery Corps), "Optical Image Guidance Technology," in *Zhidao yu Yinxin*, in *Chinese Astronautics and Missilery Abstracts* (hereafter referred to as CAMA), Vol. 2, No. 3, January 1995, pp. 34-37.

11. "Kongjun yu haihang zhuangbei fazhan" (Air Force and Naval Modernization) in *Zhonggong junshi xiandaihua* (PRC Military Modernization), Taipei: Ziyou Publishing, June 2000. One should note,

151

however, that the PAC-3 could engage an incoming MRBM if the missile was targeted directly against the fire unit itself.

12. Use of ballistic missiles in support of a naval blockade and for use against carrier battle groups is a key theme of a recent internal publication on blockade operations. See Hu Wenlong (ed), Lianhe fengsuo zuozhan yanjiu (Study on Joint Blockade Operations), Beijing: National Defense University Press, 1999. A PAC-3 interceptor could, under certain conditions, engage a DF-21C given sufficient early warning and if the missile was targeted directly against the PAC-3 fire unit.

13. Among numerous references on conventional Second Artillery doctrine, see Wang Houying and Zhang Xingye, *Zhanyixue* (*Campaign Studies*), Beijing: National Defense University Press, 2000, pp. 375-385.

14. A brigade consists of at least four battalions, probably with three to four companies each. Each brigade would be equipped with approximately 100 SRBMs. Each company likely is responsible for at least one launcher. If one assumes a notional structure of four battalions per brigade with four companies/launchers each, then a brigade would be able to execute a raid size of at least 16 SRBMs at one time. In a major campaign, seven Second Artillery brigades notionally could achieve a raid size of at least 112 theater missiles. Three salvos would utilize 336 missiles. Remaining theater missiles in the PLA arsenal would likely be kept in reserve for other contingencies and/or to support naval operations and amphibious landings. See Bill Gertz, "China Adds To Missiles Near Taiwan," *Washington Times*, August 28, 2001, p. 1; and Will Young, "Shenmi de zhongguo daodan budui," (The Development of the Chinese Second Artillery), *Shijie junshi luntan* (World Military Forum), internet edition in Chinese (*www.wforum.com*), January 2000.

15. See Tony Walker and Stephen Fidler, "China Builds Up Missile Threat," *Financial Times*, February 10, 1999, pg 1; and "Taiwan Boosts Defenses With Live Fire Test of Patriot System," *AFP*, June 20, 2001.

16. *Lianhe zhanyi di erpaobing zuozhan* (PLA Second Artillery Joint Campaign Operations), unpublished manuscript, 1996, p. 10. The document is believed to be an internal PLA academic paper, but its authenticity has not been established. However, a number of sources have corroborated much of the paper's content. PLA writings indicate that the mission of the Second Artillery's conventional ballistic missile force is deterrence; the second mission is to achieve the "Three Superiorities"—information dominance, air superiority, and maritime superiority.

17. See Wang Jixiang and Chang Lan, "Guowai jidong dandao daodan dimian shengcun nengli yanjiu" (Study on Survivability of Foreign Mobile Ballistic Missiles), in Xu Dazhe, *Guowai dandao daodan jishu yanjiu yu fazhan* (Study and Development of Foreign Ballistic Missile Technology), Beijing: Astronautics Press, October 1998, pp. 96-108. Wang and Chang are from CALT's systems integration department.

18. *Lianhe zhanyi di erpaobing zuozhan*, p. 17.

19. Xu Minfei, Zhu Zili, and Li Yong, "Feasibility of Technologies for Use of Ballistic Missiles to Counter Aircraft Carriers," *Guofang Keji Cankao*, 1997, 18(4), pp.126-130, summarized in CAMA. Also see Feng Jianbao, "Feasibility Study of Conventional Ballistic Missiles Attacking Aircraft Carriers," paper presented at the Annual China Astronautics Society UAV Specialists Conference, April 1998, summarized in CAMA, Vol. 6. No. 1.

20. Wang Guobao, "Initial Discussion on Tactical Ballistic Missile Electronic Warfare," *Hangtian dianzi duikang*, April 97, pp. 1-7, summarized in CAMA. China's interest in millimeter wave (MMW) technology is best exemplified by a Chinese firm's illegal acquisition of a MMW traveling wave tube amplifier in 1996. A special MMW laboratory was established in 1995.

21. See Wang Jixiang and Chang Lan, p. 107. Most vulnerable would be Kadena AB and Yokosuka Naval Base in Japan.

22. Duncan Lennox, ed. *Jane's Strategic Weapon Systems*, Issue 24, May 97, Surrey, England: Jane's Information Group.

23. George Lindsey, *The Information Requirements for Aerospace Defense: Limits Imposed by Geometry and Technology*, Bailrigg Memorandum 27, CDISS, Lancaster University, p. 18. If moved closer to its target, the DF-15 likely would be launched on a lofted trajectory that would increase the flight time outside the atmosphere, thus increasing the missile's vulnerability to upper tier systems. On the other hand, a lofted trajectory could increase the missile's reentry speed, reducing the footprint, or defended area, of lower tier systems such as PATRIOT.

24. Zhao Yunshan, *Zhongguo daodan jiqi zhanlue, jiefangjun de hexin wuqi* (China's Missiles and Strategy: The PLA's Central Weapon), Hong Kong: Mirror Books, p. 232. Other sources credit the DF-15 with only as good as a 150-meter CEP. See "Missiles! China Has Them Too!," *Wen wei po*, June 1, 1999, p. A5, in *Foreign Broadcast Information Service* (hereafter *FBIS*)-*CHI*-00169, June 22, 1999.

25. Brian Hsu, "M-Class Missiles' Bark Worse Than Bite: Military," *Taipei Times*, Augist 16, 2000.

26. Zhao Yunshan, *Zhongguo daodan jiqi zhanlue, jiefangjun de hexin wuqi* (China's Missiles and Strategy: The PLA's Central Weapon), Hong Kong: Mirror Books, p. 232. Informed sources assert the Mirror (*Mingjing*) series of books have a mixed record of reliability. However, development of a longer range version of the DF-15 is also alluded to in Bill Gertz, "China Adds To Missiles Near Taiwan," *Washington Times*, August 28, 2001, p. 1. Zhao states that the expanded range DF-15 incorporates a more advanced propellant. There is often confusing reporting on an unidentified 1000 kilometer system—the M-18—that may in fact be the rumored extended range DF-15.

27. Zhao, p. 234.

28. Department of Defense, *Report to Congress on Theater Missile Defense Architecture Options for the Asia-Pacific Region*, Washington, DC: U.S. Department of Defense, 1999.

29. See Department of Defense, *The Security Situation in the Taiwan Strait* (Report to Congress Pursuant to the FY99 Appropriations Bill), Washington, DC: U.S. Government Printing Office, 1999. Also see Bill Gertz, *The China Threat*, p. 232.

30. Hui Zhong, "Meiguo Kongjun Shishi Jiguang Fandao Jihua" (USAF Implements Laser Missile Defense Plan), *Zhongguo Hangtian* (*China Aerospace*), February 1996, pp. 38-39; and Zhang Yaping, "Jiguang Wuqi de Zuozhan Xiaoneng yu Fazhan Qushi," (Capabilities and Trends in Laser Weapon Development), *Zhongguo Hangtian*, July 1997, pp. 37-40. Presence of longer range surface-to-air missiles could force the ABL to operate further out. As a high value asset, the ABL would require fighter escort for protection. If based on Haitan Island, the S-300/PMU1 coverage extends out to central and northern Taiwan's west coast.

31. *Ibid.*

32. See special briefing on missile defense programs and testing by Lieutenant General Ronald T. Kadish, July 13, 2001.

33. *National Missile Defense: A Candid Examination of Political Limits and Technological Challenges*, Cambridge, MA: Institute for Foreign Policy Analysis, Inc., 1998, pp. 21-22.

34. Federation of American Scientists website, *Ground based Interceptor, www.fas.org / spp / starwars*.

35. According to the Federation of American Scientists, the basic "threshold" threat that drove the C1 architecture is said to consist of an attack of five single-warhead missiles with unsophisticated decoys that could be discriminated, plus chaff, obscurant particles, flares, jammers, and other countermeasures.

36. According to the Federation of American Scientists, a C2 architecture would have defended against any authorized, unauthorized, or accidental attack by sophisticated payloads at the basic threshold level, said to consist of an attack of five single-warhead missiles, each with either a few (about four) credible decoys that could not be discriminated (and would have to be intercepted), plus chaff, obscurant particles, flares, jammers, and other countermeasures.

37. According to the Federation of American Scientists, the C3 architecture would have defended against any authorized, unauthorized, or accidental attack by sophisticated payloads at the "objective" level. The "objective" level is said to consist of an attack of twenty single-warhead missiles, each with either a few (perhaps as many as five) credible decoys that could not be discriminated [and would have to be intercepted], or a larger number of less sophisticated decoys that could be discriminated, plus chaff, obscurant particles, flares, jammers, and other countermeasures.

38. Charles Swicker, "Ballistic Missile Defense From the Sea: A Commander's Perspective," *NWC Review*, May 1997.

39. A third lower tier capability, the cancelled Navy Area Defense system, was to be a near term capability for lower tier area defense of ports, airfields, and forces ashore. The centerpiece of the Navy Area Defense System—the SM-2 Block IVA area defense interceptor—is an evolution of the Navy's Standard Missile and is one of the Ballistic Missile Defense Organization's core programs. The SM-2 Block IVA is a high speed, solid fueled system with a dual mode (infrared and semi-active radiofrequency) homing and a blast-fragmentation warhead specifically designed to enhance the ballistic missile defense mission. The combination of precise guidance with a powerful explosive proximity fused warhead makes this interceptor highly effective augmentation to the PAC-3's kinetic-energy hit-to-kill systems. Its footprint, or defended area, was larger than the PAC-3. Naval Area Defense systems generally are most effective if they are located near the assets they are supposed to protect. At-sea testing was expected to begin in late 2003/early 2004. Taiwan has requested four AEGIS-equipped destroyers that could, in the future, provide some limited missile defense should Taiwan decide to pursue such a capability. However, Taiwan's current pursuit of AEGIS-equipped destroyers is driven by the

need to defend against airbreathing threats, such as cruise missiles and strike aircraft.

40. J. R. Wilson, *THAAD: In The Eye Of The Storm*, unpublished paper, 1996; and BMDO Fact Sheet, "Theater High Altitude Area Defense (THAAD)," *https://www.acq. osd.mil/bmdo/bmdolink/pdf/ thaad,* May 1999; and THAAD Program Office Home Page, *https:// lmmg.external.lmco.com/thaad/.*

41. See Li Feizhu, "Taikong daodan genzhong xitong dui tufang cuoshi de yingyong (Influence of Space and Missile Tracking System on Penetration Measures), unpublished China Academy of Engineering Physics paper, April 1999.

42. J.R. Wilson, *THAAD: In The Eye Of The Storm*, 1996.

43. Statement of Lieutenant General Ronald T. Kadish, USAF Director, Ballistic Missile Defense Organization, Before the House Armed Services Committee Subcommittee on Military Research & Development, Thursday, June 14, 2001, *http://www.acq.osd.mil/ bmdo/bmdolink/html/kadish14jun01.html.*

44. The Guidance Enhanced Missile (GEM) is sometimes referred to as the "PAC-2+." The GEM incorporates improvements to the front end of the PAC-2 missile receiver to enhance its effectiveness and lethality against ballistic missiles.

45. Zhang Lide, "Woguo goujian feidan fangyu yu yuanju gongji feidan xitong de pinggu," (Analysis of Taiwan's Missile Defense and Long Range Attack Missile Systems), in *Jianduan Keji*, (Defense Technology), March 2000, p. 66.

46. Federation of American Scientists homepage, PATRIOT, (*www.fas.org*).

47. Lu Te-yun, "A Patriot Anti-Missile Defense Umbrella is Forming in the Greater Taipei Area," *Lien-ho Pao*, August 24, 1998, p. 1, in *FBIS-CHI*-98-246; and Yuen Lin, "Probing the Capability of Taiwan's Antiballistic Missiles," *Kuang Chiao Ching*, August 16, 1998, pp. 54-61, in *FBIS-CHI*-98-252. To counter a DF-15 traveling at 2km/sec, MADS operators have 25-40 seconds after radar acquisition to fire and intercept the incoming missile. With cueing data, reaction/intercept time would increase to 50 seconds or more.

48. "Military May Join Theater Missile Defense Project," *The China Post*, November 19, 1998, p.1.

49. For a discussion on the potential impact of DSP support for PATRIOT operations, see Yuen Lin, "Probing the Capability of Taiwan's Antiballistic Missiles," Hong Kong *Kuang Chiao Ching*, August 16, 1998, pp. 54-61, in *FBIS-CHI-98-252*.

50. *National Missile Defense: A Candid Examination of Political Limits and Technological Challenges*, Cambridge, MA: Institute for Foreign Policy Analysis, Inc., July 1998, pp. 21-22. Chinese interest in this "staring" capability was reflected in at least one study,; see Qiu Yulun, "Staring Focal Plane Array Imaging for Missile Early Warning," *Kongjian Jishu Qingbao Yanjiu (Space Technology Information Studies)*, May 1995, pp. 150-160, in CAMA, Vol. 4, No. 2, 1997.

51. "Spectrum Astro/Northrop Grumman Complete SBIRS Low Review," *SpaceDaily* (internet version), 7 May 2001. Very hot objects radiate high quantities of short wave infrared (SWIR: 1-3 microns); warm bodies radiate significant quantities of medium wave infrared (MWIR: 3-8 microns); cold objects primarily radiate long wave infrared signal (LWIR: 8-14 microns); while very cold objects emit very long wave radiation (VWLIR: 14-30 microns). Different options for focal plane arrays include mercury-cadmium-telluride (HgCdTe) or silicon based sensors. HgCdTe arrays, which will be used on SBIRS-Low satellites, can detect infrared signatures up to about 12 microns (LWIR) but are very difficult to manufacture and susceptible to radiation and EMP effects. However, a key advantage of HgCdTe arrays is that they do not require cooling to the extreme low temperatures that other infrared materials do. For a detailed Chinese evaluation of SBIRS-Low, see Li Feizhu, "Taikong daodan genzhong xitong dui tufang cuoshi de yingyong (Influence of Space and Missile Tracking System on Penetration Measures), unpublished China Academy of Engineering Physics paper, April 1999.

52. *National Missile Defense*, pp. 21-22.

53. *Ibid.*

54. *Ibid.*, pp. 25-26.

55. *Ibid.*, p. 26.

56. *Ibid.*, pp. 26-31.

57. *Ibid.*

58. See the Cox Report (Vol. I, Chapter 4). Also see Li Bin, "The Effects of NMD on Chinese Strategy," *Jane's Intelligence Review*, March 1, 2001.

59. John Wilson Lewis and Xue Litai, *China's Strategic Seapower: The Politics of Force Modernization in the Nuclear Age*, Stanford, CA: Stanford University Press, 1994.

60. Bonnie S. Glaser and Banning N. Garrett, "Chinese Perspectives on the Strategic Defense Initiative, *Problems of Communism*, March-April 1986, pp. 28-44.

61. *China Today: Defense Science and Technology*, Beijing: National Defense Industry Press, 1993, pp. 149-150.

62. *Ibid*, pp. 152-153; also see Richard P. Suttmeier, "China's High Technology: Programs, Problems, and Prospects," in *China's Economic Dilemma*, pp. 546-564. The senior engineers responsible for the 863 Program included Wang Daheng, a preeminent optics expert who played a role in China's space tracking network; Wang Ganchang, one of the founding fathers of China's nuclear program; Yang Jiachi, a satellite attitude control expert; and Chen Fangyun, an electronics engineer and leader of program to develop China's space tracking network. To focus R&D investment for the longer term, Hong Kong media sources reported that the State Council authorized a new initiative, similar to the 863 Program, that ostensibly will emphasize six key areas: 1) aerospace technology; 2) information technology; 3) strategic defenses; 4) deep strike technology; 5) optics and laser technology; and 6) advanced materials. The project, dubbed the 126 Program, allegedly was formally proposed during the 26 January 2000 Annual COSTIND National Conference in Beijing. The effort, to be overseen by Wu Bangguo, Wang Zhongyu, Cao Gangchuan, and Liu Jibin, is to funded over the next 12-15 years. See Wen Jen, "Jiang Orders High Tech Aerospace Weapons Development—'126 Program Signed and Placed Under Hu Jintao's Command," *Tai Yang Pao*, in *FBIS-CHI*-0040, March 21, 2000, p. A19.

63. Lu Hongquan and Yang Liandong, "Zhanlue he zhanshu dandao daodan de tufang" (Penetration of Strategic and Tactical Ballistic Missiles), published in an unknown journal in March 1999. Lu and Yang are from the China Academy of Engineering Physics (CAEP); also see Bai Hande, "Ganraodan de zhonglei he zuozhan fangshi" (Types and Operational Styles Associated with Jamming Warheads), *Xiandai bingqi* (Modern Weaponry), 1995, pp. 152-153.

64. Gan Chuxiong and Liu Jixiang, *Daodan yu yunzai huojian zongti sheji* (General Design of Missiles and Launch Vehicles), Beijing: Defense Industry Press, January 1996, p. 45.

65. Wang Guobao, "Initial Discussion on Tactical Ballistic Missile Electronic Warfare," *Hangtian dianzi duikang*, CAMA, April 1997, pp. 1-7.

66. "Kongjun yu haihang wuqi zhuangbei fazhan," (Development of the Air Force and Naval Aviation Equipment) in *Zhonggong junshi xiandaihua* (PRC Military Modernization), Taipei: Freedom Publishing, June 2000; also see Bai Hande, "Ganrao de zhonglei he zuozhan fangshi" (Types of Jamming and Operational Methods) *Xiandai wuqi* (Modern Weaponry), 1995, pp. 152-153.

67. Lu Hongquan and Yang Liandong, "Zhanlue he zhanshu dandao daodan de tufang" (Penetration of Strategic and Tactical Ballistic Missiles), published in an unknown journal in March 1999. Lu and Yang are from the China Academy of Engineering Physics (CAEP).

68. For example, Cai Yi, "Status and Development of Two Color Infrared Detectors," *Hongwai jishu*, (Infrared Technology), 1997, 19(5), summarized in CAMA, Vol. 4, No. 6, details the indium-based (InSb) infrared detectors used on the THAAD missile; and the mercury-cadmium-telluride (HgCdTe) detectors that are part of the Raytheon EKV sensor system.

69. Lu Hongquan and Yang Liandong, "Zhanlue he zhanshu dandao daodan de tufang" (Penetration of Strategic and Tactical Ballistic Missiles), published in an unknown journal in March 1999. Lu and Yang are from the China Academy of Engineering Physics (CAEP).

70. Bill Gertz, *Betrayal*, p. 254.

71. Lu Hongquan and Yang Liandong, "Zhanlue he zhanshu dandao daodan de tufang" (Penetration of Strategic and Tactical Ballistic Missiles), published in an unknown journal in March 1999. Lu and Yang are from the China Academy of Engineering Physics (CAEP).

72. Wang Jixiang, "Fast Burn Boost Strategic Ballistic Missile Technology," *Aerospace S&T Intelligence Studies Abstracts (2)*, 92 (4), pp. 68-78, in CAMA, Vol 3, No. 6, 1996. Wang is from the Beijing Institute of Space Systems Engineering (Beijing yuhang xitong gongcheng yanjiusuo); also see Qin Guangming, "Application of Slotted Tubular Grain in Fast Burn Solid Motors," *Bingong xuebao* (Ordnance Journal), Vol. 18, No. 2, 1996, pp. 41-43, in CAMA, Vol. 3, No. 6. Qin is from the Xian Institute of Modern Chemistry.

73. See *National Missile Defense*, p. 16. The Topol-M is believed to change directions during the last phase of its ascent.

74. Gan Chuxiong and Liu Jixiang, *Daodan Yu Yunzai Huojian Zongti Sheji* (General Design of Missiles and Launch Vehicles), Beijing: Defense Industry Press, January 1996, p. 42.

75. *Foreign Missile Developments and the Ballistic Missile Threat Through 2015*, Unclassified Summary of a National Intelligence Estimate, Director of Central Intelligence, January 2002.

76. Stokes.

77. Gan and Liu, p. 46; Gui Yongfeng, "Penetration of Tactical Ballistic Missile's Decoy," *Hubei Hangtian Keji* (Aerospace Hubei), February 1994, pp. 36-38, in CAMA, 1995, Vol. 2, No. 1; and Li Hong, "Motion Characteristics of Atmospheric Reentry Ballistic Missile Warheads and Their Applications To Heavy Decoy Design," *Jiangnan Hangtian Keji* (Jiangnan Space Technology), 1997 (1), pp. 26-30, in CAMA, 1997, Vol. 4, No. 3.

78. Gan Chuxiong and Liu Jixiang, *Daodan yu yunzai huojian zongti sheji* (General Design of Missiles and Launch Vehicles), Beijing: Defense Industry Press, January 1996. p. 42-43; and Wu Ganxiang, "Guowai fanjichang wuqi," (Foreign Antirunway Weapons), in Xu Dazhe, *Guowai dandao daodan jishu yanjiu yu fazhan*, Astronautics Publishing House, 1998, pp. 65-76. The control maneuver may be necessary to slow down the reentry speed to allow acquisition of the target image in the ballistic missile's seeker.

79. Gan and Liu, p. 43. Also see Cai Yuanli, "Research on Trajectory Recovery in Exo-Atmospheric Flight," in *Daodan Yu Hangtian Yunzai Jishu* (Missiles and Space Vehicles), March 1995, pp. 10-15, in CAMA, Vol. 2, No.5; and Zhao Hanyuan, "Simulation, Analysis of Maneuverable Reentry Vehicles," *Yuhang Xuebao*, January 1, 1997, pp. 96-99, in *FBIS-CST*-97-012. Zhao is from the National University of Defense Technology.

80. Zhang Minde, "Simulation Research of Defenses Against Conventional Ballistic Missile Reentry Vehicles," *Xitong gongcheng yu dianzi jishu*, Vol. 19, No. 4, 1997, pp. 45-49. The simulation was conducted by CASCs Beijing Optoelectronic Engineering General Design Department. For general background on saturation, see Harshberger, pp. 169-170.

81. David Fulghum, "China Exploiting U.S. Patriot Secrets," *Aviation Week and Space Technology*, January 18, 1993, pp. 20-21.

82. Zhang Demin and Hou Shiming, "Simulation Research of Offensive and Defensive Capability of Conventional Manuevering Reentry Missile," *Xitong Gongcheng Yu Dianzi Jishu*, Vol. 19, No. 4, 1997, pp. 45-49, in CAMA, 1997, Vol. 4, No. 5. Full translation in *FBIS-CHI*-97-272. Zhang is from the Beijing Electromechanical Engineering Design Department, also known as the CASC Fourth Systems Design Department. According to one evaluation, PAC-2 has a probability of kill of 10-25 percent against an unidentified tactical ballistic missile. See Zhao Yuping, "Probability of PAC-2 Intercepting a Certain Tactical Ballistic Missile," paper presented at the November 1997 conference of National Missile Designers Specialist Network, in CAMA, Vol. 5, No. 3.

83. Meng Daikui, "Simulation of Control and Guidance of Spinning Missiles," *Xitong Gongcheng yu Dianzi Jishu*, Vol. 5, No. 3, 1994, summarized in CAMA, Vol. 2, No. 1, 1995; Wan Chunxiong and Yang Xiaolong, "Identification of Flight Disturbances on Spinning Missiles," *Zhanshu Daodan Jishu* (Tactical Missile Technology), March 1995, pp. 1-8, in CAMA, Vol. 2, No. 3. For a general assessment on methodologies to protect missile systems against high powered lasers, see Ji Shifan, "Protection of Missiles Against Lasers," *Daodan yu Hangtian Yunzai Jishu*, Vol. 5, 1996, pp. 35-42, in CAMA, Vol. 4, No. 1. Ji's research concentrated on the effects of high powered lasers on a variety of materials and opto-electronic systems.

84. Li Qiang, "Current Status and Follow-On Development of Laser Cladding Wear-Resistance Coatings," *Yuhang cailiao gongyi*, January 1997, pp. 13-18. At least one institute involved in the testing is Harbin Institute of Technology. Also see Ji Shifan, "Laser Resistant Protection of Missiles," *Daodan yu hangtian yunzai jishu*, May 96, pp. 35-42.

85. Lewis and Hua, p. 17.

86. Gan and Liu, p. 44.

87. Du Xiangwan, "Ballistic Missile Defense and Space Weapons," in *Quanguo Gaojishu Zhongdian Tushu, Jiguang Jishu Linghuo*, (National High Technology Key Reference - Laser Technology Realm). Use of depressed trajectories may incur costs associated with accuracy.

88. Lu Hongquan and Yang Liandong, "Zhanlue he zhanshu dandao daodan de tufang" (Penetration of Strategic and Tactical Ballistic Missiles), published in an unknown journal in March 1999. Lu and Yang are from the China Academy of Engineering Physics (CAEP).

89. Gong Jinheng, "High Powered Microwave Weapons: A New Concept in Electronic Warfare," *Dianzi duikang jishu*, February 95, pp. 1-9. Gong is from the Southwest Institute of Electronic Equipment (SWIEE), China's premier electronic warfare research entity.

90. For a comprehensive overview of the technologies associated with HPM weapons, see Carlo Kopp, "The E-Bomb - A Weapon of Electrical Mass Destruction," in Winn Schwartau, *Information Warfare*, New York: Thunder's Mouth Press, 1994, pp. 296-297; Also see J. Swegle and J. Benford, "State of the Art in High Power Microwaves: An Overview," paper presented at the 1993 International Conference on Lasers and Applications, Lake Tahoe Nevada, December 6-10, 1993. Swegle and Benford point out that the US, Russia, France, and the United Kingdom have HPM programs in addition to China. Zhu Youwen and Feng Yi, *Gaojishu tiaojianxia de xinxizhan*, (Information Warfare Under High Technology Conditions), Academy of Military Science Press, 1994, pp. 308-310; "Beam Energy Weaponry: Powerful as Thunder and Lightning," *Jiefangjun bao*, December 25, 1995, in *FBIS-CHI*-96-039; Outlook for 21st Century Information Warfare," *Guoji hangkong*, (International Aviation), March 5, 1995, in *FBIS-CHI*-95-114; "Microwave Pulse Generation," *Qiang jiguang yu lizishu*, May 1994, in *JPRS-CST*-94-014. CAEP's Institute of Applied Electronics, University of Electronic Science and Technology of China, and the Northwest Institute of Nuclear Technology in Xian are three of the most important organizations engaged in the research, design, and testing of Chinese HPM devices. The PRC appears to have mastered at least two HPM power sources—the FCG and vircator. The greatest challenge is the weaponization process.

91. See Liu Shiquan, "A New Type of 'Soft Kill' Weapon: The Electromagnetic Pulse Warhead," *Hubei hangtian jishu* (Hubei Space Technology), May 1997, pp. 46-48. Liu is from the Sanjiang Space Industry.

92. Chung Chien, "High Tech War Preparation of the PLA: Taking Taiwan Without Bloodshed," *Taiwan Defense Affairs*, October 2000, pp. 141-163.

93. See John Wilson Lewis and Xue Litai, *China's Strategic Seapower: The Politics of Force Modernization in the Nuclear Age*, Stanford: Stanford University Press, 1994, for information on the 640 program. As a side note, leading U.S. experts have noted that ABM systems generally have inherent capabilities as ASATs, but the converse is not always true.

94. Gao Fuli, "Development Strategy and Serial Research of Anti-Tactical Ballistic Missiles," in *Foreign Missile Technology Development in 2000*, October 1994, pp. 48-59, in CAMA, Vol. 2, No. 4. The three phase approach (*sanbuzou*) for China's missile defense development is also discussed in Yang Chunfu and Liu Xiao'en, "Research Study on U.S. Ballistic Missile Development Plan," Aerospace Information Paper HQ-96009, 1996, in CAMA, Vol. 4, No. 2.

95. See Zhu Zhenfu and Huang Peikang, "TBM IR Radiant Signature, Selection of Optimum Operating Band for Anti-Missile IR Seekers," *Xitong gongcheng yu dianzi jishu* (Systems Engineering and Electronics), January 1996. Zhu is from CAMEC's Second Academy 207th Research Institute. Wu Jianwen, "Do We Have TMD?" *Jiefang ribao,* December 8, 1999, in *FBIS-CHI-0987.*

96 "Centers Established In, Universities Of China," (no source listed) in *FBIS-CHI-0983-95*, September 9, 1995. Director of the state key lab is Professor Sun Zhongliang.

97. Wu Guanghua, "Dual-Mode Millimeter Wave-IR Seeker for An Endo-Atmospheric Interceptor," *Danjian jishu* (Projectile and Rocket Technology), Vol. 9, No. 3, 1996, pp. 15-20, in *FBIS-CHI*-97-261. The key component is a 35GHz Ka-Band traveling wave tube amplifier.

98. See Zhao Jiufen and Wang Minghai, "Yujing weixing dui daodan yujing moxing de fangzhen" (Modeling and Simulation of Ballistic Missile Early Warning Satellites), *Guti huojian jishu* (Journal of Solid Rocket Technology), Vol. 24, No. 3, 2001, pp. 1-3. The authors are from the Second Artillery's Engineering Academy in Xian.

99. AMS and defense industry officials consistently advocate missile early warning satellites in concepts for a national reconnaissance network. Leading institutes for infrared detector R&D include Beijing Institute of Remote Sensing Equipment, Shanghai Institute of Technical Physics, North China Research Institute of Optoelectronics, Kunming Institute of Physics, and Shanghai Xinyue Instruments Factory. CAST's Lanzhou Institute of Physics is a key provider of cyrogenic equipment for cooling the infrared sensors. See Liu Jintian, "Hongwai Qijian Guoneiwai Fazhan Dongtai" (Developmental Prospects of Chinese and Foreign Infrared Devices), *Zhongguo hangtian*, March 1992, pp. 41-45; and Wu Runchou, "Hangtian linghuo hongwai jishu de fazhan" Development of Space Infrared Technology), *Zhongguo hangtian*, March 1993, pp. 19-23. For other references to China's space-based infrared/ultraviolet telescope designs, see Chen Longzhi, "New Developments in Space Cryogenic Optics," *Diwen gongcheng* (Cyrogenic Engineering), March 1994, pp. 9-13, in CAMA,

Vol. 1, No. 5; and Ma Pinzhong, "Woguo kongjian wangyuanjing fazhan" (Development of China's Space Telescope), *Zhongguo hangtian*, July 1994, pp. 29-32.

100. For information on Chinese missile early warning systems and associated technology, see Lu Mingyu, Yi Kui, Yang Junfa, and Deng Ruzhen, "Development of Signal Source for Real-Time Infrared Earth Sensor," *Zhongguo kongjian kexue jishu*, June 1996, pp. 63-70. in *FBIS-CST-96-016*; and Qiu Yulun, "Staring Focal Plane Array Imaging for Missile Early Warning," *Kongjian jishu qingbao yanjiu*, May 1995, pp. 150-160, in CAMA, 1997, Vol. 4, No. 2. One should not discount the possibility of Russian assistance should Beijing have an interest in highly elliptical Molniya orbits.

101. Stokes, pp. 118-119. One should note that in the 1980s, the United States considered modification of the Pershing-2 for ASAT missions, a system similar to the DF-21.

102. For references to control problems, see Deng Zichen, "Problems in High Precision Computation for Nonlinear Control of Space Interceptors," *Feixing lixue*, Vol. 16, No. 1, 1998, pp. 85-89, in CAMA, Vol. 5, No. 5. Yang Yingbo, "Control Research on a Space Interceptor in the Terminal Guidance Phase," unpublished BUAA paper, May 1994; Shi Xiaoing, "Study on Pulse Guidance Law for Space Interception," in *Zhidaoyu Yinxin*, No. 4, 1994, pp. 1-4, in CAMA, Vol. 2, No. 3. Shi is from the Harbin Institute of Technology's Simulation Center. Deng is from Northwest Polytechnical University. For other studies, see Li Zhongying, "Study on Mid-Course Guidance for Aerodynamic Control of Anti-Missile Defense," unpublished paper (BH-B4774), Beijing University of Aeronautics and Astronautics (BUAA), May 1996, in CAMA, Vol. 5, No. 5; and Li Zhongying, "Approximative Estimation of Optimal Guidance for Frontal Ballistic Missile Intercepts," unpublished BUAA paper (BH-B4776), in CAMA, Vol. 5, No. 5; and Li Zhongying, "Mathematical Modeling of Optimal Guidance for Anti-Tactical Ballistic Missiles," unpublished BUAA paper (BH-B4854), May 1996, in CAMA, Vol. 5, No. 5.

103. Cheng Ho, China Eyes Anti-Satellite System, *Space Daily*, January 8, 2000.

104. Xu Hui and Sun Zhongkang, "Temperature Differences Between Satellites and Satellite Decoys," *NUDT Journal*, Vol 16, No. 3, 1994; also see Li Hong, Identification of Satellites and Its Decoys Using Multisensor Data Fusion," *Xiandai fangyu jishu*, June 1997, pp. 31-36. Li is from the NUDT Electronic Technology Department.

105. Li Hong'an, Wei Xuhui, and Sun Zhangkang, "Duo chuanganqi shuju ronghe shixian weixing jiqi xiliu xiu'er de zhibie" (Multi-sensor Data Fusion To Discriminate Satellites and Decoys), *Xiandai fangyu jishu* (Modern Defense Technology), November 1997, pp. 31-36.

106. DoD Report to Congress, *Security Situation in the Taiwan Strait*.

107. "Hangtian guti yunzai huojian youxian gongsi chengli" (Aerospace Solid Launch Vehicle Corporation Established), *Zhongguo Hangtian*, June 2000 (internet version). The corporation will be jointly administered by at least four key entities involved in the development of the DF-21 and its sea-launched sister, the JL-1: Beijing Electromechanical Engineering Design Department (4th Department); Academy of Space Solid Rocket Engine Technology (4th Academy); Beijing Institute of Control and Electronic Engineering (17th Research Institute); Nanjing Chenguang Factory (307 Factory); and the China Aerospace Electromechanical Corporation. For a complete history of the DF-21/JL-1 program, see Lewis and Xue, *China's Strategic Seapower*. Also see Zhang Dexiong, "Guowai xiaoxing weixing de guti huojian tuijin xitong" (Solid Rocket Propulsion Systems for Foreign Small Satellites), in Hangtian qingbao yanjiu, HQ-93011, pp. 139-155; Wang Zheng, "Screening Studies and Technology for All-Solid Space Launch Vehicles," *Guti huojian fadongji sheji yu yanjiu* (Solid Rocket Engine Design and Research), April 1996, pp. 63-73, in CAMA, Vol. 3, No. 6, 1996; and Zhang Song, "Design and Optimization of Solid Launch Vehicle Trajectory," *Guti huojian jishu*, Vol. 20, No. 1, 1997, pp. 1-5; and Zhang Dexiong, "China's Development Concept for Small Solid Launch Vehicles," CASC Fourth Academy Information Research Reports, the Fourth Edition, October 1995, pp. 1-11, in CAMA, Vol. 5, No. 2.

108. Cheng Yuejin, "Information Transmission System of Data Relay Satellites," *Kongjian jishu qingbao yanjiu*, July 1994, pp. 185-193, in CAMA, Vol. 1, No. 6. Cheng is from the Xian Institute of Radio Technology. Also see Tan Liying, "Selection of Wavelength Region for Optical Intersatellite Communication," *Haerbin gongye daxue xuebao*, Vol. 26, No. 3, 1994, pp. 24-27, in CAMA, Vol. 1, No. 6; Chen Daoming, "Frequency and Orbit of Data Relay Satellites," in *Zhongguo kongjian kexue jishu*, Vol. 16, No.1, 1996, pp. 26-31, in CAMA, Vol. 3, No. 3.

109. Department of Defense, *Future Military Capabilities and Strategy of the People's Republic of China* (Report to Congress pursuant to Section 1226 of the FY98 National Defense Authorization Act), Washington, DC: U.S. Government Printing Office, 1998.

110. Jin Weixin, "Mathematical Modeling of Tactical Surface to Surface Missiles Against TMD," in *Systems Engineering and Electronic Technology*, Vol. 17, No. 3, 1995, pp. 63-68, CAMA, Vol 2, No. 3, 1995.

111. Senior Colonel Wang Benzhi, "Didi changui daodan huoli yunyong de jige wenti," (Some Questions Related to the Use of Conventional Surface-to-Surface Missile Firepower), in *Lianhe zhanyi yu junbingzhong zuozhan*, (Joint Theater and Service Operations) Beijing: National Defense University Press, 1998, pp. 236-241. As of 1998, Wang was the Chief of Staff of the Second Artillery Huaihua Base (80305 Unit). The concept of synchronized, multi-axis strikes is a fundamental principle of Second Artillery conventional doctrine (*duodian, duofangxiang, tongshi tuji*). Other important operational concepts discussed by Wang from Huaihua include "*xushi bingyong, shengdong xiji,*" (literally "use reality, make a noise in the east, but strike to the west"); and "*xiaojiange, duoboci tuji*" (literally "cut time and strike in multiple waves"). The first calls for integration of simultaneous launches from different launch azimuths and use of infrared radiation "disruption" to confuse enemy satellite early warning systems and complicate enemy attack operations. The second includes use of two strike waves, the first "screening" the second by exploiting "time lags" (*shijiancha*) in missile defenses.

112. Gan and Liu, p. 45. Also see Zhang Demin, "Study on Penetration Techniques on New Generation Ballistic Missiles," in *Xinjunshi gemingzhong daodan wuqi fazhan qianjing*, November 1996, pp. 18-24, in CAMA, Vol. 4, No. 2.

113. Si Xicai, "Research on Long Range Antiradiation Missile Passive Radar Seeker Technology," in *Zhanshu daodan jishu* (Tactical Missile Technology), Vol. 2, 1995, pp. 42-52; other studies on specific approaches to ARM technology include Yang Huayuan, "Study on Superwideband High Accuracy Microwave DF System," in *Daojian yu zhidao xuebao*, February 1995, pp. 7-12. At least one Second Academy entity that has conducted work on anti-radiation missile seeker technology is the Beijing Institute of Remote Sensing Equipment (probably the CASC 25th Research Institute).

114. Wang Chunyuan, *China's Space Industry and Its Strategy of International Cooperation*, Stanford University Center for International Security and Arms Control, July 1996, p. 4; Marat Abulkhatin, "Official on Prospects for Space Cooperation," *Itar-Tass*, October 10, 1996, in *FBIS-SOV-96-198*; and author's 1994 discussions with Chinese space officials responsible for international cooperation.

115. "Wang Liheng fujuzhang lutuan fangwen E'Wu liangguo (CASC Deputy Director Wang Liheng Leads Delegation to Russian and Ukraine), *Zhongguo hangtian bao*, April 11, 1994, p. 1.

116. See Li Feizhu, "Taikong daodan genzhong xitong dui tufang cuoshi de yingyong (Influence of Space and Missile Tracking System on Penetration Measures), unpublished China Academy of Engineering Physics paper, April 1999.

117. This point is made by Dr. Li Bin from the Institute of International Studies, Qinghua University in "The Effects of NMD on Chinese Strategy," *Jane's Intelligence Review*, March 1, 2001.

118. Federation of American Scientists estimates that the DF-5 could accommodate six warheads similar in size to those used on the DF-21 Mod 2.

119. See Stephen Van Evera, "Offense, Defense, and the Causes of War," *International Security*, Vol. 22, No. 4, Spring 1998, pp. 5-43.

120. U.S. joint doctrine notes that attack operations are the most effective and efficient means of countering the theater ballistic missiles. Joint Chiefs of Staff, Joint Publication 3-01.5, *Joint Doctrine for Countering Air and Missile Threats*, Washington: GPO, 1999.

CHAPTER 6

CHINESE REACTIONS TO NEW U.S. INITIATIVES ON MISSILE DEFENSE

Eric A. McVadon

INTRODUCTION

The author of this chapter describes and analyzes Chinese views of U.S. missile defense initiatives, based largely on interviews, meetings, lectures, and conversations with various Chinese officials, People's Liberation Army (PLA) officers, think tankers, academics, and other strategic studies and security specialists in China.[1] The core research was done during 3 weeks on the mainland in July and October 2001, plus other meetings held and materials obtained in the weeks before and after those visits. In general, it was not necessary to raise the missile issue with Chinese interlocutors; there was eagerness among these Chinese contacts to address the topic, describe Chinese positions, and raise questions. Given the similarity of many of the responses, it was clear that the topic has received ample attention, that the same material had been read all over China, and that there was universal support among officials and academics for the central objections to U.S. missile defense initiatives, albeit with interesting modifications.

PRC VIEWS OF THE UNITED STATES IN MID-2001

Some observers in the United States have concluded that 2001 is a bad year for U.S.-China relations, that Washington's drive toward missile defense and more arms for Taiwan, coupled with many other bilateral strains, has left Beijing unready, even unwilling, to deal with Washington. Chinese observers have a different view. Chinese diplomats in Washington asserted as early as the spring of 2001 that Beijing is, at the outset of the George W. Bush presidency, exercising restraint and being accommodating—despite many U.S. administration statements, including those on missile defense, that might be considered offensive to China.

The frequently expressed hope was that the anticipated meeting between Presidents Jiang Zemin and Bush in Beijing, coincident with the Asia-Pacific Economic Council (APEC) session in Shanghai in October 2001, would result in much enhanced understanding and a steadily improving bilateral relationship. This expectation was particularly evident among interlocutors in China in July and encompassed a publicly expressed willingness, even desire, to discuss missile defense issues. This was in contrast to an earlier Chinese attitude of making righteous public pronouncements in opposition to missile defense programs but largely avoiding serious discussion, especially any form of discussion that would suggest Chinese behavior might be the subject of legitimate concern or reproach. As a consequence of the September 11, 2001 attacks on the World Trade Center and Pentagon, the Beijing meeting between Bush and Jiang did not occur, and missile defense was not prominent in their brief talks in Shanghai on the periphery of the APEC forum.

Amidst this alleged Chinese willingness to accommodate[2] and to await patiently the outcome of what is seen as a developing U.S. policy for China (and, more broadly, for Asia), there were seeming contradictions. These contradictions prominently included the arrests and trials (and subsequent deportations) of ethnic Chinese scholars with American connections, the continuing harsh crackdown on the Falun Gong movement, the sharp Chinese reaction to the reductions of military-to-military contacts initiated by the U.S. Department of Defense in 2001, and the handling of the April 2001 downing of the U.S.

EP-3 surveillance aircraft. These topics could not be addressed fruitfully by the author in most open discussions in mid-2001; however, points were made by the Chinese, mostly in private discussions, that these should be understood as exceptional situations and kept in context (the Chinese context, of course). The Chinese side, they suggested, did not link these events to the Bush administration policy toward China or missile defense initiatives; and it was hoped that an American understanding of the factors involved would insure that discussions of missile defense issues would not be prejudiced by these unrelated events.

The implications were that these events reflected three primarily *domestic* factors:

1. *An obsession with the Taiwan issue that overrides considerations of how it might affect relations with the United States.* The state security organs had doggedly sunk their teeth into the issue of scholars "misusing" information about the mainland, especially in such matters as making comparisons with Taiwan society and the like. In a written response to questions submitted to Jiang by the *New York Times*, it was asserted that the scholars were "members of Taiwan espionage organizations" and had "engaged in spy activities on many occasions on the mainland of China."[3] Discretion overrode valor for those Chinese officials who recognized the negative effects on China of such actions. Moreover, American reactions to the detentions and trials were not given high priority in evaluating the crusade; the audience for the actions was the body of ethnic Chinese scholars abroad who are inclined to undertake such work—and the Chinese public. As Senator Joseph Biden, Chairman of the U.S. Senate Foreign Relations Committee, said after meeting with Jiang and other officials at Beidaihe in August 2001, "They [the Chinese] are sending a not-so-subtle message. You [Americans] have a problem with [Chinese actions toward] Pakistan, with Iran; we have a problem with [American actions toward] Taiwan." Biden

171

said Jiang appeared preoccupied with the fate of the island Beijing regards as a rebel province.[4]

2. *Paranoia about the Falun Gong on the part of Jiang.* Jiang, personally, was still firmly convinced that the regime was threatened by the Falun Gong "cult," and no one with influence thought it prudent or useful to try to convince him of the counterproductive character of the actions; moreover, the campaign to discredit the movement and persuade the Chinese people of its evil nature was, indeed, succeeding—so why relent now?[5]

3. *Insecurity of Jiang about his future, especially as Chairman of the CMC.* Jiang, although misled by the military as to the antecedent and proximate causes and circumstances of the collision between the PLA Navy F-8 and the U.S. Navy EP-3, did not think it prudent to take on the PLA leadership about the post-accident events or the their anger about the military relationship machinations by U.S. Secretary of Defense Donald Rumsfeld. Jiang was reluctant to ignore their ranting against the United States because this might complicate his expected retention of the position as Chairman of the Central Military Commission after his upcoming retirement from the positions of President of China and Communist Party General Secretary. Thus avoiding confrontation with the military leadership is a major part of Jiang's effort to ensure that he retains an influential position and protects his aspiration to gain "paramount leader" status comparable to that enjoyed by Deng Xiaoping and Mao Zedong. He, consequently, was not inclined to confront the military and in both instances let the PLA have its way.

In short, these events that seemed to be avoidable incidents, almost gratuitously harming the relationship with the United States, were characterized by the Chinese as Jiang and others playing primarily to domestic—not international—audiences. There is another important aspect to this somewhat oblique explanation of contradictory conduct offered by Chinese specialists. These complications in the relationship were not in any way a reaction to U.S. missile defense initiatives, neither those against long-range nuclear missiles nor short-range conventional missiles, according to these Chinese sources.

China Is the Target of Nuclear Missile Defense.

Chinese specialists suggest that, indeed, their government is taking a measured, reasonable approach to U.S. missile defense initiatives. They do, nevertheless, argue, rather righteously (as usual), that U.S. statements about national missile defenses not being intended for use against China's intercontinental ballistic missile (ICBM) force are not credible. One interlocutor pointed out that China has been a factor in U.S. concerns about defending itself against or deterring missile attacks since the middle of the last century. Moreover, most Chinese experts do not take seriously the expressions of U.S. concerns about missile threats from the "rogue states," arguing generally that North Korean missile forces are not now, and will not become, significant, and that North Korea and other rogue nations have been and will continue to be deterred by the overwhelming U.S. conventional and nuclear capabilities.

The geography of the proposed defense sites (in Alaska) seems to the Chinese to be a placement specifically chosen to protect the United States against China's long-range missiles—which they term a minimal deterrent arsenal. Based on the prevalent Chinese assertion that North Korea is not a real present or potential threat to the United States, the argument that the placement is to defend against a Pyongyang threat is discounted, even scorned. The *Chinese believe firmly and state publicly* what several hawkish Americans have stated (some more publicly than others): *Regardless of what is said, China is the target of U.S. missile defenses.* If the United States succeeds in developing a small interceptor force, Washington will inexorably move to a larger, more capable force, they assert. Less loudly spoken is that Beijing does not trust Washington as a world player with such a force any more than Washington trusts Beijing with its small (but probably increasing) and obsolescent (but modernizing) ICBM arsenal, allegedly useful only as a deterrent.

It all depends on Washington, as the Chinese see it. In the eyes of the Chinese, much of the to-and-fro on the missile defense issue depends on the state of the bilateral relationship and the degree of mutual trust, a factor that could erode badly, remain stagnant, or improve significantly. They consider that the quality of the relationship depends almost wholly on Washington's thinking and actions. From their perspective, an important factor is whether Washington has, indeed, made, or is in the process of making, a fundamental change in its strategic outlook with respect to China. A prominent Chinese thinker in talks in Washington in early summer 2001 opined that he thought his government had taken a wait-and-see attitude. For him and others, there is the hope that the U.S. adheres to a one-China policy and that the bilateral relationship returns to a less bumpy track, but there is no conclusion yet. The apparent warming of Sino-U.S. relations after September 11 and the cordial, if truncated, Bush-Jiang meeting in Shanghai, have most Chinese wondering if the enhanced relationship will persist or return to bickering over the same old disputes as time passes.

In mid-2001 another Chinese strategist and specialist in American studies described two schools of thought in China on U.S. strategy. One is the conviction that U.S. strategy is "aimed at China." The other is that U.S. strategy is more globally directed (aimed at much more than China). He noted that, predating Bush administration pronouncements, President William Clinton had stated the U.S. shift to a focus on Asia. These and other such arguments made by other interlocutors seemed to hold out the prospect that U.S. policy for China and Asia was not yet in concrete, and that it was still in the process of formulation, implying an opportunity for those in Beijing and elsewhere to influence it. This, coupled with the events in September and October, encourage Beijing's hopes that, despite U.S.-Russian deal-making, it has not been relegated to an altogether passive role on the missile defense issue.

A well-connected academic remarked that hearing U.S. Secretary of State Colin Powell and Rumsfeld talk about issues relating to China or about which China was concerned was like listening to two governments. He made this observation on the day that Powell arrived in Beijing in July 2001 to prepare for the meeting between the two presidents, then 3 months in the future. The Chinese are convinced that they have taken the rational position and that it is the Bush administration, in its early pronouncements about favoring Japan and Taiwan and being firmer on China, that was producing uncertainty and instability in the bilateral relationship—and could return to that once Beijing's support is seen as no longer needed in the war on terrorism. Furthermore, the Chinese do not believe that their conduct warrants such harsh treatment and insulting affronts by Washington. They refuse, for example, to recognize that Beijing's firm position on the Taiwan problem including its refusal to renounce the use of force, plus other issues such as human rights, makes Washington conclude that Beijing is the culprit.

CHINESE REACTION TO DEFENSES AGAINST ICBMS (NMD)

Although the Bush administration has merged the concepts of national missile defense (NMD) and theater missile defense (TMD) into the common term missile defense system (MDS)[6], China's reactions can best be described and analyzed while preserving the distinction of defenses against ICBMs and defenses against short-range and medium-range ballistic missiles (SRBMs and MRBMs). For the most part, China, while acknowledging the blurring of the distinction, continues to object to the two in different ways and on different grounds, and there are also specific objections to the concept of MDS—the merging of the two concepts into some sort of layered defense of wide areas.

Measured Chinese Opposition.

Beijing is not ranting about NMD. It is not using alarmist expressions and is not engaging in name-calling, as it so often does on other issues—and as it did earlier on this one. There is little, if any, rhetorical excess, as was the case in the fall of 2000 when the Defense White Paper described the Taiwan issue as "complicated and grim." Absent in missile defense discussions are the terms *hegemonism* and *power politics*, and the accusations, like those from the White Paper, that "certain big powers are pursuing 'neo-interventionism' [and] neo-gunboat diplomacy." In Jiang's written responses to the *New York Times* questions in August 2001, the points on missile defense are only that (1) China does not favor the proposed U.S. move that it fears would jeopardize strategic stability, (2) it wishes to discuss solutions that would not harm the security of any side, and (3) China needs to maintain the effectiveness of its "self-defense" nuclear force.[7]

NMD Can Be Overwhelmed or Defeated.

That was the tone struck by Chinese interlocutors. In June, a prominent Chinese think tanker went so far as to suggest (a bit simplistically) that China could tolerate ten interceptor missiles because that would not defeat China's 20 ICBMs and that China could, in any case, build additional ICBMs in the 10 or more years before such a system could be deployed—if it works. On the matter of NMD efficacy, many Chinese specialists think that it will not work and that it certainly will not work soon. Several referred to NMD as Great Wall or Maginot Line thinking. A PLA general officer, who is considered a strategic thinker, commented on the analogy that missile defense is a train that has already left the station. He said that might be true but that the tracks are not yet complete; effective missile

176

defense, in his view, simply may not be feasible, especially in the short term.

NMD Will Cost a Lot and Not Work.

Some put a positive spin (for China) on this argument, suggesting that China will not follow the Soviet example of reaction to President Ronald Reagan's Strategic Defense Initiative (SDI, or Star Wars) but could easily maintain sufficient missiles to overcome the defenses while the United States expends enormous resources on its ineffective obsession. China, they say, will increase and improve its ICBM arsenal, but U.S. NMD will not be a central impetus for that undertaking because NMD is not expected to work very well. Some Chinese go so far as to argue that fewer resources than planned need now to be expended on ICBM modernization because NMD, by whatever name, will not be effective, that minor offensive changes will continue to overcome difficult defensive modifications.

The PLA general officer strategist, when pressed, tempered his argument a bit. He said that although effective missile defenses may be infeasible, if the technology is present, they would be built; no American president could refuse to do so. However, he forecast that NMD could not be developed before the end of this decade, so China has time to ensure its nuclear forces are effective. It is, of course, hard to determine if this theme of NMD ineffectiveness is mouthed in order to discourage its development or because the Chinese have, indeed, convinced themselves that it will not work. The latter seems most likely.

No Nuclear Arms Race.

China, it was said, does not want to expend resources on building up a much larger ICBM force; it wants both economic development and a deterrent. That combination seems feasible to the Chinese specialists. A PLA general officer suggested that China's response would be proportional and would not result in an arms race or even a priority item in the Chinese defense budget. China, he said, would do extra things, but just enough; it would not go overboard. Others said China would not react strongly to NMD and would not build a large number of missiles. Nuclear weapons, one civilian specialist argued, are just for deterrence, not real weapons. China will not waste its resources on a useless system.

There has a bit of gloating among some of the specialists that the United States would likely proceed headlong and spend an enormous amount of money on a system not likely to work and that, putting a finer point on earlier arguments, offensive missiles and imaginative penetration techniques were far easier and cheaper to devise and produce than defensive missiles and complex target discrimination technologies. However, none of the interlocutors, even in response to provocative questioning, took a position that the United States would rue the day it undertook NMD against the wise and wily Chinese, or anything resembling that position. Other threats and bluster were not offered. The tone of the conversations resembled that taken by Sha Zukang, Director of the Arms Control Department in China's Ministry of Foreign Affairs, in March 2001 when he said that, even if NMD were developed by the United States, China would not necessarily take radical steps such as withdrawing from the Comprehensive Test Ban Treaty [implying also ending its moratorium on nuclear weapon testing], as had been threatened previously.[8]

NMD Would Reduce Security.

Instead, the gentler suggestion was made often that the United States and China might both be less secure as a result of NMD. The general officer strategist and a civilian specialist in Beijing said China is concerned about the ramifications for outer space, fearing a U.S. move to put missile defenses in space would invite others to employ weapons in space or to react unpredictably to one country's "weaponizing space." In the short term, there would be an increase in the capability of the United States to defend itself; but in the long term the United States will "repent." The general went on to argue that the United States spent many years building a nonproliferation regime and now seems to be throwing all that away and inviting proliferation. The crux of his argument was that the national security of one country cannot be based on increased insecurity of others, and that absolute security cannot be achieved. Defenses, he suggested, sometimes invite proliferation rather than stop it. As did others, he pointed the finger at countries other than China, forecasting that, in reacting to U.S. missile defense, China will do just a few things; others will do much more.

Others elaborated on this theme. An arms control specialist said some countries would react to NMD by developing an improved capability to penetrate defenses; others would turn to other methods of delivery or to alternatives such as biological weapons. He then made a less familiar argument. He said NMD would lead to a sense of false security. If it were to work, the United States would feel secure against North Korea, for example. Yet Washington would, in building missile defenses, not only have further antagonized Pyongyang but also would have failed to give the appropriate attention to resolving the underlying problems in relations with North Korea—and probably further exacerbated them. To bolster his argument, he said Pyongyang has reacted favorably to overtures from Beijing and Moscow to curtail its missile program. A tough message from Washington about missile defense would be counterproductive, he argued. Almost in passing, he added that all this is about a country that does not, in the view of China, pose a credible nuclear missile threat to the United States—a country that wants and needs better relations with the United States.[9]

A specialist in Beijing gave it a geopolitical twist. He said that if Bush's plan for missile defenses were completed, the world would be divided into two parts: that covered by MDS, and that left uncovered. That returns us to a bipolar world. The real security problems in the world are based on lack of trust. MDS would exacerbate the underlying problem of lack of trust between various countries and work counter to the concept of confidence-building measures (CBMs), he argued.

North Korea No Threat.

As mentioned previously, the Chinese argue frequently and with conviction that North Korea is not now, and will not become, a threat to the United States. As one civilian specialist put it, North Korea's territory is too small to develop a nuclear weapon system that would include launching facilities, force protection, etc. North Korea cannot develop the technology to get missiles even to the western United States, he asserted. In any event, North Korea could only launch, not survive; it would be a real suicide, he said emphatically. Several others pointed out that North Korea's failure to initiate military action over half-a-century makes the point that the leaders in Pyongyang are not irrational. Chinese press this argument about the lack of credible threat from North Korea in significant measure to support their belief that U.S. defenses against ICBMs are ultimately intended to negate China's nuclear deterrent.

Piling On.

One gains the sense in talking to Chinese specialists on the missile defense issue that a great deal of time has been spent contriving and cataloguing arguments against missile defenses, apparently in the belief that the number of arguments made will count in the debate. As an example, a think tanker in Beijing said that China is worried about the prospect of an arms race but not between China and the United States. He feared that, if the United States builds missile defenses, other countries could build up their missile forces in response and then later could turn those missiles on China, or at least those missiles would be a threat to China. Nevertheless, most of the arguments offered are along similar lines and often employ precisely the same words and phrases, such as the comparison of NMD with the Great Wall and the Maginot Line mentioned previously. At a minimum, one must conclude that the specialists have all read the same material or heard the same spiel.

The Second-Strike Issue.

Two quite different views were offered (quite clinically) by two interlocutors on the issue of Chinese interest in a second-strike capability (after an initial U.S. nuclear strike on China). A Chinese strategist speaking (not for attribution) here in the United States said that China needs a second-strike capability—in addition to the ability to overwhelm a U.S. defense against ICBMs.[10] A Beijing civilian specialist suggested it was all moot. He argued privately (and gravely) that Chinese leaders would be unable to find a single major American city where close relatives of important Chinese leaders do not now live. He concluded on that basis that there is no realistic utility to China's ICBMs; they have only deterrent value, no real value as weapons. This was offered, not frivolously, but as a serious appraisal. He also noted that the United States had, for very different reasons, elected not to use nuclear weapons in Korea in 1953, suggesting that neither country has the stomach to employ them.

THE ABM TREATY ISSUE

Most of the interlocutors predicted, in one way or another, that Moscow would not, in the end, stand firmly with China on the matter of opposition to any meddling with the 1972 Anti-Ballistic Missile (ABM) Treaty that might permit missile defenses desired by Washington but prohibited by the treaty. At least as early as June 2001, a prominent specialist said that he expected Russia to concede its opposition to NMD and that China should be ready to go its own way. A civilian specialist in Beijing, noting that Russia must for economic reasons reduce the size of its nuclear arsenal, said in advance of the July 2001 Putin-Bush meeting in Genoa that Russia would compromise on the ABM Treaty issue. He explained further that on a scale of 1-10 Russia was at 10 in its concern about NMD and 5 about TMD; China was at 5 on NMD and 10 on TMD. He translated that into an expectation that Moscow would compromise with Washington and enter into some form of cooperation on NMD and warhead numbers.

After Russian President Vladimir Putin stated publicly with Bush in Genoa in late July 2001 that offensive missiles and missile defense would be treated as a set, Chinese specialists uniformly took the position that we were later to hear from Jiang in his *New York Times* interview: the matter could be worked. Possibly their concern was less than most American analysts expected, they expected that Putin had another card up his sleeve, or Beijing decided to put the best face on their disappointment. A retired senior PLA officer now with a strategic studies institute told a small international audience in Hong Kong in very late July 2001 that he had expected Russia to make a deal with the United States on the matter, or at least thought it was possible. Not even the Bush-Putin November 2001 meeting on this issue seemed to discourage the Chinese.

A well-connected senior think tanker put it this way: China's preference was to stand solid with Russia in opposition to change to the ABM Treaty that would permit NMD, but China had seen very early the prospect for change in Russia's position. He said that there are in this matter "gray areas." China, he asserted, could still work with Russia and talk with the United States. Noting that China's former principal arms control official, Sha Zukang, has said he wants to discuss missile defense with the United States, he said there could be talk on the "merits" of missile defense and on overall relations; maybe there is room for maneuvering, he ruminated. He concluded with the hope that Jiang and Bush, in Beijing in October 2001, would discuss the issue and find some way out. Although that meeting did not take place, it still seems that Beijing wants to finesse the issue, make the best of it, or at least not to give the impression that China is panicky over the unfavorable development—whatever precise form it may take as Bush and Putin continue to talk without a representative from Beijing present.

CHINA'S VIEWS ON THEATER MISSILE DEFENSE (TMD)

TMD to Protect U.S. Forces and Bases Is Okay.

Ambassador Sha Zukang, who has now left his post as China's primary arms control official, has for half a decade voiced his assertion that TMD intended to shield U.S. forces and bases in Asia were understandable to Beijing and would not draw a radical reaction from China. He has referred to this as "pure" TMD, implying apparently that it did not involve Japan or Taiwan or threaten Chinese strategic missiles. He repeated that position in March 2001 in response to questioning about U.S. plans to deploy systems to protect U.S. forces based in Asia. He said, "There is a gray area here. China is not opposed to [theater missile defense]. . . to protect troops and military bases." Nothing has been heard from a successor on this issue, affirming or denying the position. This may be in part because of the uncertainty about where the United States TMD program is headed as major changes are made in the overall U.S. missile defense program and Washington's attention and resources are concentrated on the war on terrorism.

For the Republic of Korea (ROK).

Chinese officials and specialists are generally relaxed about TMD and South Korea because Seoul has, so far, chosen not to participate. There is satisfaction among the Chinese that part of the reason Seoul does not want to obtain a TMD system is that Koreans do not want to "poke China in the eye." South Koreans have expressed the view that TMD is not an effective defense against their biggest concern: North Korean artillery and other forces just north of Seoul, that the North Korean threat may in any case go away, and that then the ROK would be stuck with a very expensive system seemingly suitable only to defend against Chinese missiles. Chinese are not giving much attention yet to the rumblings among some ROK military leaders that it would be a mistake for them to get left behind in missile defense technology—technology that many think will be an integral part of any modern armed force in coming decades.

For Japan.

China's objections to TMD for Japan persist. Various concerns are expressed with various degrees of seriousness.[11] The earlier arguments that TMD would provide a militaristic Japan with the shield behind which it could, in a matter of months, develop and deploy nuclear missiles is heard infrequently now. Nevertheless, there remain concerns that the technology shared with Japan as a result of Japanese participation with the United States on TMD research and development will aid a future Japanese ballistic missile program. One specialist pointed out that Japanese Aegis-equipped ships could be used in the Taiwan Strait, obviously thinking that he had made a telling point which would cause even Americans to recoil at the very thought of such a thing. The Chinese have been attentive to the Japanese sending of destroyers to the Indian Ocean in noncombat support of the U.S. effort in Afghanistan. At least in part because of this Chinese angst, Aegis-equipped ships, although already a part of the Japanese Maritime Self-Defense Force, were not dispatched by Prime Minister Junichiro Koizumi.

More generally, the Chinese argue that TMD is yet another American mistake in dealing with Japan. Beijing argues that Japan is the real future threat to regional stability and that the United States is aiding the potential resurgence of Japanese militarism by many of the things it is doing to aid the Japanese Self-Defense Forces (JSDF). The aspect of the U.S.-Japan alliance that has been seen as controlling Japan or curbing Japanese militarism has led in the past to Chinese acceptance that the alliance was, on balance, favorable for China, but TMD is seen as part of a shift toward the alliance making the JSDF more capable and more likely to threaten China, even to come to the support of Taiwan in some way in a conflict—especially one with U.S. involvement.

Some Chinese interlocutors will acknowledge that the real root of their concern about TMD for Japan is that the Japanese, while wringing their hands about North Korean Taepodong missiles, are actually looking over their shoulders at Chinese missiles. The essence of the concern, then, is that China wants to be able to hold at risk with its ballistic missiles Japan and, of course, U.S. bases in Japan and yet does not want to make loud public pronouncements to that effect. TMD for Japan would spoil that.

For Taiwan.

Beijing continues to express in the strongest terms its opposition to TMD for Taiwan. It has said it will react harshly to the transfer of missile defense from the United States to Taiwan. There has been no diminution of this opposition to providing defenses for Taiwan, even as Beijing has seemed to take a more measured outlook with respect to NMD. The drumbeat has intensified on the assertion that TMD for Taiwan is bad enough in itself but that the introduction of real missile defense there will mean far greater and closer coordination between the armed forces of the United States and those of Taiwan. That is described as a greater concern by far than the acquisition of the various TMD systems.

There is also in China now a more intense concern than expressed previously about the prospect of the transfer of

Patriot Advanced Capability 3 (PAC-3) ground-based air and missile defenses to Taiwan. This is the most likely real TMD that Taiwan might obtain, although it is still a rudimentary capability against short-range ballistic missiles. Previously, Chinese concerns over PAC-3 had been muted in favor of decrying the prospective transfer of ships equipped with the U.S. Navy Aegis air and missile defense system, a system that is expected eventually to have a TMD capability. The Chinese are still more wrought up about Aegis than PAC-3, but now both are of considerable concern.[12]

A well-informed Chinese think tanker has suggested that the deployment (already) by China of 300 or more short-range ballistic missiles (SRBMs) in Fujian, with about 50 more missiles coming each year, might be stopped or reversed were Taiwan to accept the one-China principle. (He went on to say that Beijing could not now make such a move because it would redound to the benefit of current Taiwan President Chen Shui-bian and aid his political party, the hated Democratic Progressive Party [DPP].[13]) Furthermore, other Chinese interlocutors now at least accept the fact that these missiles threatening Taiwan are indeed being deployed by their military. They now assert that all should understand that the purpose of these missiles is only for deterrence of a Taiwan move toward autonomy, not for use as weapons. Previously, even senior PLA officers have often denied the missile deployments or refused to discuss the subject. They simply said that everything concerning Taiwan was purely an internal affair. It is not that these developments signal that a solution to the issue is at hand, but at least, when conditions for removing missiles are raised and the fact of deployments by the hundreds is acknowledged, the prospects for reasonable discussion and even negotiation are enhanced.

Might the Door Be Open a Crack?

Because of the intertwining of TMD and Taiwan, Beijing's concerns about TMD clearly exceed those about NMD. Nonetheless, Chinese official and unofficial spokesmen, as has been described, have at least acknowledged that TMD for U.S. forces in Asia is reasonable and that their SRBMs threatening Taiwan exist and are part of the problem and an element in its possible solution.

CHINESE REACTIONS TO THE MERGING OF NMD AND TMD INTO MDS

Chinese Confusion: Real or Feigned?

There is among Chinese specialists confusion (or professed confusion) about the Bush administration's merging of NMD and TMD. Beyond the uncertainty, acknowledged by Rumsfeld, about just what the new concept of a missile defense system (MDS) implies,[14] the Chinese ask questions about Japan and Taiwan. Does MDS means that the Japanese TMD cooperation with the United States would have, as part of MDS, an NMD component against China's long-range missiles? Others raised the issue of whether PAC-3 would then be a part of MDS, thinking that it was absolute anathema to any logical person to suggest that Taiwan (which may get PAC-3) could be a part of MDS. Underlying many of the concerns expressed was the profound worry: Beyond the direct implications for China's ICBM force, would Taiwan be construed as part of MDS, meaning an even greater degree of coordination between U.S. and Taiwan armed forces? It is difficult at this early stage in the "MDS merger" to ascertain the degree to which the Chinese confusion is real or whether the MDS matter is being used as a peg on which to hang more Chinese arguments against missile defenses and to offer up more concerns about Taiwan.

187

MDS Could Negate All China's Ballistic Missile Arsenals.

There is inherent in this inchoate MDS concept the specter of a worldwide system, including sea-based and land-based interceptor missiles of various sorts and an airborne laser (to kill missiles in their boost-phase ascent), that would put in jeopardy China's ICBM deterrent arsenal, its SRBMs, and even medium-range ballistic missiles (MRBMs). Powell's visit to Beijing in late July 2001 did not assuage Chinese concerns on this issue. His arguments that the U.S. missile defense system would be limited and no threat to Chinese long-range missiles was, for the Chinese, drowned out by noises from elsewhere outside (but close to) the administration that send other signals and the silence within the administration, based on acknowledged uncertainty, about how the concept will evolve.

The Taiwan Complication.

A young researcher at a strategic institute in Shanghai summed up the Chinese view of MDS: The Bush administration's blurring of NMD and TMD is apparently a program to cover more countries with a missile-defense blanket. This complicates the Chinese view of missile defense with respect to Taiwan and gives China more reason to object to any form of missile defense for Taiwan. This is not a positive development from the Chinese military viewpoint. Coupled with the announced U.S. focus on Asia, this will give Chinese hard-liners a stronger argument. As with other arguments concerning Taiwan, the speaker considered that his point had been made tellingly when he said even Taiwan might be protected by MDS.

THE CHINESE DESIRE OR WILLINGNESS TO TALK ABOUT MISSILE DEFENSE ISSUES

For some American observers, it appears that Beijing and Washington are so firmly entrenched in mutually irreconcilable positions that there might seem to be no hope for negotiation of a positive outcome or any other form of resolution. Yet Sha, then head of the arms control department of the Chinese MFA, in March 2001 agreed to talks on NMD that he hoped would "narrow . . . differences," and he welcomed Assistant Secretary of State James Kelly to Beijing in May. In Kelly's departure statement after those talks, he said he had explained the overall American strategy and that there was agreement to a continuing dialogue.

Beijing Wants Both Economic Progress and Deterrence.

Although this statement by Kelly may have had an understandably optimistic tilt, there are other positive signs. As is well known, China is already testing a modern ICBM, the DF 31, to replace its obsolescent DF 5A force, but Beijing does not want to expend the resources to build hundreds of missiles (enough to overcome any NMD envisioned) or to greatly improve its missiles to make them less vulnerable to intercept. As alluded to previously, a responsible Chinese specialist on this issue has suggested that Beijing might be able to tolerate the 10 NMD interceptors recently mentioned by Rumsfeld, but that China could not tolerate 250 interceptor missiles. According to Chinese sources, when Kelly met Sha, Sha did not indicate a readiness to compromise so far; however, if China's core interest is respected "to some extent," China may be flexible, according to this well-informed security specialist. China, it was suggested, wants both economic development [unfettered by a need for a large nuclear buildup] and to maintain a deterrent. This speculative tidbit about possible Chinese compromise is certainly not a breakthrough, but it does reflect, it seems, a desire by China to talk and offers Washington a bit of negotiating room.

The talks with Kelly were viewed in China as successful only in that they held out the promise of further talks. The

Chinese were apparently unhappy at the level of seniority—an assistant secretary rather than the deputy secretary of state who had visited other Asian countries (and Australia) on the tour that included Kelly. It was noted that Bush administration very senior people talk to Russia and other countries, as did the Clinton administration; but that there had been, as of mid-July 2001, no such talks with China. An arms control specialist pointed out bluntly that Bush has personally spoken to other presidents on missile defense (by phone and in person, he volunteered), but he had not, to that point, spoken to Jiang on that topic. Yet Powell was in Beijing in late July, he reported that, although missile defense was a major agenda item for his session with Foreign Minister Tang Jiaxuan, there had been no in-depth discussion about missile defense. The Chinese had only "listened and responded with a question or two."[15]

Chinese Suggestions about Missile-Defense Talks with the United States.

In any event, the Chinese were, in the weeks preceding the expected Bush-Jiang October meeting, indicating a readiness to talk and making suggestions about how that might proceed. They now have the prospect of a summit in 2002, and the prospect that Sino-U.S. relations may be much improved over early 2001. The arms control specialist in Beijing explained what Americans should understand before the United States talks to China on the missile defense issue. He said that Americans need to understand more fully the Chinese political situation. Jiang has to contend with pressure from public opinion. He has to convince the Chinese people and the Chinese media[16] that the United States is not to be feared.

He then suggested that, in developing an agenda for talks, it is important for China to know what form of missile defense the United States contemplates because missile defenses are seen in China as a form of U.S. hegemony. Next, talks should turn to the threat missiles pose to the

190

United States and to China and Russia. Options other than missile defenses that could reduce the threat should be discussed, as well as options with respect to the issue of the ABM Treaty.[17] Then, options for missile defense systems to be deployed would be appropriately discussed. He added that, in the Chinese view, there is now no real threat that warrants a national missile defense.

Viewed cynically, this carefully laid out proposal for an agenda illustrates that what China, in the view of this well-informed specialist in Beijing, wants to do is force the United States to describe the concept in at least some detail, talk about options other than missile defense to cope with the threat, and then argue that national missile defense is neither needed nor appropriate and that abandoning the ABM Treaty is unwise.

Another interlocutor suggested that the United States and China should begin now to exchange views at other than the very senior level, that an early diverse dialogue would be beneficial. He said that it is important to find a way to discuss missile defense issues seriously at senior levels, expert levels, and in Track 2 (nongovernmental channels) or other such unofficial venues. His reasoning was that, if the United States deploys missile defenses, China would have to increase the number and quality of its nuclear forces. The United States should use all these diverse opportunities to persuade China that NMD is not intended against China. [This suggestion by a somewhat senior PLA reserve officer at a strategic institute is noteworthy primarily because he was the only specialist who seemed to take seriously the United States position that missile defenses are not ultimately intended to be able to defeat China's ICBM force.]

Does China Want To Share in Missile Defense?

On the issue of the Americans possibly offering to share missile defense technology with China, there were two divergent views: An arms control specialist at a Beijing

191

institute opined that China may, contrary to previous positions, be interested in having the United States share missile defense technology with China. China is concerned that the United States may react to a Chinese attack on Taiwan with a first strike, and that the United States could then defeat a Chinese retaliatory strike with its missile defenses. He rushed to add that he did not consider the scenario realistic, but that such theoretical scenarios were the stuff of arms control strategic thinking.

The other view was offered by a civilian specialist and former diplomat associated with the State Council. Chinese officials, he said, think that the United States is not inclined to share missile-defense technology with China but believe the United States is more likely to share that technology with Russia. Moreover, he asserted, the examples of disaster with military technology transfers from the United States in 1989, after events at Tiananmen Square, serve as a lesson for Chinese who might consider a program of U.S. transfer of important technology. After more than a decade, the Tiananmen sanctions are still in place. China cannot risk cooperation with the United States, he stated flatly and without acrimony.

China Wants To Be Heard.

An arms control specialist who is currently working on precisely the topic of how China should react to the Bush administration missile defense issues made a hopeful observation. He said that, propitiously, there have been no final decisions yet by the United States on missile defense. He expects [or maybe hopes and is, in effect, making a plea to Americans to whom he talks] the United States to talk to China and not present China with a fait accompli on the issue. It is not good, he said plaintively, for Americans to say that missile defenses will be deployed regardless of the views of others, "no matter what." A senior and well-connected figure at a prestigious think tank summed up China's reaction to the Bush program saying that China wants to talk more on missile defense issues and wants the United States to leave room in its policy formulation for the legitimate concerns of China. China, he reminded, has small but "legitimate" nuclear forces. If MDS works and these forces are neutralized, what is China to do? he asked, apparently rhetorically, seeming to know that there would be no answer forthcoming.

Nurture the Good or Attack the Bad?

Professor Yang Jiemian at the Shanghai Institute for International Studies used the analogy of Western and Chinese medicines in explaining his view of how Beijing and Washington approach the missile defense issue and the root problem of the threat of missile attacks. He said Western medicine is like missile defense in that it vigorously attacks a specific aspect of the problem, concentrating potent, even dangerous, medication or therapy on a certain component of the situation that seems to be producing the symptoms. By contrast, Chinese medicine more broadly attempts to nourish the positive aspects of a situation to create steady improvements that overcome or resolve the narrow problem and prevent its recurrence.

Prognosis.

It was made quite clear that a central theme of any discussions the United States may have with China on missile defenses will be the Chinese conviction or assertion that such a protective shield, even if successful technologically and militarily, will ill serve the overarching security interests of the United States, its allies and friends, and China. If Washington wishes to respond to that criticism, the reply would probably begin with an argument that the United States can find a way to have adequate missile defenses and, at the same time, improve or sustain its bilateral and multilateral relationships and demonstrate that it will not be hegemonic. That argument would almost certainly fall on deaf ears, because the

Chinese have convinced themselves that missile defenses are "false security," counterproductive, and even obstacles to resolving international security problems; many Chinese strategists have also convinced themselves that the United States increasingly acts in an interventionist and hegemonic fashion.

Nonetheless, it appears that, if desired by Washington, there is a real prospect of having meaningful discussions with China on missile defenses because Beijing is sending the clear signal that it is willing to talk—or at the very least that it wants to be heard. It will be left to the patience and skill of the negotiators and to other unpredictable factors whether avenues for progress and understanding will open during the talks, if they are held, or whether both sides will simply bog down in their deeply rutted tracks—or maybe they should be termed "preset trajectories."

ENDNOTES - CHAPTER 6

1. Although it is not appropriate to mention the individual interlocutors, spokesmen, and questioners, the organizations represented in the discussions included: in Beijing, the Division of Arms Control and Security Studies at the China Institute of Contemporary International Relations (CICIR), the Institute for Strategic Studies at the PLA National Defense University, the School of International Studies American Studies Center at Beijing University, and the the Institute of World Development of the State Council of the PRC, Institute of American Studies of the Chinese Academy of Social Sciences (CASS); in Harbin, the Heilongjiang Provincial Academy of Social Sciences; in Shanghai, the Shanghai Institute for International Studies (SIIS), Shanghai Institute for East Asian Studies, and the Shanghai Center for RimPac Strategic and International Studies; in Hangzhou, Zhejiang Academy of Social Science; in Guangzhou, Center for Asia Pacific Studies (CAPS) and Institute of Southeast Asia Studies of Zhongshan University, Institute of Southeast Asian Studies at Jinan University, and the Institute of International Studies of the Guangzhou Academy of Social Sciences; in Xiamen, Institute of Southeast Asian Studies of Xiamen University. Additionally, the topic was discussed extensively at the three-day 2001 Hong Kong Convention of International Studies sponsored by the International Studies Association (ISA) and the University of Hong Kong 26-28 July.

2. There was more than rhetoric to the Chinese assertion that, despite affronts by the Bush administration, China would turn the other cheek. For example, Chinese officials announced in early August 2001 that China would buy 36 Boeing 737 jetliners that could be worth up to $2 billion. Martin Fackler, "China Airlines to Buy Boeing Jets," *Associated Press* wire report, August 9, 2001. In contrast to this announcement, China has in the past made decisions not to buy American commercial aircraft to demonstrate its annoyance with Washington's actions on various matters. China quickly offered its support of the U.S. response to the September 2001 terrorist attacks. This likely stemmed from both a desire to enhance bilateral relations, express outrage at the attacks, and gain U.S. support (or at least more understanding and acceptance of China's problems with terrorism in Xinjiang—where it has long warned of the dangers of Islamic fundamentalism).

3. "Jiang's Responses to Questions Submitted Prior to Interview," *New York Times*, August 10, 2001.

4 Jeremy Page, "China's Jiang Preoccupied with Taiwan—U.S. Senator," *Reuters* wire report, Beijing, August 9, 2001.

5. "Jiang's Responses to Questions Submitted Prior to Interview," *New York Times*, August 10, 2001. Jiang asserted in the written response to a *New York Times* question that the Falun Gong did not have the capacity to be a serious threat to China. In defending his harsh crackdown, he focused on the harm that Falun Gong does to its followers and Chinese society. The tone and intensity of the response tends to confirm, despite the defensive words to the contrary, that Jiang is, indeed, irrationally fearful of the power of the Falun Gong organization. It also reflects his apparent belief that his anticult campaign is working, having the desired effect, so that the Chinese people are convinced the Falun Gong is an evil cult that does harm and should be eliminated by government action.

6. The abbreviation MDS (missile defense system, implying a merging by the Bush administration of various elements of missiles defenses so as to provide layered, wide protection) should not be confused with the abbreviation GMDS (ground-based mid-course defense segment), roughly synonymous with the earlier term NMD—knocking down ICBMs after boost phase and before re-entry, roughly put. Some, seeing the letters GMDS have assumed incorrectly that it meant *global* missile defense system.

7. Questions are asked about why China is concerned about U.S. NMD if it does not intend to launch those missiles against U.S. targets.

Chinese might ask the same question about the United States and its ICBM arsenal. Most Americans would answer as the Chinese do: We have no intention of attacking any country with nuclear missiles, but we feel we must maintain a deterrent force.

8. John Pomfret, "Beijing Eases Stand on Missile Defense," *Washington Post*, March 15, 2000, p. A21.

9. Given the tone of these arguments and private comments offered after the terrorist attacks, it seems only a matter of time before the Chinese will, gently or harshly—depending on the state of bilateral relations at the time, suggest that missiles defenses would not have stopped the September 11 attacks.

10. With the advent of the mobile, solid-fueled Dongfeng 31 ICBM, and especially the anticipated longer-range follow-on version, the problem of survivability of Chinese ICBMs (against a first strike) would seem to be appreciably lessened. Beijing may feel adequately confident that at least some of its ICBM arsenal would survive if they are not pinned to a fixed (and probably known) location. Use of mobile decoys could, of course, further complicate U.S. targeting.

11. For a detailed examination of China's objection to ballistic missile defense for Japan, see the recently published Michael D. Swaine, et al., *Japan and Ballistic Missile Defense*, RAND, Santa Monica, 2001, pp. 79-83.

12. Neither Aegis-equipped ships nor PAC-3 missiles have yet been approved by the United States for transfer to Taiwan.

13. The Democratic Progressive Party of President Chen Shui-bian had traditionally been known as a pro-independence party, although Chen has not embraced that concept during his time in office.

14. Vernon Loeb, "Rumsfeld in Moscow for Talks," *Washington Post*, August 13, 2001, p. A9. Rumsfeld acknowledged, as reported in this article, Russian complaints that they did not understand the kind of missile system envisioned by the Bush administration and was quoted as saying, "It's not knowable, what we're going to deploy, because we're in a testing mode."

15. U.S. State Department transcript of a press conference held by Powell on July 29, 2001. The transcript was entitled "Sec. Powell Outlines Results of Visit to Asia-Pacific Region."

16. He reduced his credibility a bit by explaining how independent the Chinese media had become.

17. This arms control specialist raised a point that no one else mentioned. He said that, rather than talk about abrogating or modifying the ABM Treaty, unidentified Europeans are suggesting that it would be preferable to try to impose some broad version of restrictions on missiles, possibly something similar to MTCR. He went on to describe it rather vaguely as an "international court" on missiles. The idea, it seemed, would be the establishment of an international body to impose restrictions or prohibitions on the development and deployment of missiles. The concept, crudely put, was that, rather than building missile defenses, missiles would be outlawed.

CHAPTER 7

EAST ASIAN REACTIONS TO U.S. MISSILE DEFENSE: TORN BETWEEN TACIT SUPPORT AND OVERT OPPOSITION

Taeho Kim

In light of the September 11, 2001, terrorist attacks on the United States homeland, it is increasingly certain that the George W. Bush administration's initial policy priorities and future visions will go through a reappraisal, readjustment, and reconfirmation. It is also true that war in Afghanistan, together with the broader international antiterrorist efforts, has significantly altered the administration's working definition of its friends and foes around the world—at least for the time being. There is also little doubt that antiterrorism will remain a priority agenda in future U.S. foreign policy.

It is equally likely, however, that given its recent origin and its varying degrees of significance to other governments, the antiterrorism agenda will be severely contested by other compelling U.S. priorities and budgetary concerns that have been put on hold during the war in Afghanistan. The Bush presidency's initial policy priorities and future visions, albeit at a reduced scale and a slower pace, will be back on the front burner sooner rather than later.

Ranging from future national security threats to the United States to the future possibility of armed conflict in international politics to U.S. relationships with such major powers as Russia, China, and Japan, they—if fully implemented—would have constituted a sharp departure from those of the William Clinton presidency. In particular, the administration strongly intended to not only slash the size of its nuclear arsenal but also develop both defensive and offensive missile systems.

Thus, missile defense (MD) stands tall as a premier defense issue in the Bush administration's larger "military transformation" with the basis of defense planning now being shifted to a future "capability-based" approach from the previous "threat-based" one.[1] One of the key questions for U.S. policymakers is how to mesh America's MD program with East Asian security—now in the larger context of international antiterrorist efforts.

In this chapter, I argue that in light of the political sensitivities, technological challenges, and budgetary constraints associated with U.S. MD, as well as the diverse defense requirements of major East Asian states, there is no such thing as a uniform, "one-size-fits-all" approach in coupling American MD with East Asian security, and that those states, as the MD issue inches toward the central place in their crowded security agenda, are highly likely to take a bifurcated and polarized position with some different nuances and shades—that is, between tacit support and overt opposition.

At present and for the foreseeable future, no single regional security issue seems more multifaceted and potentially divisive than MD. It touches upon a variety of issue areas ranging from regional stability, power balance among major states, and arms control to U.S. alliance ties. As such, a great many factors intervene in each state's calculus before any actual MD deployment within the region, while an equally great number of consequences are possible as well. To better understand the complex calculations the regional states must factor in, it is necessary to identify and prioritize some major variables that affect the debate and the likely courses of action by individual regional states. At a minimum, four major considerations stand out:

- Their primary sources of current and likely future threat and the relative weight of MD in their security calculus;

- The evolution of domestic politics and their relationships with the United States, including an assessment of the latter's future role in and commitment to regional security;

- Technological feasibility and budgetary considerations as the MD plan takes a more concrete shape in the years ahead; and,

- Possible reactions (either positive or negative) by neighboring states, especially major powers, to their decision to develop and deploy MD.

Among the four, the first factor falls within the realm of reasonable prediction, as it concerns geography, familiar threats, and the availability of defense measures. Both lateral and vertical proliferation of missile and other WMD technologies over the past decades have almost invariably increased the need to deter this type of security threat. The domestic variable is far more complex and more uncertain than the first factor and involves many unknowns and unknowables down the road. The relationship with the United States, which would normally be treated as separate from domestic considerations, is often an issue of critical importance in the vortex of politics in Japan, Taiwan, and South Korea, as all three depend to a varying extent on the United States for their security. Regarding the third variable, a thick cloud of technical uncertainties overshadow the MD architecture, especially national missile defense (NMD), while Japan, Taiwan, and South Korea, the so-called economic powerhouses, now look pale in the face of grim economic prospects. The regional reactions, of which China's appears the most important, are likely to be mixed, complicated, and nested so that they may defy a simple prediction, even if recent developments and existing trends are extrapolated.

As befits a premier defense issue in the Bush administration's "military transformation," MDs have attracted enormous attention within a short period of time on both sides of the Pacific Ocean. While there has not been a shortage of conference proceedings, edited volumes, and policy papers, they tend to highlight certain aspects of theater missile defense (TMD) and/or NMD only.[2] This much more brief essay is no exception. In particular, as other observers have pointed out, the debate has already incurred diplomatic costs prematurely: Even if program feasibility has yet to be proven by repeated test results, many observers have assumed the most effective system.[3] I would further argue that America's current ad hoc, on-and-off approach to explain its MD program overseas is not sufficient and has yet to be replaced by a more frequent and institutionalized one that aims at addressing each state's defense requirements, its political as well as technical issues, and finally, future regional stability and prosperity.

With the above considerations in mind, this chapter throws some light on each of the four Northeast Asian powers' perceptions, reactions, and likely future actions toward missile defense. It is intended to be a think piece highlighting select aspects of the MD debate in Japan, Taiwan, South Korea, and North Korea only, as China's position and its likely actions are addressed in greater detail by Eric McVadon and Mark Stokes in this volume and by others.[4] As the author is technologically uninitiated, this chapter will forgo any arcane talk about the world of science except to invoke the relevant authorities, but will address in some depth South Korea's perspectives, which have often attracted scant attention. It concludes with an assessment of the potential regional consequences of the MD program and a set of policy proposals that might enhance the prospects for coupling missile defenses and regional security.

Japan: Limited Research and Development (R&D) Commitment and Alliance Consideration.

As an island nation, Japan is particularly concerned with a missile threat. The North Korean missiles, especially their currently deployed *Nodongs*, figure prominently in Japan's security planning. While the possibility is very low, China's potential threat to use its medium-range ballistic missiles (MRBMs) in various contingencies also cannot be ruled out. For instance, in the context of an inter-Korean or a cross-Strait conflict, Japan would remain worried about a potential or actual missile threat by North Korea and/or China and the collateral cost of being a host to U.S. Forces Japan (USFJ) as well as a close ally of the United States.

As compelling as the perceived missile threat is the consideration of alliance maintenance. Even if Japan's decision to commit to a limited joint R&D program on TMD was precipitated by the August 1998 flight-test of the North Korean *Taepodong-1*, the American request for Japan's participation in MD harkens back to the Strategic Defense Initiative (SDI) program in 1983. As long as Japan regards its alliance relationship with the United States as *vital* to its national interest, its limited participation in MD should be taken as a measure to strengthen the U.S.-Japan alliance in the post-Cold War era. Thus, alliance considerations, together with a potential missile threat, constitute a primary rationale influencing Japan's decision to join the R&D program, which is also in line with Japan's overall strategic tilt toward the United States in the post-Cold War era.

At present, Japan participates in a joint R&D program on four technical areas of the Navy Theater-Wide (NTW) missile program, but has not committed itself to development or deployment of TMD.[5] It currently operates six battalions of 24 enhanced Patriot Advanced Capability-2 (PAC-2 Plus) fire units, which, under the 1975 agreement with the United States, are part of Japan's air-defense role for U.S. military installations. As of the end of 2001, Japan is likely to acquire PAC-3 as part of its force improvement plan and/or an upgraded PAC-3 Configuration-3 system to fully function as part of a layered TMD architecture. In addition to the current four *Kongo*-class AEGIS-equipped destroyers, the Japan Maritime Self-Defense Force (JMSDF) plans to acquire two additional ships in the new Mid-term Defense Program (2001-2005), with the decision likely in 2003. For reasons related to Japan's requirements and system characteristics, other TMD components, such as theater high altitude area defense (THAAD) and naval air defense (NAD), are not likely to be seriously considered.

Before moving beyond the current R&D stage, however, Japanese policymakers need to pay attention to a host of major domestic and external factors. First, as the Japanese economy suffers from nearly 0 percent growth for a decade, coupled with growing nonperforming and underperforming loans and a record-high unemployment rate of 5 percent throughout 2001, the JSDF is doomed to engage in an uphill battle against the national level social programs and economic restoration efforts, as well as within its three services.

Second, Japan's MD debate is subject to well-known bureaucratic in-fighting and legal constraints. It is the complex and divisive nature of MD that brings to bear upon the debate the continued competition among the ideological camps (left vs. right), interest groups (anti-China groups vs. arms control supporters) and government agencies (Ministry of Finance vs. Japan Defense Agency). The weakening of the traditional left and the new "Koizumi factor"—as Japan's wider security role in the wake of the war in Afghanistan demonstrates—could make a stronger case for missile defense, although a fragile political coalition and the ensuing frequent change of government could steer the debate back into a more familiar bureaucratic tug-of-war among the ministries concerned with the issue.[6] As Stephen A. Cambone has pointed out in a perceptive study, the MD program is set to stir domestic debate in Japan as it touches upon such sensitive issues as the peaceful use of space, the right of collective defense, and the export of defense-related technologies.[7]

Third, Chinese reactions will have an important role to play. Japanese policymakers will remain concerned with the negative impact of its MD decision on Sino-Japanese relations, even if China's relations with both the United States and Japan are likely to be strained for the foreseeable future regardless. As to the most sensitive issues involving Japan in the eyes of Beijing—that is, Japan's potential role in a Taiwan contingency, Japan has no practical option other than taking an ambiguous stance. For this reason, Japan will be very cautious and remain mindful of the so-called "international security situation," in which the China factor occupies a central place. Aside from political developments in cross-Strait and inter-Korean relations that many American officials and analysts often believe to be important variables, the positions by Taiwan and South Korea on TMD acquisition could significantly affect the Japanese decision as well.

Fourth, even if the PAC-3 low-tier and AEGIS-based NTW upper-tier systems were eventually to be acquired by Japan, it would leave no role for the Japan Ground Self-Defense Force (JGSDF). Not only does the army still remain the most dominant service in Japan—as well as in Korea—but inter-service rivalry among the services, with each trying to secure its respective crown jewels (e.g., tanks, ships, and aircraft), does not bode well for TMD funding. Under such circumstances a real opportunity cost exists between major platforms and TMD.

Fifth, and closely related to the fourth factor, interoperability and command and control problems will arise sooner rather than later. As the JSDF is not structured to operate under a combined forces command with the United States, unlike the U.S.-Republic of Korea (ROK) case, it needs to address such complex questions as the level of interoperability, surveillance and cueing, adjustments of force structure, and operational control.

Taken together, these issues confront Japan with diverse challenges, which it must face before moving beyond the current R&D phase. If Japan ever takes that course of action, it would transpire in the context of domestic politics and an external environment characterized by a dramatic departure from the past patterns. In order to prepare for such an eventuality, as one Japanese observer noted, a political decision based on the criticality of the U.S. alliance as well as public education intended to provide a better understanding of this arcane issue will be a good beginning.[8]

Taiwan: In Search of a Political Shield.

A missile threat from mainland China, together with a limited naval blockade, constitutes a primary source of concern to Taiwan, especially at the opening stages of a large-scale cross-Strait conflict. Besides its longer-range missile inventory, China is reported to have deployed a minimum of 150-200 short-range ballistic missiles (SRBMs) opposite Taiwan and doubtless has a capability to significantly increase its existing missile arsenal.[9] Short warning time further complicates any missile defense scheme by Taiwan.

Even if Taiwan possesses a limited missile defense capability consisting of three PAC-2/Modified Air Defense System (MADS) fire units with 200 missiles as well as of Tien Kung (Sky Bow) surface-to-air missiles (SAMs), it by no means possesses sufficient measures to counter the large and apparently growing Chinese missile threat. For this reason, Taiwan has considered other options, such as development of longer-range missiles that can reach the targets inside the mainland and has implemented various passive defense measures. None of them are likely to be very effective against the Chinese missiles, however.

As many observers in Washington, Beijing, and Taipei have pointed out, Taiwan's search for a missile defense capability centering on the United States is primarily aimed at securing political, rather than military, deterrence. As the need to counter the mainland's threat and to maintain relations with the United States is a well-established fact of life among politicians and the general public in Taiwan, it is natural for Taiwan to consider joining U.S. MD to an extent and in ways that maintain stability in the Taiwan Strait.

The danger lies, according to Thomas J. Christensen, in the false sense of safety MD might create for Washington as well as for Taipei. In his words, "The acquisition of missile defenses thus may perversely make the island appear safer than it actually is in the eyes of the American public and leadership, to the detriment of Taiwan's security."[10] Furthermore, as a Stimson Center report has persuasively argued,[11] any TMD components transferred to Taiwan that are interoperable and linked with U.S. forces would not only invite a strong reaction from China, including tensions in the Taiwan Strait, and in U.S.-China relations, but could actually send another wrong signal to the Taiwan people, as noted before.

For its part, Taiwan made an official call for common defense against the growing Chinese missile threat to itself as well as to the United States and Japan. In a recent interview, Taiwan President Chen Shui-bian argued that "A PRC [missile] threat against Taiwan is something that the United States, Japan and Taiwan must jointly deal with through the division of responsibility and cooperation."[12] In a similar vein, Taiwan's Ministry of National Defense made clear that if invited it would "seriously" consider joining U.S. MD.

While Taiwan's reactions to U.S. MD will very much depend upon the level of missile and other threats from mainland China, the Chinese leadership, for its part, remains worried about any possible connection between U.S. TMD and the Taiwan question. China's reactions to TMD transfers to Taiwan will be most serious. As MD would compromise its ability to coerce Taiwan not to move beyond the limits set by Beijing, the PRC is very opposed to Taiwan

TMD. In particular, as a recent study by the Monterey Institute of International Studies (MIIS) has pointed out, a TMD linked with Taiwan—especially the AEGIS-equipped destroyers—would severely impair China's ability to deter the United States or the United States and Japan in a major Taiwan contingency and would constitute a quasi-alliance between Taiwan and the United States.[13] It may thus further reinforce a circle of containment against China.

In light of both Taiwan's need for a political shield in the face of a clear missile threat and of China's strong reactions against closer ties between Taiwan and the United States, any viable future for Taiwan would fall between the opposite positions. This also points to the fact that any resolution in cross-Strait relations will and should be of a political, and hopefully peaceful, nature. However, continued stalemate in the cross-Strait talks, coupled with the highly limited scope of the MD debate in Taiwan,[14] would continue to make the issue a dormant yet highly consequential one in the three-way relationship among Beijing, Taipei, and Washington.

South Korea: Self-reliant Now, Linked with the United States Later?

Countering missile threats in South Korea's overall defense requirements should be seen in a different context from those of Japan and Taiwan. For one thing, the kaleidoscopic changes in post-Cold War global and regional security notwithstanding, the crux of the Korean security problem has remained remarkably unchanged to date: a land-based military threat from North Korea. Even without a Nuclear, Biological, and Chemical (NBC) capability, North Korea's conventional military capability in general and the size, deployment, and equipment of the North Korean People's Army (NKPA) in particular pose a significant threat to the defense of South Korea. Not only is the NKPA numerically superior and highly mechanized, but 65 percent of its offensive elements are currently concentrated within 60 miles north of the Demilitarized Zone (DMZ). Since Seoul, the South Korean capital and home of 12 million people, is located less than 30 miles south of the demilitarized zone (DMZ), the South Korean forces would have little strategic depth and warning time. While it is true that the South Korean forces, backed by the United States forces and by their own industrial infrastructure, do retain a substantial technological edge, the NKPA's quantitative and geographical advantages could well lead to unacceptable damage upon the South, especially upon Seoul.[15]

Throughout the 1990s, moreover, North Korea's accumulation of an NBC capability posed an additional threat to South Korean security. North Korea's consistent efforts to develop various types of missile systems were manifest in at least three flight tests: the May 1993 test of the *Nodong* missile (an improved version of *Scud-C*) with the range of over 500 miles; the June 1994 test of two 60-mile antiship missiles; and the well-publicized three-stage *Taepodong-1* Medium-Range Ballistic Missile (MRBM) in August 1998.[16] North Korea is believed to possess 300-500 *Scud* Short-Range Ballistic Missiles (SRBMs) of various types and about 100 *Nodong* MRBMs.

However, most worrisome, especially at the opening phases of war, is the threat of barrage tactics by North Korea's 11,500-strong artillery. In particular, the 240-mm Multiple Rocket Launchers (MRLs) and 170-mm self-propelled guns, with a range of 65 kilometers and 45 kilometers, respectively, can literally shower Seoul with thousands of rounds within a few hours—a fact pointedly made in an apocalyptic statement in March 1994 by North Korean negotiator Park Young Soo who threatened his counterpart that, in case of a war, Seoul would become a "sea of fire." As an additional reminder of this artillery threat, the NKPA's two artillery corps are currently deployed below the Pyongyang-Wonsan line. Thus, it can be concluded that North Korea's missile capability constitutes a significant, but not the primary, threat to South Korean security.

The relative weight given to missile threats in South Korea's overall defense requirements was a major factor in the ROK government's March 1999 announcement that it would not participate in a U.S. TMD system on the ground that "South Korea's geographical characteristics and its limited strategic depth as well as our technical capability and economic conditions would not allow us to join it at this stage."[17]

ROK policymakers are well aware, however, that missile defense is an issue that could critically affect the health of its alliance relationship with the United States. Besides its alliance ties, South Korea remains central to an overall U.S. MD plan and its regional components: the North Korean missile as a primary rationale, the Mutual Defense Treaty (MDT)-mandated deployment of U.S. weapons in and around South Korea, and the presence of U.S. Forces Korea (USFK).

It would be an exaggeration to say, however, that in South Korea there has been an extensive debate on the MD issue at either the public or government level.[18] The government's position has largely been confined to that of the Ministry of National Defense (MND), while any in-depth discussions on the pros and cons of missile defenses in South Korea have so far been held only by a handful of policy institutes, universities, and nongoverment organizations (NGOs).[19] From those limited debates, a few emerging perspectives can be discerned that could affect South Korea's likely course of action.

First, how could peace and unification, the primary national objective of South Korea, be reconciled with missile defenses? Would the peace process on the peninsula be inversely correlated with U.S. missile defense, as Michael Green and Toby Dalton, among others, have posited?[20] Or would missile defense constitute a part of South Korea's preparation for its future security environment regardless?

Second is the possibility for a change of government in the December 2002 presidential election. Unlike the incumbent government, which puts a heavy emphasis on reconciliation with North Korea, Lee Hoei Chang, the current chairman of the opposition Grand National Party, who was defeated in the 1997 presidential election by a narrow margin, is known to have a much tougher policy stance toward North Korea in general and toward the latter's missile and weapons of mass destruction (WMD) capability in particular.[21]

It should also be noted parenthetically that much of the confusion in the ROK's North Korea policy stems from the tension between a progressive government and conservative society in South Korea, while the opposite—that is, a conservative government and progressive society—has long been the case in post-war Korean politics.

Third, while the ROK government decided not to join U.S. TMD, it does not necessarily mean that it will be deprived of any missile defense capability in the future, a point frequently raised by the inquisitive media and the critical NGOs.

While it is rare for senior ROK officials to make public statements on MD, one of the most explicit statements was made by the defense minister in early 2001, which deserves a long quotation.

> The U.S. NMD plan, which is still at a conceptual stage, needs to cope with technical problems, budget appropriation, consultations with allies including NATO, and Russian and Chinese responses and will therefore take some time to be finalized. The [ROK] government, when the Bush administration's NMD plan becomes more concrete, will cautiously clarify our position after taking a comprehensive view of our capability and other security considerations. Regarding TMD, the government is not considering to participate in it at this stage in light of our geographical characteristics, economic capability, and the urgency of [our] responses to North Korea's long-range artillery and short-range threats [Scuds?]. Over the longer term, given the

211

current North Korean missile threat and future battle environment, we are reviewing to construct a missile defense system suitable to our own [security] environment.[22]

Furthermore, the South Korean military is now in the middle of making five major weapons procurement decisions: the F-X, the AH-X, the E-X, the SAM-X, and KDX-III.[23] Among the five big-ticket items, totaling over $10 billion ($1=1,200 won), the SAM-X, the KDX-III, and the E-X (Airborne Warning and Control System) programs are relevant to an MD architecture, even if the eventual form of any ROK missile defense system is a matter of conjecture at this time.[24] For the SAM-X program the PAC-3 Configuration-3 is a serious contender, while the KDX-III includes two destroyers with the AEGIS system. As for the remaining three platforms, it seems safe to say that they are still being contested by American and European defense bidders.

While the government still insists—only when asked by the inquisitive Korean and foreign media—on an MD system that fits into South Korea's needs, it begs the question of how the ROK would ever acquire and operate the surveillance, cueing, and Battle Management/Command, Control, and Communications (BM/C3) capability, which immediately puts a big question mark on its technical feasibility and funding availability. At present, USFK operates only one battalion of Patriot missiles with six firing batteries, which can barely defend its key installations— again a pointed reminder of the ROK government's future need for a larger missile-defense system.

Finally, like many other states in the region, South Korea will also factor in the impact of its MD decision on its larger neighbors, especially on China. This is quite understandable, as peace and security on the peninsula is as much an international issue as an inter-Korean one and the majority of the South Korean public perceives, rightly or wrongly, that China will play a growing and benign role in peninsular affairs in the future.[25] To make a long story short, however, the China factor, while important, will not dominate the decision, as a combination of factors including South Korea's defense needs, its elite perceptions, and the emerging strategic configuration in the region all point to the prolongation of the existing "strategic prioritization" with the United States in the decades to come.

North Korea: A Matter of Regime Survival.

Being singled out as a primary rationale for U.S. MD, North Korea adamantly opposes the plan. North Korea's visceral reaction to MD, however, should be seen in the context of its fundamental goal: regime survival. Its nuclear and missile capability is a multipurpose enabler that helps to keep the Kim Jong Il regime afloat.[26] Militarily, for one thing, it deters the United States or the ROK-U.S. combined forces from attacking the North in case of a contingency as its *Scuds*, *Nodongs*, and possibly *Taepodongs* could threaten South Korea, Japan, and the United States, respectively. Diplomatically, for another, its missile capability helps North Korea to maintain its own leverage and prestige in the international arena. For still another, its missile capability is a major hard currency earner in its overall declining outside trade.

For these reasons, while taking a "diplomatic united front" against U.S. MD with Moscow and Beijing, Pyongyang has offered the most acerbic phrases in its official *Rodong Shinmun*, which says that the United States has intended to "run over the Republic [DPRK] by MD," "push to death those who do not surrender," and "aim at the whole world as its strategic coordinates."[27] It further argues that the "so-called theory of the North Korean missile threat is an unashamed casuistry," and that the United States is now threatening North Korea by military means and would launch a preemptive strike at it at the right moment.[28]

Among a long list of negative impacts of MD unto itself, MD waters down and may eventually neutralize the utility of North Korea's nuclear and missile program as a bargaining chip (if it was ever intended to be so) in its negotiation with the United States. It is also possible and even likely, however, that the North Korean leadership has already understood the fact that despite its repeated hostile rhetoric, TMD/NMD is not an issue to be bargained away at any price. North Korea's perspectives and positions on MD are similar to those of China in that it sees U.S. MD as having a political motive based on military and technological prowess and that MD is aimed at "rogue states," "states of concern," "missile proliferators"—in other words, the dislikes of the United States.

While the Bush administration has confirmed the resumption of negotiations with Pyongyang, the latter understands full well that unless its WMD capabilities, missile proliferation and conventional forces are addressed, there will be little hope for improved relations between itself and Washington. Notwithstanding Secretary of State Colin L. Powell's call for a resumption of U.S.-North Korean talks "anywhere, at any time,"[29] the new U.S. administration's demand for an "improved implementation" of the 1994 Geneva Agreement, "verifiable constraints" on missile programs as well as the conventional force issue—which are significantly different from those of the Perry Process—are seen by North Korea as tantamount to giving up its trump cards.

North Korea's possible reactions to U.S. MD deployment and particularly South Korea's future involvement in it are by no means certain. A limited range of options North Korea might take, such as expansion, improvement, and sophistication of the existing missile arsenal, development of new types of missiles or countermeasures, and increased missile sales, would be prohibitively costly and/or diplomatically unwise. In their stead, North Korea's short-term solution is a diplomatic clarion call with China and Russia, while waiting for a change of atmospherics in a recalcitrant Washington. As long as Seoul and Tokyo remain vulnerable to its missile and NBC capability, North

Korea may take a coercive option combined with separate negotiations with the United States and South Korea.

It was, however, in this constricted external environment of North Korea that the September 11 attacks intervened. For one thing, North Korea had never held a priority in the Bush administration's long foreign policy agenda—at least before September 11. For another, now is not the time for North Korea to draw world attention by making its time-proven provocations or incidents, which are nonetheless necessary for a continued flow of international assistance onto itself.[30] For still another, as Russia's ostensibly moderate response to U.S. withdrawal from the ABM Treaty might indicate, North Korea's strong opposition to MD may end up with a chorus of one— arguably the worst situation in the eyes of Pyongyang. In short, North Korea's limited military and diplomatic options as to MD would likely result in delaying tactics in separate talks with the United States and with South Korea over the longer term.

Conclusions and Implications for East Asian Security.

In the closing pages of this chapter, it is appropriate to sum up the findings and arguments with respect to the questions raised at the outset. First, in light of the varying consequences of U.S. MD on regional security and of equally diverse reactions to it by individual states, it is critical to address the specific defense requirements of U.S. regional allies and friends and their concerns with regard to the MD issue. This is all the more necessary because—even if U.S. regional allies and friends generally support the MD program—there will be nuances in policies, shades in commitment, and delays in implementation in their reactions.

Second, as the highly circumscribed nature of the MD debate in the three countries—at both public and governmental level—strongly indicates, more regular and more systematic efforts on the U.S. part are necessary to explain its MD plan to regional states. Focused discussions on the different levels of missile threat to individual states and consideration of their domestic politics—the two most important factors driving their individual responses to MD—would be a good starting point. An institutionalized discussion of the MD issue in regular U.S. defense talks with its allies would be another approach enhancing mutual understanding on the subject.

This also undergirds the third recommendation, which is that the sooner the United States copes with the major defense and strategic concerns of regional states on MD, the easier it will be to tackle the specific technical and even budgetary issues later. Without a semblance of thought, for instance, on the future possibility of possessing either individualized MD assets or those of an integrated Northeast Asian MD system, the regional states would continue their own soul-searching with significant waste of political and budgetary resources likely down the road. For another, the China factor, and more specifically America's understanding with China on the MD issue, should be conveyed to regional states so as to allay their concerns about China's potential reactions to the MD issue and to their respective bilateral ties. This would be particularly pertinent as China enters the critical period of the generational change in leadership and of projecting benign images to the outside world.

Fourth, while there is little doubt in America's need and determination for a MD plan, a more sensible and more balanced approach is necessary to cope with other types of international and regional sources of threat. As the September 11 attacks have vividly shown, a fuller spectrum of threats to national security is now the order of the day for most nations in the world. They include, but are not limited to, biological and chemical attacks, border/homeland infiltration, computer viruses, and international terrorism.[31] In brief, a viable MD program should complement, not supplant, other compelling defense requirements of a nation.

Finally, it is trite, but true, to note that MD ultimately intends to enhance *both* U.S. security and regional stability. Neither goal should be pursued at the expense of the other. Nor should the MD issue be taken as a litmus test for "making or breaking" U.S. bilateral relationships with its allies and friends in the region. Barring any unforeseen developments or regional shocks, it is certainly possible for U.S. regional allies and friends to adjust their respective defense requirements for the sake of regional stability and prosperity. Whether or not the MD issue will open up a new possibility for this goal will hinge on a renewed effort and mutual understanding on both sides of the Asia-Pacific.

ENDNOTES - CHAPTER 7

1. "Military transformation" is the key word of the *Quadrennial Defense Review (QDR) Report* released by the Pentagon on September 30, 2001. For the operational goals of the military transformation, see p. 30 of the *QDR Report*. See also Kim Burger, "QDR Report Blurs Edges on Specific Strategy," *Jane's Defence Weekly*, October 10, 2001, p. 10; Andrew Koch, "QDR Aims to Transform US Forces," *Jane's Defence Weekly*, August 22, 2001, p. 6.

2. For a fuller discussion of U.S. MD and East Asian security, see Michael D. Swaine, Rachel M. Swanger, and Takashi Kawakami, *Japan and Ballistic Missile Defense,* Santa Monica: RAND Corporation, 2001; Evan S. Medeiros, ed., *Ballistic Missile Defense and Northeast Asian Security: Views from Washington, Beijing, and Tokyo*, Monterey: The Stanley Foundation and the Monterey Institute of International Studies, 2001; Michael J. Green and Toby F. Dalton, *Asian Reactions to U.S. Missile Defense*, NBR Analysis, Vol. 11, No. 3, November 2000; *Theater Missile Defenses in the Asia-Pacific Region*, Working Group Report No. 34, Washington, DC: A Henry L. Stimson Center, June 2000. See also the conference papers presented at the "Partnership for Peace: Building Long-term Security Cooperation in Northeast Asia," *http://www.nautilus.org/nukepolicy/workshops/shanghai-01/paper s.html*, and "East Asian Regional Security Futures: Theater Missile Defense Implications," *http://www.nautilus.org/nukepolicy/TMD-Conference/index.html*.

3. See, for example, Medeiros, p. i.

217

4. For China's official positions on MD, see a series of statements by Ambassador Sha Zukang at the PRC Foreign Ministry's web page, *www.fmprc.gov.cn*. See also Yan Xuetong, "TMD Rocking Regional Stability," *Korean Journal of Defense Analysis*, Vol. 11, No. 1, Summer 1999, pp. 67-86; Xie Wenqing, "US TMD and Taiwan," *International Strategic Studies*, Serial No. 57, July 2000, pp. 25-31; Xia Liping, "Prospects for Cooperative Security in East Asia: From Chinese Perspectives," a paper presented at the "Partnership for Peace: Building Long-term Security Cooperation in Northeast Asia," *http://www.nautilus.org/nukepolicy/workshops/shanghai-01/paper s.html*; Li Bin, "The Effects of NMD on Chinese Strategy," *Jane's Intelligence Review*, March 2001, pp. 49-52.

5. The four areas of cooperative research based on the August 1999 Memorandum of Understanding between Japan and the United States are the lightweight nose cone, the infrared sensor, advanced kinetic warhead, and second stage propulsion. See *Defense of Japan 1999*, p. 84.

6. Michael Swaine and his colleagues have offered by far the most detailed examination of the Japanese bureaucratic actors on the MD issue. See Swaine, *et al.*, *Japan and Ballistic Missile Defense*, esp. chap. 3.

7. For further details, see Stephen A. Cambone, "The United States and Theatre Missile Defence in North-east Asia," *Survival*, Vol. 39, No. 3, Autumn 1997, pp. 68-69.

8. This comment is attributed to Satoshi Morimoto in *Plutonium*, No. 33, Spring 2001, in Japanese.

9. The most recent figure is 350 missiles. See Bill Gertz, "China Increases Missile Threat," *Washington Times*, August 28, 2001.

10. Thomas J. Christensen, "Theater Missile Defense and Taiwan's Security," *Orbis*, Vol. 44, No. 1, Winter 2000, p. 89.

11. Taiwan's reactions to MD are best analyzed in The Henry L. Stimson Center, *Theater Missile Defenses in the Asia-Pacific Region*, esp. pp. 41-60.

12 Quoted in Brian Hsu, "Military Says US National Missile Defense an Option," *Taipei Times*, July 18, 2001.

13. Medeiros, p. 19.

14. A series of interviews with defense officials and security analysts conducted in Taiwan indicate there is no serious public debate

on the MD issue, which is still regarded as an arcane issue of technological and military nature. Interviews, Taipei, December 2001.

15. For a succinct yet focused overview of the military situation on the peninsula, see "2000 Report to Congress: Military Situation on the Korean Peninsula," September 12, 2000, available at *www.defenselink. mil / news / Sep2000 / korea09122000.html*.

16. See *Chosun Ilbo*, June 16, 1993; *New York Times*, June 1, 1994.

17. See *Sisa Journal*, April 8, 1999, pp. 64-65. For an objective assessment on the relative weight of MD in South Korea's overall defense needs see The Henry L. Stimson Center, *Theater Missile Defenses*, esp. pp. 33-39.

18. In Japan and Taiwan as well, any in-depth discussions over MD are confined to a small group of security experts inside and outside of their respective governments and generally do not extend to the wider public or throughout the government. Interviews, Taipei, December 2001. See also Swaine, *et al.*

19. One of the most vocal NGOs is the Civil Network for a Peaceful Korea. See its web page at *www.peacekorea.org*, which is available in both Korean and English.

20. Green and Dalton, pp. 21-25.

21. Wook-Shik Chung, "Why Should We Oppose MD?" a paper presented at the KIDA Policy Forum on "The MD Plan and [Our] Security Interest," KIDA, Seoul, July 13, 2001, p. 17.

22. Unofficial translation by the author. Defense Minister Cho Seong-Tae's statements on the ROK's position on NMD and TMD at the 218th provisional session of the ROK National Assembly, February 20, 2001. In a similar vein, an ROK foreign ministry official argues that South Korea should maximize the "benefit of ambiguity" until MD feasibility is proven, but nonetheless support U.S. efforts in the end. See Shin, Kak-Soo, "The Implications for South Korea of the United States Missile Defense," *New Asia*, Vol. 8, No. 4, Winter 2001, pp. 178-207.

23. They are Fighter-Experimental, Attack Helicopter-Experimental, Early Warning Aircraft-Experimental, Surface-to-Air Missile-Experimental, and Korean Destroyer- Experimental-III, respectively. See Shim Jae Hoon, "South Korean Projects May Face Further Delays," *Jane's Defence Weekly*, April 19, 2001, p. 20; Darren Lake, "South Korea Announces Record High Budget," *Jane's Defence*

Weekly, July 4, 2001; John Larkin, "Dogfight over Seoul," *Far Eastern Economic Review*, July 5, 2001, pp. 16-18, 20.

24. For a report that South Korea plans to acquire MK-41 VLS, see *http://www.state.gov/p/eap/rls/prs/cfm?docid=2856*. For South Korea's introduction of the 300-km-range ATACMS Block-IA SRBM, see *Dong-a Ilbo*, January 5, 2002, p. A2.

25. For details on the South Korean public perception of China and its role on the peninsula, see Taeho Kim, "South Korea and a Rising China: Perceptions, Policies, and Prospects," in Ian James Storey and Herbert Yee, eds., *The Dragon Awakes: Perceptions and Prospects of the China Threat*, London: Curzon, forthcoming in 2002.

26. For an in-depth discussion of the various purposes of the North Korean missiles, see Chung Min Lee, "North Korean Missiles: Strategic Implications and Policy Responses," *Pacific Review*, Vol. 14, No. 1, 2001, pp. 85-120; *idem.*, "North Korea and Its Missiles," *Far Eastern Economic Review*, July 29, 1999, p. 26.

27. *Rodong Shinmun*, North Korea, August 15, 2001, available at *http://www.hani.co.kr/20010816*.

28. *Ibid.*, and North Korea's official announcements via Chosun Central News (*Chosun jungang tongshin*) and Pyongyang Broadcasting (*Pyongyang bangsong*), at *http://www.hani.co.kr/20010805*.

29. See "Transcript: Powell Discusses Korean Peninsula, Missile Defense," *Washington File*, No. 2890, July 27, 2001, available at *www.usinfo.state.gov*.

30. L. Gordon Flake has noted the current North Korean dilemma between its need to lie low when the cost for its provocative action is high and its equally compelling need to draw world attention for the sake of international assistance and aid. See his "North Korea's Options After Sept. 11," *PacNet* No. 47, November 23, 2001.

31. A perceptive study is available on the issue of balancing MD with other defense requirements. See Michael E. O'Hanlon, "Beyond Missile Defense," *Brookings Policy Brief*, No. 86, August 2001.

PART III: IMPROVEMENTS IN PLA CONVENTIONAL CAPABILITIES: FORCE PROJECTION AND AIR FORCE LOGISTICS

CHAPTER 8

ROUGH BUT READY FORCE PROJECTION: AN ASSESSMENT OF RECENT PLA TRAINING

Susan M. Puska

Introduction.

Over the last 3 years,[1] the Chinese People's Liberation Army (PLA) has significantly advanced its near-periphery power projection capability through concerted experimentation and adaptation of modern warfighting capabilities during threat-based training and exercises among targeted army, navy, air, and missile forces.[2] This experience base now reaches into all seven of its Military Regions (MRs),[3] and includes a growing number of younger, innovative military thinkers and fighters who are versed in modern operational art.

Against a potential threat that closely resembles the advanced capabilities of the U.S. military, the PLA has shown a determination, particularly since Kosovo, to enhance its confidence and competencies with the means and resources that are presently available. To maximize what it has now, the PLA has more concertedly used training as the warfighting laboratory in which to develop creative ways to compensate for its own relative weaknesses, while it aggressively and innovatively seeks ways to exploit the vulnerabilities of an advanced, information-dependent opponent.

During 2000-01 training, in particular, the PLA's warfighting training aimed at maximizing its offensive and defensive operations within the PLA's area of operation, including its maritime periphery, through a combination of threat-based military training and civilian augmentation.

The author of this chapter examines these developments in terms of mobility; joint operations; logistics; missile operations; coastal/maritime operations; communications, electronic warfare (EW), and Computer Network Attack (CNA); and special operations. The materials used for this examination are primarily Chinese national and regional military newspapers, although some recent journal articles and books have also been consulted.

Background.

The last 3 years have been a particularly dynamic period in the modernization of the PLA. The results of experimentation and innovation during this time have been summed up in the seventh generation of military training and examination programs, which will be implemented during 2002.[4] These programs will concentrate on seven areas—ground, naval, and air forces; Second Artillery; scientific research and test units; reserve units; and the People's Armed Police.[5]

During the last 3 years, the scope of military exercises has steadily increased to include out-of-sector MR forces performing increasingly complex tasks in parallel and increasingly joint operations. Maritime (individual and unit) training has been stressed during this time and culminated in major near periphery exercises during the summers of 2000 and 2001 near Dongshan Island in southern China opposite Taiwan.

Then in the fall, the PLA sought to showcase its accomplishments in applying science and technology to training up to that point by conducting concurrent drills and exercises on October 13-16, 2000.[6] Foremost among those was a "grand military show" said to be the first since 1964, which was held near Beijing at the foot of the Yanshan Mountain.[7] Jiang Zemin, as the Central Military

Commission (CMC) Chairman, inspected the Beijing exercise on October 13. This exercise was said to demonstrate primarily defensive measures to counter stealth technology, aerial surveillance and reconnaissance, precision guided weapons, and EW. It also employed various concealment and deception measures, such as "infrared decoys," to interfere with enemy operations and conceal combat operations.[8]

Concurrently, selected ground units trained in Inner Mongolia, while naval units conducted training in the Bohai Sea, and Second Artillery strategic missile forces exercised in Jilin Province in northeast China.[9] Elsewhere in China on October 13, a Chengdu MR unit conducted a sabotage raid against vital enemy targets, while a naval helicopter-borne Marine unit attacked an enemy rear command center. PLA digitized artillery, armored corps, and mechanized infantry demonstrations were held, while the "first successful" multi-direction airborne operation (including personnel and gear, rockets, and vehicles) was conducted against an enemy on the march.[10]

Throughout 2000-01, the Nanjing and Guangzhou Military Regions (MRs) led the PLA for their innovations in training and operations. Since both MRs play key roles in potential force projection against Taiwan, as well as into the South China Sea, their training appears to have had greater emphasis and perhaps, resources.

A 2000 assessment of the Guangzhou MR's training reflects the progress its units made in training during 2000-01. The report noted that MR training in 1999 focused on company and battalion level training. During 2000, it progressed to training in Joint Operations, during which Army, Navy, and Air Force units fought under high-tech conditions.[11]

This assessment also observed that achievements in training during 1999 depended on innovations in equipment. In 2000, however, over one-half of all innovations related to methods of operations, military

225

theory, and methods of training, accomplishments that depend upon the ability of personnel to apply concepts and new ideas. While training in the Guangzhou MR solved "common" problems in 1999, during 2000 the MR units could solve more complicated and important problems. Further, most of the 1999 training achievements came from combat units; while in 2000, the majority of training achievements were in joint logistics and armament.[12]

Regarding joint operations, the graduated mobilization response (GMR) assessment described pre-2000 Service relations in military exercises as "friendly support" or "guest performances" through negotiations. By 2000, the training among the Guangzhou MR's three Services was assessed as more joint and extended from individual level training up to operational, tactical, and technical training, and, finally, to unit training.[13]

Although the Guangzhou MR and the Nanjing MR training have been most extensive, improvements in training within the other five MRs, as well as the Strategic Rocket Forces, have also been significant, particularly out-of-sector support and support to cross-sea operations, which have been stressed throughout all seven military regions.

Building on the 2000 priority on "three strikes and three defense,"[14] PLA training and operational priorities during 2001 concentrated on rapid mobility operations,[15] including combat use of helicopters;[16] emergency logistics support;[17] special operations;[18] sea landing and cross-sea operations;[19] maritime denial (anti-submarine and blockades);[20] air combat and support;[21] mobile missile operations; and EW and countermeasures.[22] Cover and concealment, psychological training to counter battle and operational stress, and enhancing confidence in PLA equipment, operational strategy and doctrine, were also stressed. Based on Chief of the General Staff General Fu Quanyou's direction, the training objective during 2001 was no longer to simply "fight" a local regional war under high-technological conditions, but "fight to win" against a qualitatively superior force that was based on U.S. military capabilities.[23]

In the General Staff Department (GSD) training plan for 2001 PLA units were specifically asked to deepen advances in science and technology (S&T) training.[24] Priority was placed on the following guidelines and tasks:

- Innovate in light of actual conditions;

- Achieve rapid advancement in fighting capacity;

- Further upgrade the quality of officers and men;

- Apply research results to training;

- Deepen research on military theory;

- Closely study adversary operational concepts, equipment, and weaponry and develop counter-measures;[25]

- Accelerate innovation in training;

- Carry out realistic, warlike training;

- Expand the use of computers, simulators, and online training; and,

- Exert greater effort in Joint Operations training.

While the GSD 2001 training plan continued to stress the "three strikes, three defenses," night training and physical fitness were also emphasized. Operationally, the 2001 plan specifically called on units to make greater efforts to solve problems in the following areas: defense penetration and counter-penetration; destruction and counter-destruction; sea and air control; and electronic warfare.[26]

Fu, in an address to an enlarged party committee meeting of the GSD, stressed that 2001 military work must be based on the basic requirement to "win in battle."[27] He said the PLA must strengthen studies of the international situation, high-tech local war, and the application of rule of law to military management during 2001. He called on the PLA to organize and coordinate all efforts between units, schools, academies, research centers and test units. He urged that the process of transforming research accomplishments into policies, training, war-readiness, and combat strength be accelerated. He also stressed the importance of science and technology to enhance combat capability throughout the entire Armed Forces. He called on the PLA to enhance command and control, Joint Operations, and combat effectiveness, and stressed the importance of training a large number of "new-type" high-quality military personnel.[28] The March 2001 National People's Congress added a sense of urgency to the need to modernize the PLA to conduct "military struggle" as soon as possible.[29]

Rapid, Long Distance Mobility: Land, Air, and Sea.

Military training conducted during 2000-01 emphasized the need for rapid mobility across long distances by air, sea, and land. Air movement, for example, continually stressed long-range air raids and various air combat missions. In mid-March 2001, a Nanjing air regiment was highlighted for flying 3,000 km across five provinces to conduct a surgical raid on enemy radar, guided missiles, and AAA positions, using live ammunition. The unit was credited with successfully penetrating enemy electronic interference, radar tracking, and guided missile attacks.[30] In early March, one Second Artillery equipment inspection regiment (Zhuang Jian Tuan) demonstrated its enhanced rapid delivery capabilities during an exercise in which units simultaneously delivered equipment to several launch positions over long distances via highway and railway networks.[31]

A Beijing MR motorized infantry brigade held rapid reactions maneuvers that covered 1,000 km within Inner Mongolia during late 2000. These maneuvers also stressed information countermeasures, coordinated operations, field defense, and comprehensive logistics support.[32]

Reserve units have also stepped up mobility training. On April 20, 2001, for example, a reserve regiment on Hainan Island held a rapid mobilization and assembly exercise following the release of the EP-3 crew. It was reported to be the first ever reserve exercise held between four provinces and one autonomous region in south China. All pre-appointed officers, specialized technical soldiers, demobilized soldiers, squad leaders, and assistants answered the call up within 1 hour from notification. Among them were 168 reservists working in Haikou, Shenzhen, and Zhuhai.[33]

Logistics mobility, which will be essential to support of any force projection, was also tested. In the Guangzhou MR, for example, mobile command, control, and logistics support modules were developed. The Guangzhou MR reportedly invested two million yuan during 2000-01 to reform its command and control and logistics support in the field. At least one unidentified Guangzhou MR Group Army and division were equipped with mobile command systems that can be disassembled and moved within 1 hour. The same unit's logistics and armament technical support facilities also were made mobile for field operations. Modular barracks were developed, which can accommodate ten bunks presumably for command and operations personnel.[34]

Joint Operations: A Work in Progress.

Joint operations continued to develop slowly. The PLA consequently has not yet realized the full potential of joint operations. Nonetheless, substantial progress has been made, particularly at the operational level of each Military Region.

At least three problems inhibit the PLA's transformation to joint operations so far. First, the PLA views "joint" in unique and flexible terms which allow for independent interpretation that undermines synergy of effort. Second, there is resistance, perhaps even confusion, about what "joint operations" means and why they should be conducted. Finally, the command and control of the PLA under a Military Region system and an Army-dominated General Staff perpetuates combined arms operations, at best augmented by parallel air, navy, and missile forces operations, rather than facilitating joint integration. But PLA leaders and defense intellectuals recognize these problems, and appear committed to achieving sufficiently joint operations to suit the PLA's operational needs.

To address these challenges and enhance understanding of joint operations within the PLA, military scholars and commanders published several articles and books on joint operations during 2000 and 2001. Yang Zhiqi, director of the GSD, Military Affairs Department, in late 2000,[35] for example, urged the PLA to accelerate changing from a combined arms command system to a joint operations command system, which is an essential link to realizing joint operations. He argued that a joint command system could not be established at the last minute during a crisis, but must be put in place during peacetime. Although Yang observed that the PLA has made substantial progress to achieve greater joint coordination between Services during operational level training, he noted, all the Services tend to fight in different ways once an exercise begins. Yang attributed this deficiency to a fundamental lack of an "authoritative" joint command.[36]

In a National Defense Publication entitled, "New Theory of Joint Operations,"[37] the authors argue that despite similarities in its nature to combined arms, joint operations represents a great, even radical, change for the PLA.[38] Through joint operations, they wrote, the Armed Forces will unify combat capabilities through coordination to defeat the enemy.[39]

In December 2000, a symposium entitled "War Patterns and War Theory in the Early 21st Century" was held in Beijing.[40] The meeting was sponsored by the Beijing Military Region and the Strategic Studies Department, Academy of Military Sciences (AMS). It was attended by representatives from the seven military regions, the National Defense University (NDU), and the Air Force Command Academy. The Beijing MR Chief of Staff, Yu Chenghai, presided over the meeting, which was reported to be the first joint activity held between the PLA's highest-level strategic studies department and a theater command. The purpose of the meeting was to promote transformation of military strategic research into combat strength throughout the Armed Forces. Development trends in joint operations were among the topics discussed.

On December 29, 2000, the Nanjing Military Region published an article that also stressed the importance of forming a joint operations command system.[41] The article identified several problems that centered on command and control. Specifically, it criticized "factionalism" (parochialism) between Services. The article argued for the need to establish truly separate units under Joint Operations Groups (JOG), in order to eliminate command and control interference by the units' parent Services. The article stressed that Services should only provide combat support and coordination to units assigned to a JOG.[42] Other writings discussed the need to significantly reduce the layers of command—changing from a "tree-type" command structure to a "flat" one.[43]

Training within all Services of the PLA has stressed joint operations. Air Force training, for example, increasingly emphasized joint support to both ground and navy forces. In March 2001, a Guangzhou Military Region Air Force aviation regiment was highlighted for its joint operations. This unit is equipped with a "new-type fighting aircraft" (probably SU-27) to conduct blue water combat patrols, combat escort missions, and military exercises. The regiment had recently shifted from technical to tactical

231

training on the new equipment. It reportedly had achieved an all-weather offensive and defensive flying capability. Its capabilities included low-altitude and ultra low-altitude flying, the ability to attack ground targets at great speed, live bomb operations, deep sea interception, and over-the-horizon air combat during electronic countermeasures (ECM).[44]

During 2000-01, PLA training focused on Taiwan-like scenarios within all seven military regions. Priority was given to sea-crossings, island seizures, and special operations behind enemy lines. The threat-based scenarios employed forces that were modeled on the advanced technology of the U.S. military, including armed helicopters; cruise missiles; sophisticated reconnaissance; EW capabilities; stealth technology; and extensive maritime assets.

The intent of this training seems to have been multifold—first, it gave PLA units experience against a Taiwan and U.S.-type opponent, which provided a better understanding of the strengths and weaknesses of potential opponents. Second, more realistic training focused on likely scenarios helps to build confidence in PLA equipment, as well as defensive and offensive operations. Finally, more realistic training exposes PLA weaknesses that can be solved or avoided before actual combat.

Logistics: Flexibility and Forward Support.

Progress in the Joint Logistics System benefited from the stress on war preparation, which revealed the need for more field logistics support and mobility. During 2000-01, consolidation of common garrison functions, such as military hospitals, which have been opened up to civilians as well as other Services, and consolidation of key commodity items, such as bulk petroleum, continued. Emergency stockage of generic, dual-use items were also developed. In some cases, emergency supplies were integrated into civilian warehouses to provide emergency and training replenishment to military forces through contracted or other support arrangements.

During 2000-01 emphasis was placed on components of operational level logistics, such as field feeding, field medical support, forward maintenance, and on-site repair and re-supply. Rapid reaction and emergency support units were tested to provide multiple types of support to combat forces in near-combat field conditions. Throughout the Air Force, Navy, Army, and Second Artillery units, logistics support emphasized enhancements of core support capabilities. In addition, within the Nanjing and Guangzhou MRs, civilian augmentation to military logistics was stressed. This support included the coordinated use of the civilian air, land, and sea infrastructure; acquisition of maritime vessels; access to civilian telecommunications; and acquisition of materiel and supplies.

While much of the logistics support is managed by the General Logistics Department (GLD), the new General Armament Department (GAD), created in 1998,[45] played the central role in ammunition replenishment and maintenance of weapons and armor. Like Second Artillery, GAD made a concentrated effort to enhance the quality and expertise of its personnel through greater cooperation with civilian and military institutions. In November 2000, General Cao Gangchuan, director of GAD, noted that reforms in armament, national defense science and technology, and industry now are reaching an unprecedented level in China. He encouraged further reform and innovation, citing a Party and CMC directive to raise the rate of success in scientific testing.[46]

In October 2000, GAD hosted an all-Army symposium at the Armored Force Engineering Academy, commanded by Major General Wang Hongguang, in Changxindian, Beijing, with the stated purpose of enhancing comprehensive armament support.[47] During October 2000, GAD initiated a 1-month rotational course, open to the entire PLA command cadre, to take advantage of peacetime to improve armament management and raise the level of comprehensive armament support for wartime. The main focus of this training was on the science of armament and wartime armament support.[48]

In 2000, Guangzhou MR set up a "theater command center for armament support," which was the first in the PLA.[49] The center provides mobile command posts for field armament support to the MR, army, and divisional levels. Additionally, the MR has developed a command automation system for the Guangzhou War Zone. This system links information vertically and horizontally between armament and support units and higher headquarters. It greatly enhances command and control over ammunition assets, and facilitates decisionmaking and operational management.[50]

During February 2001, the GAD convened a symposium in Beijing to discuss its military training tasks for the year. These included: (1) assess training achievements and transform these into training capabilities; (2) strengthen guidance and theoretical studies, and regulate the scientific development of military training; (3) renew training content, methods and quality; (4) train high-quality personnel to achieve leapfrogging development in armament; and (5) strengthen infrastructure construction and maintain the sustained development of military training.[51]

In the summer of 2000, the Jinan MR conducted an emergency logistics support drill based on a flood relief scenario.[52] Materiel, POL, transportation, and medical support modules were quickly mobilized. The support modules were based on warehouses, hospitals, and other specialized units, and encompassed ordnance, material, POL, transportation, medical, and maintenance support. During peacetime, these units are sent on firefighting, flood relief, and other major projects and operations. The division developed new approaches to conceal supply at fixed points, maneuver under concealment of smokescreens, and coordinate logistics support with naval and air units.[53]

Nanjing MR formed an "Emergency Mobile Logistics Support Model" that met the CMC's standards to perform combat missions without personnel and equipment replenishment and pre-battle training (i.e., no notice).[54] One brigade spent over three million yuan improving its company-level combat-readiness provisions, standard storage rooms, field medical kits, combat-readiness coffers, and wartime light sets. The brigade developed new equipment, including floating stretchers, field kitchen containers, and rapid reaction tankers, and participated in numerous exercises with the Navy, Army, and Air Force units over the past 3 years.[55]

Guangzhou MR developed multitube POL tankers for field refueling that significantly raised field support efficiency. Water tankers could support up to 20 kitchen units at one time. Field repair vehicles could perform various emergency repairs. In addition, support equipment for sea operations was also developed by GMR's Logistics Department and an unidentified GMR division.[56]

Although there has been some emphasis on field medical support, most medical support improvements, including joint logistics, have focused on reforms, as well as garrison and near-garrison support. In this regard, the Guangzhou MR medical training objectives, which varied according to a unit's level, may be representative.[57] The brigade or regiment focuses on rapid deployment of a first-aid post. The battalion or company focuses on rescue of personnel injured on the firing line. Medical units above the division hospital level focus on treatment of critical cases and research in traumatology. In recent years the Guangzhou MR has built or renovated 80 percent of its division hospitals and brigade or regiment medical teams.[58] Emergency support units have been issued "advanced" field mobile medical equipment, such as field surgery vehicles and decontamination trucks. The GMR reported that the

235

medical war-readiness of "key units" within "key combat divisions and brigades" now meets war readiness standards.[59]

By early October 2000, two-thirds of all PLA hospitals completed construction of "Project Number 1," which laid a foundation for an "informationized" medical service system that can be used by both the military and civilian medical services.[60]

The PLA's first airborne medical teams conducted battle drills during the summer of 2000.[61] Three planes airdropped medical personnel and medical supplies onto a captured airfield. The medics boarded air-dropped vehicles and set up a first aid station. Twenty medics of the First Airborne Medical Team parachute unit, made up of personnel from the PLA 457th Hospital, landed by plane. The Second Medical Unit, consisting of 50 personnel, arrived by plane and set up a comprehensive multipurpose medical post. During the exercise, transport aircraft evacuated critical personnel.[62]

The Nanjing Military Region's Fujian Military District also worked hard to improve its wartime integrated logistics support capabilities during 2000. The military district medical support forces conducted an exercise during the summer that included an evacuation of casualties brought in on an unidentified vessel "from distant seas."

A notable feature of the PLA's extended logistical system during 2000-01 was the integration of civilian fixed facilities, infrastructure, personnel, and resources into contingency operations and training. This support is established through a combination of pre-arranged contracts, legal confiscation of support and civilians, as well as integration through local reserve and militia units. The coordination and integration of civilians and domestic resources provides a "total war" logistical multiplier to PLA support, especially along China's coastal region and in the southwest, where this type of support has so far been most emphasized. The types of civilian resources, including

236

possible fiscal augmentation, are extensive and continue to develop. In addition to supplies, material, and personnel, they also include airports, ports, rail networks, expressways, and bridges that have been adapted to military specifications and support military missions. For example, the construction of some high speed roads and bridges was coordinated with the military to include extra exits and upgraded surfaces to bear the weight of military vehicles, better withstand air attack, and facilitate quick rebuild in case of an air attack. In certain areas, such as the Guangzhou MR, the military works closely with civilian authorities to capitalize on civilian assets and ensure these can easily be integrated into military operations when needed.

With a priority on cross-sea operations and island seizures during 2000-01 training, the use of civilian marine vessels was also tested. In some cases, maritime exercises were conducted with a mix of civilian vessels that have been integrated into war planning. Civilian vessels and personnel even participated in antisubmarine exercises—showing that the use of civilian assets by the PLA is not limited by either imagination or legal restrictions.

In July 2000, the Navy held a 17-day, 4,000 nautical miles wartime shipping drill across the Bohai, Yellow, East China, and South China Seas, using the National Defense Mobilization Ship, *Shichang*.[63] The exercise was the first successful drill of "wartime emergency mobilization and drafting of civilian personnel vessels." The exercise was jointly organized by the State National Defense Mobilization Committee and the PLA Navy. Dozens of military and civilians participated from the State Planning Commission, Finance Ministry, Communications Ministry, Chinese Academy of Engineering, General Staff Department, and General Logistics Department. The exercise tested and enhanced the efficiency of drafting civilian vessels into service in an emergency.[64]

Reserves and militia also have increasingly facilitated local support to military exercises and operations. For example, in Zhejiang Province a militia seaborne refueling unit was set up on April 18, 2001, at the Zhejiang Petroleum Limited Company in Yuhuan. The unit was made up of 100 militiamen whose mission is to set up permanent refueling points at ports along the eastern coastline and highways, as well as small mobile refueling teams on land, to provide POL support during peacetime and war.[65]

Missile Operations: Concealment, Mobility, and Quality.

Missile Operations, which have been a pocket of excellence in the PLA for several years,[66] continued to improve in terms of the quality of personnel, rapid mobility, concealment and deception, and logistics support. During 2000-2001, Second Artillery pushed enhancements, particularly to address key problems in rapid mobility and information countermeasures under high-tech conditions.[67]

To improve the quality and quantity of its science and technology personnel, for example, Second Artillery has actively recruited about 2,000 university students in recent years.[68] Like other elements of the PLA, it has sought not only to deepen the quality of its personnel, but also to encourage innovative high-tech solutions to its training and operations through closer cooperation with civilian institutions, as well as the recruitment of civilian-educated specialists. On March 9, 2001, for example, the Second Artillery Engineering Academy signed a cooperative agreement on research and teaching with Northwest Industrial University.[69]

Coastal/Maritime Operations: Key Focus.

With a concerted effort to enhance coastal operations, all Services emphasized sea-crossing and island seizure training. A Nanjing MR Group Army held sea training on the southern Fujian Coast during mid-July 2000 that is representative.[70] Training included infantry and tanks seizing beaches, scouts conducting reconnaissance from the sea, artillery employed on ships, amphibious armored troops seizing beaches and carrying out fire attacks at sea; and engineers clearing obstacles. The GA has been engaged in sea training since the beginning of the summer 2000. Mock ups of an amphibious landing field have also been set up in garrison so that infantry regiments could continue sea training year round.[71]

The Shenyang MR developed amphibious training in early 2000. On January 22, 2000, the division experimented with live-fire practice from a freighter, and tested several ways to secure equipment onto vessels (presumably civilian).[72] Between January and July, the division trained in loading equipment onto vessels, firing armored car guns over water, striking at aerial targets using ship-borne anti-aircraft artillery, and striking beach targets with ship-borne artillery.[73]

In June 2000, a Naval Landing Ship Unit that is attached to PLA unit 38091 at Haikou, Hainan Island, conducted training in night landing operations with troops, armored cars, and amphibious tanks against an enemy objective.[74] Because the unit's equipment was outdated, it tried to develop innovative ways to enhance its capabilities and compensate for its deficiencies. This included training during the heavy fog season (March through June) in fishing areas and narrow channels. Air defense training was also stepped up to "take advantage" of heavy air traffic in the area. During the first half of 2000, the unit conducted 42 single ship drills and eight formation landing drills, half of which were conducted at night, in heavy fog, and in other environments resembling realistic warfare conditions.[75]

A submarine flotilla that underestimated the capability of the enemy and failed a training test 2 years before stepped up its study of enemy capabilities and consequently was able to penetrate an enemy port to enforce a blockade during a summer 2000 drill.[76] The unit has focused its study on submarine attack of aircraft carrier and destroyer formations, and submarine coordination with the aviation corps and surface vessels to penetrate an enemy blockade and lay mines in a port. The unit established a file on each enemy vessel and adjusted its training to counter enemy anti-submarine capabilities.[77]

In August 2000, the Beijing MR reported on an Air Force unit that had participated in sea operations.[78] The unit, which had only trained over land before, trained for 2 months over water beginning in April 2000. During the sea training, special attention was paid to low-altitude acrobatics, formation and navigation.[79]

Communications: Connectivity, EW, and CNA.[80]

The PLA recognizes that it must enhance its command and control, EW, and counterelectronic warfare capability, as well as its computer network attack and counterattack capabilities, if it hopes to fight to win a regional war under high-tech conditions. Consequently, the PLA has taken increased efforts to boost all of these capabilities. As an example, Group Army Deputy Commander Zhang Hetian of the Nanjing MR held network warfare drills[81] on July 11, 2000 in which Blue Force (enemy) reconnaissance and attacks on Red Force targets were simulated. The Group Army achieved an initial network capability at the time of the exercise, but Zhang noted that some PLA commanders had not yet grasped the demands of "achieving victory."

The Lanzhou MR held an Electronic Warfare Defense Work Meeting on July 3-4, 2000, at a Group Army that had been a pilot for electronic defense operations during the previous two years.[82] During the meeting, the MR reviewed the accomplishments in "three anti's, one resist" (anti-reconnaissance, anti-jamming, anti-network attack, and resist destruction). The ability of commanders and staffs to organize and direct information/electronic warfare was reportedly significantly enhanced.[83]

Beijing MR (BMR) held a major electronic warfare exercise in early August 2000 in conjunction with a combined arms operation.[84] This was the first time all the new and main battle EW equipment of the ground forces were brought together and comprehensive assessments were made of the combat capability of the equipment systems and units.[85] BMR has also developed online Operational Forces (OPFOR) training for electronic warfare to enhance training.[86]

In the "Southwest 2000" Exercise, two formations separated by 500 km fought against each other in a "virtual reality laboratory" in Chengdu MR's first online test of its command and staff. This developed from online "checks" held during late 1999. Chengdu MR applied its experiences, which were ahead of other PLA units, to cooperation with NDU to develop a "Campaign Command Training Model System" that formally went into operation during the Southwest 2000 Exercise.[87]

NDU experts characterized this as the first true "War Laboratory" for PLA campaign training. The main characteristics of the exercise were:

1. Units in five southwestern provinces and regions were linked by dozens of local networks and several hundred terminals.

2. Real-time, force-on-force simulation that provided information on the campaign situation, disposition of orders, and Red Force and Blue Force postures.

3. The exercises unfolded synchronously in real-time at numerous campaign units and included sound, image, text, and data online, thanks to an emergency doubling of the transmission capability. (4) The exercise led to a significant change in network architecture, re-routing of transmission routes, renovation of equipment, and breakthroughs in achieving secure information transmission under dynamic long-range network characteristics.[88]

The PLA Air Force (PLAAF) of the BMR held an online training exercise in conjunction with a meeting on headquarters science and technology training in mid-June 2000.[89] This exercise simulated an attack on Beijing by multiple sorties of enemy aircraft flying at low altitude. The system greatly reduced training planning and preparation time and can be used to access information about enemy aircraft and meteorological information, as well as draw up plans for integrated simulated training and joint training with army units.[90]

Special Operations: Strike Deep Behind Lines.

Special operations forces have concentrated on enhancing basic skills to conduct operations deep behind enemy lines. The "Cheetahs," a model unit commanded by Colonel Liu Youchun, is one example of the accomplishments in recent Special Operations training.[91] The 56294 unit is a Chengdu MR Special Reconnaissance Dadui that has made notable progress to develop special operations soldiers. Cheetah soldiers can perform multiskills including operating light to heavy weapons, basic knowledge of foreign armies' weapons, and the ability to operate transport that ranges from ground, to tank, to helicopter, and to assault boats.

Shenyang Military Region lauded personnel improvements in one special operations unit that is commanded by Li Jizhao, and political commissar, Han Baosheng. The unit expects to train 100 officers in both command and technical tasks, and develop 100 personnel who are experts in airborne operations, island-landing and sabotage operations, psychological warfare, enhanced instructor skills (with the "four abilities"), and all-round special operations skills.[92]

One Special Operations Unit that had previously failed a spot examination in Lanzhou MR was highlighted in the MR newspaper for passing an inspection without prior notification. No advance information was provided on the subjects to be tested, which was a change from previous years. The unit had previously failed some tasks and only achieved good results in about half of the 23 test subjects. The unit had consistently performed with excellent results in yearly training.[93] The inspection reinforced the need for units to develop a no notice capability.

Overall Improvements.

PLA training has become increasingly more sophisticated and complex, incorporating evolving joint operations and national defense mobilization. Training within a core of elite and experimental units is characterized by use of more professional and capable Opposing Forces (OPFOR);[94] near-combat conditions; all-weather and night operations; sea and island force projection; and long distance deployments into unfamiliar terrain.[95] Acceptance of "failure" (i.e., defeat of the Red Force by the Blue Force), as well as more open discussion of deficiencies has also lead to a more realistic appraisal of strengths and weaknesses, with the potential for more realistic measures to correct shortcomings. In addition, training is conducted more frequently throughout the year, rather than simply relying on end-of-year training. Greater use of simulation and "online" training are becoming more wide-spread and sophisticated, providing an augmentation to field training in everything from command and control, to asymmetrical warfare, to mobile operations, to nuclear and biological warfare training.[96]

Conclusion.

The PLA lacks a sufficient budget to support faster and more extensive military hardware and technology acquisition, and is handicapped by China's deep-seated preference for independent domestic capabilities that can be obtained through reverse engineering, domestic innovation, or acquisition of technical information. Moreover, China needs to sustain an export-led economic strategy that could be undermined if the region or the West were alarmed by China's military modernization efforts before China is ready.[97] The PLA has been able to make a virtue out of necessity by focusing on software modernization. Among these are steps: (1) improving the quality of personnel through educational and recruiting reforms and initiatives; (2) instituting organizational changes that will enhance efficiency, reduce wasteful practices, including corruption, and will ultimately enhance combat force capabilities, such as adaptation of joint operations and joint logistics; (3) selectively adapting relevant foreign military management practices and modern (specifically information age) asymmetric strategies; (4) streamlining organizations; and (5) intensively studying and assessing potential threats, with particular emphasis on the United States, and more recently on Taiwan's military capability.

Relying on key units that serve as both the vanguards and testing grounds for new equipment, structures, techniques, and strategies for offensive and defensive operations in a high-tech environment, the PLA has tested a myriad of equipment, made operational improvements, and innovations to enhance its combat effectiveness in a high-tech environment. The PLA is poised to capitalize on the lessons learned to enhance its regular, reserve, and militia units. At the very least, the PLA now has developed a sound basis for continuing enhancement of the PLA's force projection capability, and has established a jump off point for modernization of the entire PLA as resources increase, modern technology is absorbed, and innovation and adaptation further develop.[98]

While hardware and technology acquisition will continue, the PLA's recent concentration on modern thinking, innovation, and experience of leaders and fighters provides a more potent base for accelerated modernization. The PLA today possesses a rough but ready force projection capability, one that will continue to steadily improve over time, which adds greater risks and costs for potential opponents in China's near periphery. The modernizing PLA increasingly provides the Chinese leadership with credible coercive strength—one that can back up the threat of the use of force and/or selective employment of force to promote China's national sovereignty and security interests along its land, air, and maritime borders.

ENDNOTES - CHAPTER 8

1. *Jiefang Jun Bao* (hereafter JJB), August 10, 2001.

2. "Modernization" of the PLA must be viewed in relative terms. This chapter does not argue that the PLA has become an "advanced" military in the past 3 years, since most PLA equipment and weaponry still remains up to 20 years behind advanced militaries. This chapter, however, starts from the firm belief that hardware-based comparisons to advanced militaries are insufficient to fully assess the growing coercive power of China's military in both real and psychological terms within the Asia-Pacific region.

3. Beijing, Shenyang, Jinan, Guangzhou, Lanzhou, Nanjing, and Chengdu Military Regions.

4. JJB, August 10, 2001.

5. *Ibid.*

6. JJB, October 14, 2000.

7. *Lanzhou Military Region Jundai Bao* (hereafter RMJD), October 17, 2000; *Nanjing Military Region Renmin Qianmin* (hereafter RMQX), October 17, 2000; *Rocket Force News*, October 17, 2000; *Guangzhou Military Region Zhanshi Bao* (hereafter ZSB), October 16, 2000.

8. *Ibid.*

9. JJB, October 14, 2000.

10. *Ibid.*

11. Guangzhou MR ZSB, October 13, 2000.

12. *Ibid.*

13. *Ibid.*

14. Reconnaissance and counterreconnaissance; air raid and counterair raid; and jamming and antijamming.

15. See, for examples, JJB, December 2000; *Shenyang Military Region Qianjin Bao* (hereafter QJB), April 4, 2001; JJB, May 7, 2001; *Beijing Military Region Zhanyou Bao* (hereafter ZYB), November 4, 2000; ZYB, November 7, 2000.

16. See, for examples, JJB, May 6, 2001; ZSB, March 6, 2001; JJB, May 16, 2001; RMJD, April 26, 2001; ZSB, March 6, 2001.

17. See, for examples, *China National Defense News*, May 21, 2001.

18. See, for examples, QJB, April 9, 2001; JJB May 4, 2001; ZSB, March 6, 2001; JJB, December 4, 2000; QJB, April 9, 2001; JJB, May 29, 2001; ZSB, March 6, 2001.

19. See RMQX, March 2, 2001; RMQX, April 5, 2001; RMQX, November 2, 2000; ZSB, November 3, 2000; ZSB, March 6, 2001; *Air Force News*, April 19, 2001; *China National Defense News*, May 21, 2001; ZSB, March 6, 2001. In addition, six of the PLA's 29 proposals submitted at the National People's Congress in March 2001 addressed maritime issues, which testifies to an increasing interest. This was said to be the largest number of PLA proposals ever submitted (JJB, March 11, 2001). For coordination of sea-land unit coordinated training, see *People's Navy*, 10 April 2001.

20. See, for examples, *People's Navy*, April 7, 2001. For People's Liberation Army Navy (PLAN) sub-chasing training in coordination with PLA army, see *People's Navy*, April 12, 2001.

21. For People's Liberation Army Air Force (PLAAF) Opposing Forces (OPFOR) support, see *People's Navy*, April 5, 2001; for long range operations (up to 3,000 kilometers), see *Air Force News*, April 19, 2001.

22. See, for examples, ZSB, April 19, 2001; JJB, May 20, 2001; *China National Defense News*, May 24, 2001; RMJD, March 15, 2001.

23. See, for examples, JJB, May 27, 2001; ZSB, March 3, 2001; JJB, May 29, 2001.

24. JJB, February 2, 2001.

25. In Chinese open source writings, "opponents" are most frequently characterized in terms of capabilities, which most frequently implies U.S. military capability. Recently, however, materials have been increasingly published that specifically identify Taiwan military

capabilities as a threat and name the United States as an opponent, or even "enemy."

26. *Ibid*.

27. JJB, January 12, 2001.

28. *Ibid*.

29. See ZSB, March 3, 2001.

30. *Air Force News*, April 19, 2001.

31. *Rocket Force News*, March 8, 2001.

32. JJB, December 28, 2000.

33. JJB, April 28, 2001.

34. Guangzhou MR ZSB, March 1, 2001.

35. JJB, October 31, 2000.

36. *Ibid*.

37. Zhou Xiaoning, Peng Xiwen, and An Weiping, *Lianhe Zuozhan Xinlun*, National Defense University Press, Beijing, 2000.

38. JJB, October 10, 2000.

39. *Ibid*.

40. ZYB, December 28, 2000.

41. RMQX, December 29, 2000.

42. *Ibid*.

43. JJB, January 9, 2001.

44. *Air Force News*, March 15, 2001.

45. *Directory of PRC Military Personalities*, October 2000, p. iv.

46. JJB, November 14, 2000.

47. *Ibid*.

48. *China Defense Industries,* November 9, 2000.

49. ZSB, October 20, 2000.

50. *Ibid.*

51. *China Defense News*, March 1, 2001.

52. JJB, August 9, 2000.

53. *Ibid.*

54. RMQX, March 8, 2001.

55. *Ibid.*

56. ZSB, March 1, 2001.

57. ZSB, July 26, 2000.

58. *Ibid.*

59. *Ibid.*

60. JJB, October 25, 2000.

61. *Air Force News*, August 17, 2000.

62. *Ibid.*

63. *China National Defense News*, August 11, 2000.

64. *Ibid.*

65. *China National Defense News*, April 26, 2001.

66. For more detailed and authoritative discussion of missile modernization, see Mark Stokes, *China's Strategic Modernization: Implications for the United States*, Carlisle Barracks, PA: Strategic Studies Institute, 1999; and "China's Military Space and Conventional Theater Missile Development: Implications for Security in the Taiwan Strait," in *People's Liberation Army After Next*, Susan M. Puska, ed., Carlisle Barracks, PA: Strategic Studies Institute, 2000.

67. *Rocket Forces News*, March 1, 2001.

68. JJB, May 10, 2001.

69. *Rocket Forces News*, March 15, 2001.

70. JJB, August 8, 2000.

71. *Ibid.*

72. QJB, July 10, 2000.

73. *Ibid.*

4. *People's Navy*, July 8, 2000.

75. *Ibid.*

76. *People's Navy*, July 15, 2000.

77. *Ibid.*

78. JJB, August 8, 2000.

79. *Ibid.*

80. Computer Network Attack.

81. JJB, August 8-9, 2000.

82. RMJD, July 11 and 15, 2000.

83. *Ibid.*

84. JJB, August 11, 2000.

85. *Ibid.*

86. *Ibid.*

87. *Ibid.*

88. *Ibid.*

89. *Air Force News*, July 8, 2000.

90. *Ibid.*

91. JJB, May 4, 2001.

92. *Shenyang MR Qianjin Bao*, April 4, 2001.

93. JJB, December 31, 2000.

94. See, for examples, ZYB, April 2, 2001; JJB, December 1, 2000; *People's Navy*, April 7, 2001; CONMILIT, October 2000; *Renmin Qianxian*, September 9, 2000; JJB, October 10, 2000; *PLA Pictorial*, January 2001; *Air Force News*, March 29, 2001; and *People's Navy*, April 5, 2001.

95. See, for examples, *Air Force News*, April 5, 2001.

96. See, for examples, ZYB, April 24, 2001; RMJD, April 21, 2001; *Rocket Force News*, April 26, 2001.

97. Michael D. Swaine and Ashley J. Tellis, *Interpreting China's Grand Strategy, Past, Present, and Future,* Santa Monica, CA, RAND, 2001, pp. 141-147.

98. Finance Minister Xiang Huiacheng announced in March 2001 that the PLA budget would be increased by 141.004 billion yuan, 17.7 pecent. Xiang attributed this defense budget increase to (1) salary increases; (2) adaptation to drastic changes taking place in the world military situation; and (3) the need for the PLA to prepare for defense and combat. (See JJB, March 6, 2001). This increase is a consistent trend—in 1998 the official defense budget was increased by 93.47 billion yuan, in 1999 it was increased by 107.67 billion yuan, and in 2000 it was increased by 121.29 billion yuan.

CHAPTER 9

LOGISTICS SUPPORT FOR PLA AIR FORCE CAMPAIGNS

Kenneth W. Allen[1]

Under today's wartime conditions, aviation troops must be prepared to deploy quickly across borders to a war zone and be prepared to fight immediately. Currently, some of China's war zones do not have many first-line airfields, so the existing airfields must support several types of aircraft. The PLAAF must also hide its aircraft by dispersing them to field airstrips and highway landing strips. Therefore, PLAAF logistics troops must have the capability to support multiple types of aircraft at different types of airfields.[2]

Logistics Support for Mobile Operations, 1997

INTRODUCTION

The purpose of this chapter is to examine what the People's Liberation Army Air Force (PLAAF) is doing to reform its logistics systems in order to fight and win high technology wars under modern conditions, employing all five of its branches. Many of these reforms have come about as a direct result of contingency planning for a possible war with the United States over Taiwan, but the reforms are applicable to the PLAAF as a whole.

In the 1990s, the PLAAF began the process of transforming itself from a force capable of employing single branches (aviation, surface-to-air missiles [SAMs], antiaircraft artillery [AAA], radar, and airborne troops) and single types of aircraft in positional defensive campaigns to one capable of using multiple branches and several types of aircraft in air force combined arms, mobile offensive operations campaigns, with the goal of shifting to operations in joint service campaigns.[3] In order to reach this goal, the PLAAF has had to implement some significant changes in its logistics system, which traditionally has not been structured for supporting mobile, offensive operations. While many of the changes are still underway, some are still only aspirational.

The chapter is divided into four sections. In Section I, I will provide the setting for changes in the PLAAF's logistics operations by discussing PLAAF operational theory. In Section II, I will define PLAAF logistics and provide a brief discussion of the PLAAF logistics structure. In Section III, I will examine PLAAF logistics theory and what types of training the PLAAF has conducted to implement this theory. In Section IV, I will provide some conclusions about changes in the PLAAF's logistics system in relation to possible campaign operations against the United States.

SECTION I: PLA AIR FORCE OPERATIONS THEORY

PLAAF Positional Defense.

The PLAAF basically has two modes of operations—positional and mobile.[4] Traditionally, the PLAAF's primary mission has been positional air defense for China's airfields, national political and economic centers, heavy troop concentrations, important military facilities, and transportation systems.[5] As a result, most fighter airfields and virtually all of the PLAAF's SAMs and AAA are concentrated around China's large cities. During the its first 3 decades, the types of weapon systems the PLAAF had and the location of the airfields made it difficult for the PLAAF to conduct any other type of operations.

According to Paul Godwin, the PLAAF's reliance on positional defense became even more apparent during the late 1970s, when the core of the PLA's new strategy of

"People's War Under Modern Conditions" was forward defense.[6] Godwin states,

> This strategy meant that China would be defended at selected critical points as close to its borders as possible to prevent Soviet forces from driving deep into China. Positional defense was not the preferred option for China's military strategists, who would have preferred a more flexible mobile defense. But, the superior arms and equipment of Soviet forces conducting joint warfare granted them such mobility, speed, and destructive power that the PLA's operations could not realistically be based on a war of maneuver.

The PLAAF's Search for a Strategy.

Serious changes in the way the PLA thought about its future took place between the 1979 border conflict with Vietnam and Deng Xiaoping's 1985 "strategic decision" that directed the armed forces to change from preparation for an "early, major, and nuclear war" to preparing for "local limited wars around China's borders, including its maritime territories and claims." Whereas the PLA Navy (PLAN) had conceptualized a change in its strategy from coastal defense to offshore defense, the PLAAF entered the second half of the decade still in search of a strategy.[7]

The PLAAF's search was driven, in part, by a desire to seek independent missions and to try to break away from its near total submission to the ground forces. This dependence was exemplified in the early 1980s when the PLA began reorganizing its ground forces into group armies, and the PLAAF was tasked to provide defense for group army positions. Specific guidance from the General Staff Department (GSD) was given that "each branch and unit of the PLAAF must establish the philosophy that they support the needs of the ground forces and that the victory is a ground force victory."[8]

Wang Hai Initiates Shift Toward Simultaneous Offensive and Defensive Operations.

Under Wang Hai, who became the commander in 1985, the PLAAF began articulating its views on mobile, offensive operations. First, in a break from the PLAAF's focus on positional defensive campaigns, Wang laid out a program in 1987 that formally set forth the *thought* (*sixiang*) of "building an air force with simultaneous offensive and defensive capabilities" (*jianli gongfang jianbei xing kongjun*).[9] Wang emphasized that the combined arms combat environment of the 1980s required a force that "could move quickly over long distances, could fight in an electronic environment, could have the capability to attack an enemy, and could keep the PLAAF from sustaining complete damage from an enemy air attack."

In the late 1980s, the PLA began experimenting with the concept of rapid-reaction units. In 1990, the PLAAF published an authoritative book entitled *Air Force Operations Research* that stated, "The rapid-reaction *strategy* (*kuaisu fanying zhanlue*) is based on the premise that China will only be engaged in local wars for the foreseeable future, and the PLA must strike to end the war quickly and meet the political objectives."[10]

Given China's military limitations compared with those of the Soviets and Americans, the study advocated the concept of deploying air defense forces according to the principle of "front light, rear heavy" along with the principle of "deploying in three rings."[11] The fixed-base logistics system that existed at that time met the PLAAF's requirements for positional defense.

Using the "front light, rear heavy" concept, the PLAAF stated it should organize its SAM and AAA troops into a combined high-, medium- and low-altitude and a far-, medium-, and short-distance air defense net. The air force would also set up many intercept lines and organize its aviation troops into a layered intercept, especially along the enemy's main routes. In deciding how to deploy its forces, the PLAAF divided the battle area into three lines, using the front line of enemy airfields as the baseline. The first line would extend to a radius of 500 kilometers (300 miles) from the baseline, within which the notional enemy will mainly use its fighters and fighter-bombers. The second line would extend to 1,000 kilometers (600 miles), where the enemy will primarily use its fighter-bombers and bombers. The third line extends beyond 1,000 kilometers, where the enemy would mainly use its long-range strategic bombers.

Information from *The Republic of China 1993-94 National Defense Report* described the situation as follows,[12]

> The deployment of the Air Force is aimed primarily at defending against Russia and secondarily at defending against the Republic of China and Vietnam. Their deployment adopts the principle that 'a minimum number of troops are deployed on the front line while the main forces are mobile.' Currently (1994), within 250 nautical miles (450 kilometers) from Taiwan, Mainland China has 13 airbases capable of accommodating more than 1000 aircraft. However, there are only about 100 fighters stationed there now. In the second line, which is 250-500 nautical miles (450-900 kilometers) from Taiwan, there are more than 20 airbases with over 1500 [PLAAF and Naval Aviation] combat aircraft of various types.

The *Republic of China 1998 National Defense Report* states,[13] "At present, 1,300 aircraft are stationed at airbases within 500 nautical miles of Taiwan, of which 600 have a radius of operation over Taiwan proper." The *2000 National Defense Report* states, "Already deployed within 600 nautical miles (1000 kilometers) of the Taiwan proper are about 1000 [PLAAF and Naval Aviation] planes of various types which could undertake operational missions at any moment."[14] In December 2000, Taiwan's ministry of defense stated, "There were 14 military and civil airfields within 250 nautical miles of Taiwan. They currently have 121 fighters, but could accommodate 1,279 fighters, not including Su-27s, on short notice . . ."[15]

Looking at a map, the area out to 1,000 kilometers described in Taiwan's reports starts at the Shandong Peninsula, arcs halfway through Hubei and Hunan Provinces, then goes down to the Leizhou Peninsula, covering almost all of the Nanjing MR and about half of the Guangzhou Military Region (MR). According to the Federation of American Scientists Map 1, there are 50 airfields within 800 kilometers of Taiwan, including 36 military airbases—not all of which are permanently occupied.[16]

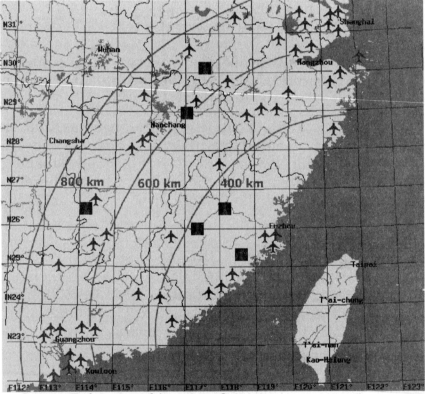

Source: Federation of American Scientists.

Map 1. Chinese Airfields within 800 Kilometers of Taiwan.

According to Taiwan military officials, since the mid-1990s, the PLAAF has been deploying small units from designated rapid reaction units from throughout the PLAAF into some of the bases directly opposite Taiwan for 6-month familiarization deployments.[17] The deployments have given the PLAAF's logistics system the opportunity to practice supporting those forces.

In using the "light front, heavy rear" concept, the air force believed it would have to deal with two important problems. The first problem was that the PLAAF's aircraft in the 1980s did not have the capability to fly to the border from their home bases, loiter for any length of time, conduct an intercept, and return home again. This problem was exemplified during the 1979 border war with Vietnam. In addition, the PLAAF believed that, during any sudden attack on China, it must be able to scramble all of its first line aircraft to meet the attack and prevent the incoming aircraft from striking any airfields.

The second, and contradictory, problem was that the most likely anticipated adversaries at that time—the United States and Soviet Union—had aircraft capable of conducting deep strikes into the heart of China. Therefore, the PLAAF believed it should station most of its air defense weapon systems in the second and third lines so they could intercept any longer-range aircraft as they converged on key targets. Furthermore, the attacking aircraft would most likely not have the proper escorts at those distances, and the PLAAF's early warning radars might be able to give enough advance notice of an attack for the air defense systems to be ready.

Several simultaneous forces are pulling on the PLAAF today. Although current PLAAF writings do not mention the "front light, rear heavy" concept, the air force still faces the same concerns about air defense and aircraft survivability at facilities near the coast. They are being told to prepare for offensive operations, possibly against U.S. forces, but they are also analyzing the types of operations and weapons, including long-range cruise missiles used during the Gulf War and Kosovo conflict that successfully targeted air defense networks and airfields.[18]

Teaching the Theories.

Beginning in the 1990s, the PLAAF began training its mid level officers in some of these new theories. According to an article in *China's Air Force* magazine:[19]

The PLAAF Command College implemented an in-depth teaching reform in 1993 to change the PLAAF's operating methodology from employing single branches and single types of aircraft to using multiple branches and several types of aircraft in an air force combined arms campaign, with the goal of shifting to operations in a joint service campaign. Prior to then, the training of middle-ranking commanders was aimed mainly at directing combat involving a single branch and single types of aircraft in warfare under general conditions. Commanders who graduated from such training were good at the tactical operations of their own types of aircraft and their own branch, but they did not know much about other types of aircraft or other branches and services. The PLAAF's joint operations consisted of aircraft flying combat air patrols and attack airplanes flying far apart from each other and not having much to do with each other.

As part of the reforms to produce "transcentury commanders," the Command College also began focusing on theories such as joint combat operations, mobile warfare, information warfare, and electronic warfare.[20] The new combat theory embodied "four changes" as follows:

1. Change from studying air combat under general conditions to studying air combat under high-tech conditions.

2. Change from stressing air defense to stressing air offense.

3. Change from air combat supported by joint operations with the army to air combat supported by joint operations of army, navy, and air force.

4. Change from warfare involving a single branch and single type of aircraft to combined arms warfare involving the multiple branches and types of aircraft.

The PLAAF under Liu Shunyao.

Whereas Wang Hai initiated the concept of simultaneous offensive and defensive operations in 1987, it did not receive much publicity until late 1996, when Chinese leaders, including Central Military Commission (CMC) Chairman Jiang Zemin and PLAAF commander Liu Shunyao, began to emphasize the PLAAF's need to fight offensive battles.[21] During 1997, Liu stated, "The PLAAF must improve its capabilities in actual combat by highlighting campaign and tactical training."[22] He further emphasized that campaign training involves air deterrence, air interdiction, air strikes, and participation in joint exercises.

In the February-March 2000 issue of *China's Air Force* magazine, four authors provided a candid assessment of the PLAAF's shortcomings and requirements for it to be able to conduct simultaneous offensive and defensive operations.[23] The article stated, "The PLAAF must change the direction of its strategic thinking from an emphasis on territorial air defense, primarily because the concept of modern high-tech war has changed. If the PLAAF does not change its thinking, then its development will be constrained and fall behind with the rest of the world's weak countries."

The article also stressed that the ability to attack is the PLAAF's weak link. This weakness was a direct result of the PLAAF's past operational thought, which was reflected in the air force's flight training program. The authors stated that if the PLAAF wants to develop a simultaneous offensive and defensive capability, then reforming the training system is urgent. Some of the reforms include upgrading the professional military education (PME) system, overhauling the pilot recruitment and training requirements, and focusing on realistic flight training.

PLAAF Mobile Operations.

As the PLAAF acquires better weapon systems and contemplates using its rapid-reaction units in simultaneous offensive and defensive operations, it has begun to focus more on mobile operations. In 1997, the General Logistics Department (GLD) published a series of books on logistics support of local wars under modern high-tech conditions. One of those books, *Logistics Support for Mobile Operations*, provides valuable information on PLAAF logistics.

The *PLAAF Dictionary* defines mobile operations as "Aviation troops seizing the right moment to move to the objective by air, land, or water. Normally, this entails deploying mobile *fendui* to concealed locations to conduct their attack."[24] Although this is the official definition, the PLAAF's use of mobile operations is not limited to *fendui*-size forces, not is it limited to the aviation forces. Today, all five of its branches and support units train in mobile operations. According to *Logistics Support for Mobile Operations*, the PLAAF has five types of mobile operations—long-range, air interdiction, support for other services and branches, airborne supply, and ambush—as described below.[25]

1. *Long-range operations.* According to the PLAAF's view of mobile operations, bombers and fighter-bomber aircraft are the primary means for conducting mobile long-range air attack operations. Normally, these are planned attacks on land or maritime targets by aircraft carrying specific weapons and supported by all types of escort aircraft. Therefore, in order for the PLAAF to adopt this method, it must take into consideration the current condition of its bomber units. When planning the bomber force's future attacks, the PLAAF must select the right

forward bases. Therefore, it must strengthen the ability of the airfields in peacetime to support bomber operations during wartime. The PLAAF must plan on having its bomber airfields attacked after the PLAAF's bombers conduct their attack, so the PLAAF must carefully select its targets and decide upon pre- and post-attack procedures. Based on the PLAAF's bomber and escort aircraft range capabilities, it must determine the appropriate distance for long-range attacks, so that the attacking task force will have enough time over the target to accomplish its mission and the electronic support aircraft will have enough time to support them.

2. *Air interdiction operations.* The PLAAF uses its fighters as the primary method for air interdiction operations. This method is used for air superiority, air defense over key points, and air cover missions. Operations during the Gulf War showed that an attacking force cannot completely destroy all of the opposing force's aircraft on the ground, so the best way to keep your aircraft from being destroyed on the ground is to conduct air interdiction operations against the attacking force. In future wars, the PLAAF will adopt the following methods for air interdiction: concentrate force by stressing quality and combat power to carry out emergency (*ji*), difficult (*nan*), dangerous (*xian*), and significant (*zhong*) missions as the edge of the knife; attack the aircraft that are supporting the attacking aircraft, such as airborne early warning and jamming aircraft; attack the enemy at all levels along the entire route as far out as possible; and pay attention to attacking low and super low level air targets.

3. *Aviation Support for Other Services and Branches.* The PLAAF's aviation troops will also provide support for the ground and naval forces, including airborne cover missions, airborne firepower support, aerial reconnaissance and electronic countermeasures to degrade the enemy's overall combat capabilities. This includes the enemy's campaign rear air defense system, second echelon units (or campaign reserve forces), logistics support system,

communications system, helicopters, and massing forces. It also means the PLAAF's attacking force must avoid ground or maritime corridors and guarantee friendly ground and naval forces' freedom of movement.

4. *Airborne drop operations.* The PLAAF is responsible for air transport of supplies, which can be either airdropped by parachute or brought into an airfield. Since transport planes do not have any air defense capability, it is important to consider their routes and vulnerability to air attack.

5. *Patrol and ambush operations.* The PLAAF uses its aviation, AAA, and SAM troops as the primary methods for these operations. These operations require a high degree of independence, use little firepower, are highly flexible, and usually receive good results. In order to execute these types of operations, the PLAAF will deploy small aviation elements or AAA and SAM units to areas where the attacking aircraft will pass. AAA and SAMs will be effective against low and super low flying targets, including armed helicopters.

SECTION II: WHAT IS PLA AIR FORCE LOGISTICS?

This section begins the discussion of PLAAF logistics reforms by first laying out what PLAAF logistics encompasses. Basically, the logistics system is responsible for providing all the PLAAF's general purpose supplies, construction, health services, food, shelter, clothing, fuel, and transportation, as well as managing its budget and expenditures. The *PLAAF Dictionary* defines air force logistics as the overall term for the logistics structure that supports combat, training, and air force-building.[26] PLAAF logistics consists of command, plus finance, health, armament, fuel, materials, transportation, capital construction, and airfield management support services. Logistics is organized into four operational levels— Headquarters Air Force, military region air forces (MRAF), air corps, and units. The administrative structure consists of a Logistics Department at Headquarters Air Force and each of the MRAF and air corps headquarters. In addition, each ground unit (non-aviation) division, brigade, and regiment has a Logistics Departments or Logistics Division.

The most important logistics organization for operational aviation units at the division and regiment level is the field station (*changzhan*), which is an independent logistics support unit under dual leadership of the air division and the MRAF headquarters. In the PLAAF, the field station director serves the same function as a U.S. Air Force (USAF) base commander. Prior to February 1970, the field station was called a base, and had the status of a division.[27] Today, it has the status of a regiment. The field station is responsible for organizing and supplying material and equipment, and also for providing continuous combined service support for operations and training. Each airfield housing aircraft assigned to the division has its own field station. Each airfield generally has 1-2 aircraft regiments, which determines the field station's size. For example, a field station at an airfield supporting two fighter regiments has about 930 personnel, including 170 officers and 760 enlisted troops.[28] According to *Logistics Support for Mobile Operations*, the field station will be augmented by additional logistics personnel when necessary.

The PLAAF's supply depot system is organized into a three-tier structure—first level depots are located in various military regions but are subordinate to Headquarters Air Force; second level depots are located in each military region and are subordinate to the MRAF Headquarters; and third level depots are located at and subordinate to operational units.[29] For example, each airfield has a third level depot, and the second level depots can support the third level depots when required. In addition, first level depots can either supply the second level depots or send items directly to the unit if necessary.

The *PLAAF Dictionary* states that the air force's strategic and campaign rear area depots can be divided into composite depots, where all types of materials are stored, and specialized depots for air materiel, armament, fuel, vehicles, and quartermaster articles, etc.[30]

In the past, the PLAAF's Logistics Department has also been responsible for some weapon systems maintenance. The PLAAF has always made a clear distinction between its aviation (aircraft) and air defense forces (AAA, SAM, and radar troops). This can be seen throughout the entire PLAAF's administrative, operational, logistics, maintenance, and training structure. Whereas the PLAAF has always had a separate first level department that was responsible for aviation maintenance,[31] the Logistics Department has been responsible for air defense equipment maintenance.[32] In 1998, the Logistics Department transferred its second level Air Materiel[33] Department (*hangcaibu*) and Armament Department (*junxiebu*) to the PLAAF's Equipment Department. Today, the Logistics Department is responsible for all general purpose supplies, and the Equipment Department is responsible for all special purpose supplies and all weapon systems and equipment maintenance.[34]

Finally, there are PLAAF academies, schools, and training regiments and groups to train logistics and nonaviation maintenance personnel. In addition, the PLAAF has several subordinate research institutes for aviation medicine, fuels, clothing, aviation munitions, four stations (oxygen generation, compressed air, battery charging, and power supply) equipment, and capital construction.[35]

Operational and Logistics Command Posts.

The PLAAF has identified several types of operational command posts (*zhihuisuo*), some of which are established only during exercises and wartime campaigns.[36] The PLAAF's logistics system also has a separate set of command posts, which may or may not coincide with the operational command posts. According to a report in the

South China Morning Post, the PLAAF built 100 command posts, operational offices, and aviation control centers between 1994 and 1999.[37]

Operational Command Posts. Each of the following PLAAF headquarters have operational command posts:[38] Headquarters Air Force, MRAF headquarters; air corps; aviation divisions and regiments; and AAA and SAM divisions, brigades, and regiments. The senior staff for each type generally consists of the following representatives: a commander, chief duty officer, chief of staff, and logistics support staff officer. Depending on the organization level, other staff officers include representatives from the various second level administrative offices under the four major departments (headquarters, political, logistics, and equipment), including operations, intelligence, communications, confidential (security for classified material), navigation, SAM, AAA, flight management, weather, radar, political, logistics, and maintenance.

Based on their mission, command posts can be categorized as main (*jiben*), alternate (*yubei*), advance (*qianjin*), auxiliary (*fuzhu*), or rear area (*houfang*) command posts. Main command posts are permanent command posts that are normally established at each echelon's headquarters. During campaigns, the commander is the senior officer in the command post. Alternate command posts are established before the start of a campaign at Headquarters Air Force, each MRAF, and each air corps with the responsibility of commanding units at the division and below. They are built at the same time as a main command post but are not used unless the main command post is no longer functional. Alternate command posts can also be set up for special purposes or to command lower level units.

Advance command posts are established in the operational area to assist the main command post in a general command role or to command air force units that are assisting ground and naval forces. For example, during the 1979 border conflict with Vietnam, the Guangzhou MRAF Headquarters established an advance command post at an unidentified location, which worked together with the 7th Air Corps Headquarters at Nanning as the unified authority for the PLAAF's participation.[39] An auxiliary command post is created to assist a main or advance command post in combat areas where command is difficult. In addition, depending on the type of activity, command posts can either be fixed or mobile, and depending on their physical location, they can be on the surface, underground, shipborne, or airborne.

War Zone Joint Logistics Command Posts. According to *Logistics Support for Mobile Operations*, the war zone joint logistics structure is the joint logistics command center for all of the various services and branches, and is the highest logistics command structure for the campaign.[40] Normally, the war zone logistics organization forms the base, which then incorporates people from the participating navy, air force, and second artillery campaign *juntuan* logistics organizations, and local command structures that are supporting the campaign, as well as the appropriate people from the headquarters, political, and equipment departments. When necessary, the GLD and the Headquarters Navy and Air Force Logistics Departments send representatives to participate. Under normal circumstances, the war zone deputy commander who is in charge of rear area logistics work becomes the joint logistics center commander, and the war zone logistics department director and each of the war zone service and branch logistics directors are assigned as deputy commanders.

Depending on the mission, the joint logistics command structure can organize four other types of command posts: rear area basic command post, rear area reserve command post, advance command post, and a direction command post. Normally, a rear area basic command post is located in the rear area where it is safe to conduct complete, unhindered command of joint logistics for mobile operations.

A rear area reserve command post is established early to take over from the basic command post if necessary. Normally, the reserve command post is staffed by the war zone deputy logistics commander, other required staff officers, and logistics support *fendui*. The reserve command post is located to the flank or to the rear of the basic command post. They maintain a close relationship. In the event that the basic command post is damaged or is unable to command the logistics units and *fendui*, the reserve command post immediately takes charge.

A rear area advance command post is established to strengthen the logistics command for the primary direction or for the important operations. When the war zone deploys an advance command post, the war zone logistics organization must deploy a logistics command team to be part of the advance command post, or it must establish a rear area advance command post in front of the basic command post to assist the basic command post in carrying out its command.

A rear area direction command post is established to strengthen logistics command for independent campaign directions. When the war zone creates a direction command post, the war zone logistics organization should simultaneously create a direction command post composed of a logistics deputy commander (unspecified from what logistics level he comes from) and key staff officers to assist the basic command post and to command the logistics for that particular direction. Other personnel for the advance logistics command post can come from logistics branch departments along the direction, including naval bases, from the highest campaign *juntuan* joint logistics organization, and from the war zone logistics organization.

The GLD stresses that in order to provide the best command, the command posts must remain survivable, must have good communications, and must have good camouflage. According to the requirements and capabilities, logistics mobile command posts can be placed in fast, mobile vehicles, aircraft (including helicopters), ships, and trains. In order to support command for technical (maintenance) support units and elements, each level of war zone logistics organization should also make every effort to create technical (maintenance) branch command posts.

PLAAF Logistics Command Posts. According to the GLD book, for future wars, the war zone air force logistics structure must create a "three-tiered command system" comprised of a war zone air force logistics command post, air corps and base logistics command posts, and field station basic command posts or flight logistics support command offices. The war zone air force logistics command post will be the command coordination center. The GLD book did not indicate whether this was part of the joint logistics command center. The air corps or base logistics command post or air force forward command post is responsible for managing logistics along the direction of the war, and the field station or flight logistics support office will be responsible for the lowest level of logistics command tasks.

The PLAAF stresses that the key to making this system work during a war is communications along the chain of command, since logistics is the link between a campaign and the units involved in battles. The brigade and regiment level is the basis for the *budui* logistics. Therefore, when lines of communication are disrupted, logistics along this chain are also disrupted.

SECTION III: PLAAF LOGISTICS THEORY AND TRAINING

PLAAF Logistics Support Theory.

Having looked at the PLAAF's logistics structure, this section will focus primarily on logistics support theory and applied training for mobile operations, which can be utilized in both offensive and defensive campaigns. The PLAAF has traditionally conducted its combat operations as a series of air campaigns within the PLA's overall campaign. The term "air force campaign" is a general term for all types of air force campaign operations.[41] The PLAAF describes an air force campaign as "using from one to several campaign large formations (*zhanyi juntuan*) or campaign tactical formations (*zhanyi zhanshu bingtuan*) to carry out the integration of a series of battles (*zhandou*) according to a unified intention and plan to achieve a specific strategic or campaign objective in a specified time. An air force campaign is implemented under the guidance of the national military strategy and the PLAAF's strategy."[42]

An air force campaign is also described as "a campaign conducted independently by an air force campaign large formation or with the coordination of other services and branches. An air force campaign involves various air-to-air, air-to-ground, and surface-to-air battles to achieve specific military objectives. The campaign determines the battle's character, goals, missions, and actions, and directly supports the local and overall war."[43]

PLAAF Logistics Support for the 1979 Vietnam Border Conflict.

The 1979 border conflict with Vietnam was a watershed for the PLAAF, whose operational capabilities had deteriorated significantly during the Cultural Revolution. Although the conflict clearly pointed out that the PLAAF's existing aircraft were not capable of projecting force beyond China's borders and were not capable of conducting sustained operations, it did show that the PLAAF's logistics forces were proficient at implementing their basic missions. Even though the PLAAF has corrected many of its deficiencies, a review of the PLAAF's conduct during the conflict provides some valuable clues about how the logistics forces might prepare and operate during the next campaign.

Although the PLAAF deployed over 700 aircraft to the border area, neither the PLAAF nor the Vietnamese Air Force flew any combat missions in direct support of their ground troops.[44] According to PLAAF statistics,

269

The air force flew 8,500 sorties, using 3,131 groups of aircraft during the campaign. Transport aircraft performed a very crucial logistics support function, flying 228 sorties, carrying 1,465 troops and 151 tons of materiel. The number of sorties also included a large number of helicopter sorties, including those used to transport over 600 wounded soldiers from frontline hospitals to Nanning.[45]

Several reasons contributed to the lack of Chinese air combat operations, including the fact that most airfields were not near the Vietnamese border, the existing aircraft (primarily F-5s, F-6s, and Il-28s) had short legs and limited loiter time, and the PLAAF did not train for sustained sorties, especially from airfields other than their home bases.[46] Equally important was Beijing's concern that any PLAAF air involvement would escalate the conflict, which was planned to last only 45 days.[47] Beijing met its goal of "using its aircraft to deter the Vietnamese from escalating the conflict," even though 20,000 to 30,000 PLA ground troops were killed during the 45-day campaign.[48]

The PLAAF's logistics forces were thoroughly involved from the time preparations began in the Guangxi Autonomous Region and Yunnan Province opposite the Vietnamese border about 45 days prior to the first day of operations. The PLAAF's overall preparations included establishing a command structure; preparing airfields to receive aircraft, AAA, SAMs, and over 20,000 PLAAF troops; and delivering propaganda designed to get the troops and local populace ready for the war.

The Guangzhou MRAF commander (and future PLAAF Commander), Wang Hai, was placed in charge of PLAAF troops in the Guangxi operations area.[49] The Kunming MRAF command post director, Hou Shujun, was placed in charge of PLAAF troops in the Yunnan operations area.[50] Each operations area was further divided into several operational directions, and a combined command post was established at one strategically located airfield within each operational direction to command and coordinate all matters among different branches and aircraft types within

270

that district. The Guangzhou MRAF headquarters also established a forward command post at an unidentified location, which worked closely with the 7th Air Corps at Nanning as the unified authority for the PLAAF's participation in the conflict.

Before and during the conflict, the PLAAF's logistics organizations had two primary missions—to support housing for those troops already stationed in Guangxi and to prepare housing, food, water, and electricity for the incoming troops. These organizations issued about 10,000 mobile beds, over 32,000 meters of water pipe, and 200 kilometers of electric cable; built 43,000 square meters of bamboo sheds; and repaired over 23,000 square meters of old housing. In addition, the air force used vehicles and its boat troops to transport mobile housing with the troops to Tianyang. During the conflict, the Nanning Wuxu field station dispatched over 16,500 vehicles to provide support for portions of one aviation regiment and one independent air group.

The logistics organizations also had to acquire and supply enough fuel for the incoming aircraft. Based on initial estimates of the amount of fuel required, the PLAAF's fuel supply was totally inadequate, and several depots were almost empty. Therefore, during the preparation period, fuel depots at all of the region's airfields were filled. This included the depot at Tianyang, which relied on water transport for its fuel supply. Some of the airfields did not have rail spurs, so vehicles had to bring in all the fuel. In addition, all of the combat readiness tanks available throughout the MR and some from outside the MR were quickly transferred to the frontline airfields. These expanded the amount of aviation fuel by over 50 percent. By the time the conflict began, the amount of fuel supplied to all the Guangxi airfields was 4.3 times the normal amount.

Supplying fuel during peacetime in China was difficult enough, but it proved even more difficult during wartime. Because some airfields, such as Ningming, are close to the border, their fuel storage was partially underground, and the rail lines supplying the bases were overscheduled. As a result, the PLAAF was concerned that the Vietnamese might destroy or disrupt fuel supplies. Because of this concern, the PLAAF took about 45 days to build over 50 kilometers of semipermanent fuel pipes leading to three different airfields.

Because the air force did not fly any actual combat missions during the conflict, only about one-fourth of the fuel estimated for combat was used, and the difficulties with fuel consumption were fewer than expected. However, several organizational and facilities problems were highlighted. For example, the fuel depot capacity at the PLAAF's airfields was too small, and there was no way to support several types of aircraft or the sustained combat use of fuel for several batches of aircraft. In addition, the refueling equipment was deemed backwards and incompatible—a problem the PLAAF states it grappled with through most of the 1990s but has now solved for the most part.

What Logistics Changes Have Taken Place?

As noted earlier, by the early 1990s, the PLAAF had not progressed sufficiently toward combined arms training, let alone joint service training. Because of this, the PLAAF's logistics system was still not organized to support mobile operations for long periods of time. By the late 1990s, however, that situation had begun to change.

The testing ground for the PLAAF's operational and logistics concepts has been the advanced training center at Dingxin, Gansu Province, in the Lanzhou MRAF. In 1958, the PLAAF built a large center for testing its air-to-air missiles (AAMs) and SAMs in the Gobi Desert near Dingxin.[51] During the mid 1990s, the PLAAF began expanding this base to include a large tactics training center, where multiple PLAAF units could practice the tactics developed at the Tactics Training Center at

Cangzhou, Hebei Province, and tested in individual units throughout the force. The PLAAF also established a smaller-scale "joint tactical training base" in the Nanjing MRAF in 1995.[52] A 1995 *Liberation Army Daily* article alluded to the Dingxin training center while describing a large-scale exercise as follows:[53]

> The exercise involved three categories and six types of combat aircraft, including fighters, attack planes, large transport planes, armed helicopters, and transport helicopters. Units have made efforts to turn airfield and support stations from those that provided logistic support for only one category of combat planes in the past into those that provide support for all categories and all types of combat planes. Since different categories and different types of combat planes are to participate in future air battles in one air fleet, units have worked out different types of support plans, renovated and transformed existing combat planes' service equipment and facilities, and imported advanced foreign logistic support equipment and facilities with the result that airfield and support stations can now provide logistics support for different categories and different types of combat planes.

The most important logistics changes have taken place at the field stations, which have tried to implement three basic changes in order to support mobile operations. First, the field stations have had to adapt their organizational structure to support the regiment(s) housed at their airfield when they deploy to other airfields. Second, the field stations have had to organize themselves to support multiple types of aircraft that deploy to their airfield. For example, in March 2001, several aircraft from a Guangzhou MRAF bomber division conducted a long-range mobility exercise, involving "round the clock flying for several thousands of kilometers, and stops at several unfamiliar airfields."[54] Third, the field stations have had to prepare to support operations from dispersal airfields and highway landing strips.

To assist the local field stations, the PLAAF is also trying to create central field stations that act as regional support centers. The goal of establishing central field stations is to change the current system of providing support for only one type of aircraft or one branch to a system that can support multiple types of aircraft and branches, such as AAA, SAM, and radar units in the area of an airfield. This center will have additional fuel, ammunition, and supplies for the aircraft.

In order to support aircraft deploying in or out of a permanent airfield, the PLAAF began establishing in the mid 1990s a rapid-reaction logistics structure organized of various *fendui* as follows:[55]

- Emergency mobile flight support *fendui* will deploy to field airstrips, highway landing strips, or to other airfields when needed.

- Emergency mobile transportation *fendui*, equipped with large fuel trucks, tow trucks, and container trucks, will deploy to an area quickly to supply personnel and materiel.

- Emergency field fuel pipe *fendui* will be responsible for providing fuel to airfields not serviced by rail.

- Emergency mobile field medical and rescue *fendui*.

- Emergency mobile repair *fendui* will be responsible for repairing special equipment.

- Emergency mobile airfield repair *fendui*, consisting of 150 personnel, will augment the central field station repair runways and do other required engineering tasks.

- The *fendui* can either deploy to another base with the aviation unit they support, or they can deploy to a base that requires additional support for incoming aircraft. In addition, they can be used to help prepare and support aircraft dispersing to auxiliary airfields, field strips, or highway landing strips.

According to a 1995 *Liberation Army Daily* article, the PLA moved from the theory phase to testing phase for "group contingency logistics support" to meet the requirements of local wars under high-tech conditions.[56] The article stated, "The PLAAF had already formed various mobile support battalions to be transported by air, along with creating field station contingency support *fendui*. At that time, over 90 percent of the personnel had reportedly been placed in service and over 80 percent of the major required logistic equipment was already available."

An April 2001 article in *Air Force News* described several exercises that the Nanjing MRAF had conducted since 1996.[57] Each exercise involved deploying emergency support teams of 100-300 personnel to unoccupied airfields to set up support operations for aircraft to perform combat sorties. During one exercise, four aircraft landed and took off again after 15 minutes of refueling and provisioning of ammunition.

By the end of 2000, the PLAAF felt comfortable enough to begin expanding the concept to larger units. For example, at the end of 2000 the Jinan MRAF conducted "the first organic deployment of an entire aviation division." According to a *PLA Pictorial* article,[58]

A Jinan MRAF aviation division received orders for combat maneuvers and immediately went into a state of combat readiness. Four hours later, several transports carrying an advance echelon of officers, men, and all kinds of support equipment and supplies left for the war zone. The next day, dozens of combat aircraft took off and flew across three provinces to the designated area, where support activities were quickly accomplished and an advance command post was established. Shortly after landing, the combat aircraft engaged in exercise training up to 400 kilometers away. Ten days later, the division returned home.

The Role of Transport Aircraft.

Although the use of civil aircraft is not new to the PLAAF, there are differing opinions about the PLA's ability to use civil aircraft, as well as military aircraft, to transport supplies and personnel during wartime. Unlike the U.S. military, the PLA transports almost all of its troops, equipment, and supplies by road or rail. The PLAAF's transports are used primarily for VIP support and to support the PLAAF's 15th Airborne Army. In June 1989, the PLA used civil aircraft to transport troops to Beijing prior to the Tiananmen assault. In December 1992, the PLAAF used three Tu-154 transports to ferry over 10,000 troops in and out of Xinjiang and Tibet during the annual troop rotation.[59] The aircraft flew 83 sorties and also carried 153.3 tons of supplies. In 1995, the PLAAF for the first time ordered that large transport aircraft carry support personnel and equipment to accompany large deployments of aircraft in emergency mobile combat support exercises.[60] In addition, military officials in New Delhi reported that the PLA used civil aircraft to ferry troops to Tibet during a recent exercise.[61] According to a 1999 Department of Defense report, the PLAAF's current complement of large transport aircraft is limited to about a dozen Il-76/Candids and about fifty Y-8/Cubs, the remainder of the transport force consists of smaller aircraft like the An-24/Coke, An-26/Curl, and Y-5/Colt.[62] Beijing can be expected to purchase a few additional Russian Il-76s or similarly-sized foreign aircraft. The ongoing expansion of China's civil aircraft fleet will also allow the PLAAF to use the country's civil airlines to supplement its transport capability during crises.

In September 2000, Taiwan's *Tung Sen* news quoted high level Taiwan military sources as saying that the PLA plans to use civil aircraft, which are capable of transporting 20,000 troops to Taiwan within 24 hours, to carry out a first-wave assault.[63] Regardless of what the PLA does during peacetime, there are limits to using civil aircraft to ferry troops into a hostile environment.

Since the early 1990s, the PLAAF's 15th Airborne Army's exercises have become more sophisticated in scope. For example, analysis of a 75-day offensive exercise held in April-May 2001 showed that "the PLA now has the capability to airdrop an organic regiment plus an accompanying logistics support unit, together with necessary equipment and supplies, in one airborne operation, and to sustain the operation with reinforcements in succeeding airdrops less than six hours later."[64]

In July 1999, the *Liberation Army Daily* provided information about a large-scale airborne operation in the Dabie Mountains in central China.[65] The article emphasized that the exercise included airdropping pieces of light artillery, boxes of ammunition, combat vehicles, communications equipment, and individual air defense missiles. According to the article, this was the first time heavy equipment and assault vehicles were para-dropped by the PLA airborne force, marking a historic leap of the force from sole para-landing operations to combined arms operations. The reporters stated, "This emergency logistics support unit, otherwise called an 'airborne warehouse,' carrying tens of tons of war supplies, can be air-dropped at any location according to operational needs. It can be employed in a concentrated form in one direction, or separated into small segments and dropped over scattered locations to provide supplies to the battlefield in many directions."

Fuel Support.

One of the most important challenges for the field station is maintaining sufficient materials, especially fuel, on hand before the start of a campaign, and then maintaining enough supplies to sustain the campaign. The PLA states that the cost for fuel per flying hour for the PLAAF's "comparatively advanced" aircraft can reach

10,000 renminbi (USD1,250).[66] Assuming this refers to an F-8, the cost for a regiment of 24 aircraft with each pilot averaging 100 hours per year, and 1.5 pilots per aircraft, means the regiment's aircraft would fly 3600 hours at a cost of approximately 36 million renminbi (USD4.52 million) per year. According to the PLAAF,[67]

> Fuel is 80 percent of the PLAAF's materiel. Based on PLAAF statistics, a small scale local war requires 90,000 to 140,000 tons of aviation fuel. Given this large quantity of usage, it would be difficult for the PLAAF's water and ground transportation system to supply this amount completely today. The best way to solve this problem is to build a pipeline network, which would be easy to open, could transfer large quantities of fuel, is easy to hide, and its ability to exist is high.

Given the PLAAF's historical problems with refueling equipment, in 1999, the PLAAF reportedly developed and tested a new airfield petroleum, oil, and lubricant (POL) supply system in the Jinan MR.[68] The system is an emergency mobile refueling device capable of supporting transregional air operations, and can be quickly deployed to forward airfields. It is mainly for use on sod airstrips, reserve airfields, and on highway runways opened for wartime operation. It can also be used on fixed airfields in case of damage to POL installations or power outages. During the exercise, the system was brought in and withdrawn after refueling two warplanes in 15 minutes. It can simultaneously refuel two aircraft of any model by gravity or pressure.

The importance of the PLAAF's emphasis on its fuel supply and refueling techniques was demonstrated during an exercise in Nanjing in April 2000. According to a *Liberation Army Daily* article,

> Minister of Defense Chi Haotian observed a PLAAF logistics exercise that focused on building a field oil depot capable of providing support to several hundred planes. The exercise also covered several other logistics tasks, including cleaning up after an enemy air attack on an airport, restoring the airport's

support capability, providing mobile combat support by ground units, implementing camouflage and protection for aircraft, battle positions, and oil depots.[69]

Given the PLAAF's dual concerns of supplying its forces with sufficient material in a timely manner and protecting its supplies from being destroyed, it states,[70]

> Because the PLAAF's transportation capability is weak and requirements for supplying lots of material during wartime is high, the most material should be stored at the primary war direction rather than secondary war directions. Fuel and ammunition used during battles are primary targets for the enemy, so it is not easy to store lots of material together. Therefore, the PLAAF should use campaign rear area bases as the primary with stores in several places. Airfields in the focal point direction can store some common use material, but the most important material should be stored and controlled by the war zone PLAAF logistics organization or by PLAAF Headquarters logistics for emergency purposes. When necessary, they can be air transported to the combat area units.

Logistics Support for Combat Sorties.

The PLAAF has established procedures for what it calls the "four flying phases," so that all aviation and support units train and fight from the same sheet of music.[71] This is especially important for the logistics system when aircraft deploy to a new airfield, or the receiving airfield's field station does not necessarily have the proper facilities or experience to support the new type of aircraft or equipment. Therefore, the field station is required to follow established procedures. According to the *PLAAF Dictionary*, the four flying phases are as follows:[72]

1. Advance preparation phase, which usually takes place the day before a flight.

2. Direct preparation phase, which occurs the day of the flight.

3. Flight implementation phase.

4. Flight appraisal phase.

Whereas the commander determines the missions, the political commissar's responsibility throughout the four phases is to ensure that the pilot is trustworthy enough to fly under the particular circumstances. Other people are responsible for ensuring the pilot has the proper technical qualifications to perform a particular mission, he is healthy, and the flight plan conforms with the reality of the pilot's situation. In addition, others prepare the aircraft for the mission.

Sortie Generation and Sustainability.

The key to any conflict for the PLAAF is sustained combat, and the PLAAF has not yet demonstrated the capability to conduct sustained, high intensity operations. The PLAAF does not have any real world experience in planning and executing the kind of high intensity air campaign that has proven so successful in U.S. and allied operations over the past decade. Although one should not analyze the PLAAF through mirror imaging, information about U.S. and Allied air force activities during the Gulf War and the Kosovo Conflict provide a measure of combat sortie generation and sustainability.

During the early stages of the conflict in Kosovo, allied air forces deployed approximately 400 aircraft to the area.[73] By the end of the conflict, the number of U.S. and NATO combat aircraft participating in strike delivery rose from 214 to 590 aircraft.

During the 78 days of Operation Allied Force, U.S. and NATO aircraft flew a total of 37,465 combat sorties—an average sortie-generation rate of 486 missions per day.[74] Of the total, 14,006 were strike and suppression of enemy air defenses (SEAD) missions (10,808 of which were dedicated strike sorties). According to Pentagon information, 23,000 bombs and missiles were used. In the early days of the campaign, however, the sortie rate over Yugoslavia was

280

more like 150 missions per day. The maximum intensity of operations was reached on day 57, when 1,000 sorties were flown, 800 of which were combat missions. These figures compare to 109,876 combat sorties over the 43-day Gulf War, or an average of 2,555 missions per day. Of the total flown in the Gulf, about half were strike missions, averaging around 1,600 sorties per day. These numbers do not include noncombat transport support sorties. These figures demonstrate the capability needed to ramp up and maintain high intensity operations, orchestrate operations through a unified daily air tasking order (ATO), and the need to sustain intense air operations when faced with a determined adversary.[75]

Weather affected nearly half the sorties during the Gulf War (in a desert environment), and the air offensive against Yugoslavia ground to a halt for days on end while targets remained obscured by cloud.[76] During the 78-day operation, there was at least 50 percent cloud cover for over 70 percent of the time. The need to minimize civilian casualties demanded visual identification and the use of precision weapons. Without a reasonably clear optical path, however, laser-guided bombs could not be employed.

NATO and U.S. forces were also hampered by the political decision to restrict the operating height of NATO attack aircraft to a baseline of 15,000 feet for much of the war.[77] While this kept NATO pilots beyond the range of most Yugoslav hand-held surface-to-air missile (SAM) systems and antiaircraft artillery (AAA) over Kosovo, it placed what many saw as highly artificial limits on the freedom of air campaign planners and strike crews to employ the full range of battlefield air interdiction techniques for which they had long been trained. It also, on occasion, challenged the alliance's ability to identify targets correctly, contributing to a number of targeting errors. The worst of these was an attack on a Kosovar Albanian refugee column, when high-flying USAF pilots apparently mistook tractors and other civilian vehicles for Serbian armor. These examples indicate that restrictive rules of engagement will most likely guide any future air campaign by the U.S. and possibly the PLAAF as well.

It is clear that the PLAAF has never conducted the high intensity sortie generation capability the allied forces showed in the 1990s. Based on an analysis of Chinese literature and interviews in China, it is evident that PLAAF pilots do not fly as many hours as their Western counterparts. According to interviews with PLAAF and foreign air force officials, the PLAAF's flying hours have not changed appreciably over the past 15 years, but they have changed their training techniques. Since the end of the 1970s, bomber pilots have consistently flown an average of 80 hours per year; fighter pilots 100 to 110 hours; and A-5 ground attack pilots up to 150 hours.[78] This compares to about 215 hours per year for USAF bomber, fighter, and attack crews. USAF pilots also conduct numerous hours training on advanced simulators.[79]

The PLAAF's official magazine, *Zhongguo Kongjun* [*China's Air Force*], has provided information on the number of sorties certain divisions have flown, which gives a glimpse of how the PLAAF as a whole operates. The 1994-4 issue discusses flight activity by the 39th Air Division in the Shenyang MR for a 5-year period.[80] From 1989-1994, the division flew 12,153 sorties in 1,715 *changci*, equating to 7 sorties per *changci*.[81]

A 1995 article in *China's Air Force* provided information about a fuels branch assigned to a PLAAF field station located on the Leizhou Peninsula. Based on the information contained in the article, the field station is part of the 2nd Air Division in the Guangzhou MR and supports a mix of F-6 and F-7 fighters. The gist of the article was that the Leizhou Peninsula has severe thunder storms 11 months out of the year, and the fuels branch conducted its activities safely under difficult weather conditions. The article touted the fuel branch's safety record by stating that it supported 54,506 sorties over the 8-year period of 1987 through 1994, equating to 6,813 sorties per year.[82] Based on the author's calculations of these types of articles over a 15-year period, an average sortie lasts from 45-60 minutes. It is not clear from the article whether the field station supports one or two regiments. Assuming the field station supports one regiment with a standard table of organization and equipment (TO&E) of at least 24 aircraft and 1.5 pilots per aircraft (36 pilots), this equates to 190 sorties per pilot per year, or 3.6 sorties per week. If the field station supports two regiments of 48 aircraft and 72 pilots, this equates to 85 sorties per year or 1.6 sorties per week. If there are more aircraft and pilots per regiment, then the sortie rate is lower.

According to Air Commodore Ramesh Phadke of the Indian Air Force,[83]

> Nearly 50 per cent of the PLAAF consists of ageing and difficult-to-maintain F-6s, while the remaining aircraft belong to the reasonably modern category. Maintaining operational readiness must be a difficult undertaking. It would be safe to assume that at the rate of approximately 1.5 pilots per aircraft, the PLAAF would have to provide a minimum of 120-150 flight hours annually to 4500-5000 of its active duty pilots. Allowing for those employed in staff and headquarters appointments, it would mean that at least 4000 pilots would need regular flying training. A rough calculation would show that to provide 150 hours of flying to 4000 pilots at 60-70 percent rate of serviceability, the PLAAF fleet would have to fly some 285 to 335 hours per serviceable aircraft per year, or 24-28 hours per month, which would be a huge task by any standards.

In the past, the PLAAF tried to overcome the individual aircraft sortie generation gap by having high numbers of aircraft available, such as when the PLAAF deployed over 700 aircraft near the Vietnam border in 1979. Another reason for low sortie generation rate is that most engines (F-6, F-7, and F-8) can only be used from 100 to 300 hours before they are overhauled, the aircraft availability rate would probably be reduced considerably during periods of sustained use during a conflict. Although the engines for the

Su-27s and Su-30s are much better, the PLAAF still faces the airframe serviceability. The PLAAF has facilities to overhaul all of its F-6s, F-7s, and B-6s, and their engines, but its F-8s must still return to the Shenyang Aircraft Factory to be overhauled—a process that can take from 6-12 months per aircraft.[84] Until the Shenyang Aircraft Factory has the full capability to overhaul the Su-27s and Su-30s, the PLAAF must send these aircraft back to Komsomolsk to be overhauled. It is not clear what the overhaul service period for a Su-27 is; however, assuming the original Su-27s that arrived at the 3rd Air Division in June 1992 have been flown a minimum of 150 hours per year (1.5 pilots at 100 hours each), then those airframes have at least 1,350 total hours each. The PLAAF must decide whether to fly those aircraft more or less as time progresses. Flying less means a reduced readiness capability, but flying more means more time on the airframes that cuts down the time before they must be overhauled.

The two latest examples of PLAAF sortie generation and massing aircraft come from the 1996 exercise opposite Taiwan and the sorties flown in response to President Lee Teng-hui's "state-to-state" comments in July 1999.

The PLAAF was actively involved during the PLA's large-scale exercises opposite Taiwan during March 1996. According to available open source material, "The exercise included 12,000 PLAAF and 3,000 Naval Aviation servicemen. More than 280 aircraft deployed to the exercise area and conducted total 680 sorties, including 82 transport sorties. Over 800 combat aircraft were within a combat readiness of 550 miles or were on the alert." Another report stated the PLA deployed fewer than 100 additional aircraft to the 13 Fujian airfields from other bases, raising the total to only 226 aircraft. Based on a briefing by the U.S. Office of Naval Intelligence, the PLA conducted a total of 1,755 sorties during the exercise.[85] Further press reporting stated that the PLAAF deployed aircraft from its second and third line airfields to first line airfields, where they conducted their exercise activity. It took about 3.5 hours for the

PLAAF fighters to prepare for takeoff, compared to the 10 hours they had needed previously. In addition, the PLAAF demonstrated rapid aircraft sortie regeneration of 40 minutes, which was considerably quicker than the past.[86] What was not indicated in the reporting is the number of sorties each pilot flew per day and whether they flew every day.

During July and August 1999, only twelve PLAAF aircraft were airborne at any time, not all of which were over the Strait, and the PLAAF flew only about 30 total sorties per day.[87] The air environment over the Taiwan Strait also provides limitations on the number of sorties that can be flown. Most of the airspace immediately north and south of Taiwan, flying to/from Taipei and Kaohsiung, is dedicated to civil air routes, and over 1,000 civil air flights fly through Taiwan's airspace daily.[88] Although the PLAAF did not fly that many sorties in the Strait, Beijing definitely sent a clear message that the PLAAF could fly in the Strait if it wanted to and psychologically altered the view of the PLAAF in Taiwan.

The PLAAF has classified its flying regiments into several categories as an indicator of their combat effectiveness. The highest is Category-A (*jia lei*). In 1997, Liu stated that 90.5 percent of the combat regimens were Category-A and the number of pilots capable of "all-weather" combat had reached 76.2 percent, the highest ever.[89] In 1999, Liu stated that 98 percent of the regiments were Category-A.[90]

Camouflage, Concealment, Deception, and Dispersal.

Throughout the PLAAF's writings, there are references to concerns about secrecy and early detection of its plans for offensive operations, given today's intelligence satellite and airborne surveillance collection capabilities. PLA writers have stated, "Major military operations cannot escape from such an intelligence net,"[91] so conducting frequent movement and a certain amount of dispersal is an effective concealment method.[92] "Forces should integrate the use of feints, camouflage, screening, and dispersion to conceal our command, control, communications, and intelligence systems and to deceive and jam enemy information reconnaissance."[93]

The PLAAF's logistics forces have the primary responsibility for implementing most of the camouflage, concealment and deception (CC&D) measures. While some CC&D and dispersal activities will take place during the campaign preparation phase, others will occur during the execution phase. As a result of the need to conduct undetected offensive operations, at least during the early stages of a campaign, yet provide for survivability in a counterattack, the PLAAF's logistics forces have invested considerable time and money into passive CC&D measures, such as building aircraft cave shelters, small hangars, single aircraft shelters, false targets, and "concealing the real and making the false obvious."[94] The PLAAF has identified additional measures that must also be taken to ensure survivability, such as building hardened entrances to caves, underground command posts, aircraft hangars, and personnel shelters, as well as fuel, ammunition, materiel, and equipment storage facilities.[95] Other passive CC&D measures have also been tried. For example, in an October 2000 exercise, a Nanjing MRAF airfield conducted a complete blackout as their aircraft returned from an air strike.[96]

The PLAAF has paid particular attention to trying to enhance these CC&D measures through the use of dispersing its weapon systems and equipment. The PLAAF states that the key to gaining air superiority is keeping airfields available for operations. According to *Logistics Support for Mobile Operations*,[97]

> The PLAAF must have a network of three types of runways— permanent, field, and highway. During the first ten days of the Gulf War, 40 percent of the Iraqi Air Force's aircraft were

destroyed. The majority of the aircraft survived, but they were not able to take off from their airfields for combat, so it was the same as not having them at all. Therefore, the best way to deal with this type of situation is to hide your aircraft and air defense equipment by dispersing them to field airstrips and highway landing strips from which they can continue to conduct their combat operations. The dispersal is especially important because airfield protection is weak. Currently, some war zones do not have many first-line airfields, so logistics support should be strengthened at first-line airfields to support multiple types of aircraft prior to or returning from a strike, or aircraft stopping to refuel en route to their home bases. When mobile operations units are massing and there are not enough airfields, then the war zone logistics must open up field airstrips and highway landing strips and support them with emergency logistics support *fendui*.

Over the past decade, the PLAAF has tried to increase the number of airfields, as well as to open up many of its airfields for civil aircraft. A 1996 *Xinhua* report stated, "The PLAAF had opened 71 military airports and offered 53 reserve airports to civilian airplanes since 1990."[98] According to a 1999 *South China Morning Post* article, "The PLAAF built 37 airports between 1995 and 1999. In addition, more than 100 large weaponry and equipment warehouses and war-readiness facilities had been enlarged and renovated."[99] Unfortunately, the article did not provide a list of the airfields or state whether they were strictly for military use or joint civil-military use.

In the late 1980s, the PLAAF began practicing dispersing its aircraft from permanent bases to alternate runways, including highway and sod landing strips. For example, in September 1989, three F-8 interceptors from the 1st Air Division at Anshan and one Il-14 transport used the Shenyang-Dalian highway as a dispersal runway for the first time ever.[100] The F-8s landed singly and took off quickly in a three-ship formation. The 1996-4 issue of *China's Air Force* showed several photos of a logistics fuel team setting up fuel pipes to support a single F-8-2 from the

1st Air Division landing on the Shenyang-Dalian highway during mobile operations "for the first time" in May 1996.[101]

The PLAAF has established set procedures for providing logistics support for dispersing aircraft. According to *Logistics Support for Mobile Operations*, logistics forces will follow a four-step process to prepare for aircraft to arrive at a field strip or highway landing strip.[102] The first step is the arrival of the advance team, that will coordinate with the local civilians and militia for securing the area and make an initial check of the runway, aprons, and facilities. The second step includes the arrival of the first echelon, which is responsible for setting up the logistics command post, closing the highway to civilian traffic, inspecting and clearing the runway and parking apron, assisting maintenance personnel prepare for flight operations, setting up fuel and ammunition storage, and organizing housing and health facilities. The next step includes opening the air strips and arrival of additional logistics forces. The final step is arrival of the aircraft and more logistics support troops.

Although this type of dispersal training was rarely noted in the open media until the late 1990s, an exercise in April 2000 provides a good example of recent training.[103]

> At 0615, an unidentified PLAAF airfield in the Jinan MR initiated an emergency dispersal exercise following a simulated cruise missile counterattack on the airfield. Given the scenario, the cruise missile counterattack appears to have occurred while the PLAAF's aircraft were returning from an attack. One group of support troops and over 50 special vehicles, including fuel trucks, power supply trucks, and oxygen trucks, dispersed to a designated highway landing strip to support the regiment's takeoff and landings. At the same time, a second group of emergency support personnel begin repairing bombed runways, extinguishing aircraft fires, giving first aid to injured pilots, and repairing oil pipelines.

Besides using emergency runways for pre- and post-attack dispersal airfields, the PLAAF has also gradually tried to build up the capability to provide logistics and maintenance support at auxiliary airfields for more than one type of aircraft over a sustained period of time. The PLAAF has gradually moved from supporting a few aircraft of a single type at an airfield for increasingly longer periods of time, to supporting multiple types. In doing this, they have had to tackle a number of long-standing problems that undermine support efficiency, including backward plane refueling technology and backward bomb loading technology.[104]

Support for Nonaviation Units.

Although most of the PLAAF's reporting focuses on its aviation branch, nonaviation units have also conducted CC&D and dispersal operations. A September 1999 *Liberation Army Daily* article described a North Sea Fleet Naval Aviation radar brigade exercise, that most likely represents the type of activity the PLAAF's radar units would implement during a campaign.[105] The article stated, "On receiving orders to set out, the brigade took only 40 minutes to dismantle its nonmobile radar station and begin a motorized advance of several hundred kilometers. On reaching the combat area, the radars were quickly set up to provide air situation reports to the command post. In addition, decoy radars and positions were set up at the same time to confuse reconnaissance planes." In November 2000, a Beijing MRAF SAM division equipped with three types of SAMs used "mixed deployment, concealing the real and displaying the false, and mobile ambush operations" during a live-fire exercise.[106]

Unanswered Questions.

There are many questions this chapter was not able to answer due to the lack of open source information. For example, as someone who has observed China's defense industry for decades stated,[107]

Logistics revolves basically around systems and numbers. What kind of relationships does the PLAAF have with its suppliers? What do we know about their supply chain management skills? What do we know about packaging—are consumables such as ammunition and petroleum, lubricants and oils (POL) packaged so they can be used right away "out of the box," or do they require assembly and/or processing before they can be used? What do we know about operating standards and rates, including sortie rates, ammunition and fuel consumption rates, maintenance rates (manhours of maintenance per hour of flight time), and other crucial logistics metrics?

These are just a few of the basic questions that need to be answered to really understand what the PLAAF's logistics capabilities are.

Although little open source information is available about the PLAAF's actual supply system, some generalizations can be made by looking at the way the U.S. military's logistics system manages similar responsibilities. The following information is taken from AFSC Pub 1, *The Joint Staff Officer's Guide*, 1997.[108] "The hundreds of thousands of items in the U.S. Federal supply system are categorized into one of 10 broad classes shown below. Deployment planning focuses on very broad categories, but it does subdivide the 10 classes into a total of just over 40 subclasses. For example, ammunition is subdivided into ammo-air and ammo-ground; subsistence is divided into subclasses for in-flight rations, refrigerated rations, non-refrigerated rations, combat rations, and water."

- Class 1: Subsistence

- Class 2: Clothing, individual equipment, tools, administrative supplies

- Class 3: Petroleum, oils, lubricants

- Class 4: Construction materiel

- Class 5: Ammunition

- Class 6: Personal demand items

- Class 7: Major end items; racks, pylons, tracked vehicles, etc.

- Class 8: Medical materials

- Class 9: Repair parts

- Class 10: Material for nonmilitary programs

The *Officer's Guide* further states, "Strategic movement of people, equipment, and supplies is only part of a complex logistics problem, whereby units must move, supplies must be requisitioned and delivered on time, combat force loading must be done according to the type of offloading expected, and there are always competing demands for transport resources and support facilities." Based on the author's experience with the PLAAF and aviation ministry in the late 1980s and follow up discussions with aviation business representatives since then, the PLAAF has moved closer to a fully automated logistics system, but there are still problems with standardizing parts to put into the system.

SECTION IV: CONCLUSIONS

The bottom line is what the PLAAF's logistics forces have done to better prepare the PLAAF to fight against the United States if required to do so. It is clear that the logistics forces have made adjustments in their organizational structure and operational methods to support the PLAAF's shift toward joint mobile, offensive operations, but they are not there yet.

Over the past 5 decades, the PLAAF has only been involved in three major external campaigns—the Korean War, the 1958 Taiwan Strait Crisis, and the 1979 Vietnam border conflict.[109] During those campaigns, the PLAAF deployed several hundred aircraft to a handful of airfields near the border, but their per pilot sortie rate was minimal.

More importantly, none of those campaigns involved enemy attacks against targets inside China's borders, so the PLAAF's aircraft, airfields, and troops were safe. The PLAAF has studied the Gulf War and Kosovo conflict and knows that the next war will most likely be completely different. Their aviation and air defense assets, not only near the front but also in rear areas, will not be safe from attack by Americans. stealth aircraft and long-range cruise missiles. This is why the PLAAF is concentrating on CC&D and dispersal measures, and why China has placed a higher emphasis on national military and civil air defense capabilities the past couple of years.

The current description for PLAAF fighter, bomber, and ground attack offensive air campaign operations can be summarized as "transregional rapid mobility integrated long-distance strikes at night in all weather conditions from multiple levels and different directions under unknown conditions. These attacks can be conducted against land or maritime targets, and the navigation routes can be over land or over water." Media reports discussing the PLAAF's exercises have mentioned all of the above, but from the PLAAF's perspective, one of the strongest aspects of its training program is that during exercises both antagonists are told when a war begins, but they are not told the other side's number of sorties, location, or altitude. Therefore, they must decide how to achieve victory in a completely unknown environment. An exercise conducted by a Jinan MRAF fighter regiment indicates the PLAAF's trend in training for emergency mobile transregional operations. According to a November 2000 report in *Air Force News*,[110]

A regiment of fighters consisting of over 20 aircraft departed its home base in the Jinan MR (which includes Shandong and Henan Provinces) on a rainy night "under concealment" in late October. The aircraft flew to an airfield south of the Yangzi river (probably in the Nanjing MR), to conduct air patrols and render air support to the war zone. This emergency combat mobility drill signified a new breakthrough in its capability for large-fleet, long-range, all-weather operations at all hours and in all air spaces. The regiment holds monthly simulated drills of emergency take-off and mobility, and change of alert conditions. It has switched to unfamiliar field targets for target practice, and changes ground markers frequently to enhance aviators' capabilities for independent navigation and target identification. It flies frequent low- and ultra-low altitude flights, some over sea areas under unknown conditions. It also subjects aviators to maximum daily flying time training. Training for complicated weather conditions is conducted in minimal weather conditions. On the recent maneuver, the regiment also practiced electronic countermeasures, penetrating enemy defenses from different directions, coordinated attacks from high and low altitudes, and simulated attack over water.

Throughout this chapter, there have been references to the PLAAF's requirement during the 1990s to transform itself from a force capable of employing single branches and single types of aircraft in positional defensive campaigns to using multiple branches and several types of aircraft in air force combined arms, mobile offensive operations campaigns, with the goal of shifting to operations in joint service campaigns. Within this goal, the PLAAF's logistics forces have had to change their operational structure and methods of operation from supporting single types of aircraft at their home base to supporting multiple types of aircraft at their home or deployed bases for short and long periods of time.

Based on the material available to write this report, it appears that the PLAAF's logistics system has made progress toward reaching its goal of supporting mobile forces. Organizationally, it has established emergency mobile *fendui* to support deploying aircraft into and out of airfields. These *fendui* are also responsible for helping set up mobile operations at field airstrips and highway landing strips. Although the articles reviewed discuss the need to preposition adequate material in the campaign areas before a war breaks out, they did not discuss whether this has actually happened.

From a training perspective, it appears that the PLAAF's logistics forces are applying their theory to operational exercises. The exercises involve repairing damage to airfields after notional enemy attacks, including runway repairs, taking care of wounded personnel, putting out fires, and preparing to recover aircraft that are en route home and have been damaged during their mission. At the same time, the logistics forces have deployed some *fendui* to begin preparing the field airstrips or highway landing strips for recovering aircraft or for generating follow-on combat sorties.

One of the most important issues that is not clear from the articles reviewed is how proficient the PLAAF would be during a real conflict, especially if some of the key first line airfields were destroyed—as the PLA anticipates will happen in a conflict with the United States. Would the PLAAF, in fact, be able to conduct combat sorties out of field airstrips and highway landing strips, or would they merely be somewhere to disperse the aircraft until they could fly to another operational airfield? Would the PLAAF opt to move its aircraft further to the rear as its airfields began sustaining damage? Will the PLAAF actually be able to provide logistics support to multiple types of aircraft at a single base? Many airfields have a single regiment with two types of aircraft (generally F-6s and F-7s), or have two regiments with different types of aircraft, such as one regiment with F-7s and one with F-8s. The field stations are organized appropriately to support more than one type of aircraft. But how proficient will the logistics forces at first line airfields be if they have to support several regiments of different types of aircraft? Although bombers have conducted exercises where they stopped at multiple airfields, the media reports did not specify the types of airfields they transited or the types of support they received.

Two probable weak links for the logistics forces during a campaign will be communications and transportation. *Logistics Support for Mobile Operations* states that "when lines of communication are disrupted, logistics along this chain are also disrupted. Therefore, the PLAAF needs to establish an independent command communications network, consisting of radio, landline, and computers."[111] It is not clear from the media reports or the PLA books whether this taking place.

Although the PLAAF has ordered that transport aircraft should be used to move logistics forces during campaigns, road and rail will still be the most likely means. A logistics transportation exercise conducted during summer 2001 in the Guangzhou MRAF emphasized that the PLAAF is not yet prepared to operate under poor weather conditions or non-scripted exercises. During his critique, the Guangzhou MRAF transportation director emphasized "the key is that training still consists of form without substance, including training for show to pass the test. Some units were thrown into disorder with just the slightest change in the predetermined disposition."[112]

If the PLAAF does have to engage the United States in battle sometime in the near future, the keys will be pilot proficiency, sortie generation and sustainability, adequate logistics support across the board, reliable communications and intelligence, and equipment maintenance capabilities. The PLAAF has made much progress in all of these areas over the past decade, beginning with establishing the theory, then providing the training to implement the theory. It is clear, at least from reading PLAAF writings, that much of what they want to do is still aspirational, but they are definitely putting the pieces of the administrative and operational structure in place to accomplish their goals sometime in the future. The PLAAF is also in the process of acquiring the types of weapon systems that will allow them to operate from airfields that are farther from the borders and to deploy SAMs with ranges that can reach out beyond China's borders. The logistics forces are also definitely changing accordingly to support these new systems.

ENDNOTES - CHAPTER 9

1. The author would like to thank Major Bill Belk (USAFR) for his assistance in gathering the FBIS material for this chapter, and to Ken Ashley, Jeff Goldman, and Jeremy Morrow for their comments on early drafts. The author would especially like to thank Rick Kamer for his assistance in identifying certain PLAAF units by their aircraft tail number, using his website *www.China-defense.com/aviation/numbering-system*.

2. Wen Guangchun, ed., *Jidong Zuozhan Houqin Baozhang*, [*Logistics Support for Mobile Operations*], PLA General Logistics Department Headquarters Department, PLA Press, January 1997, p. 184-185.

3. This description is a composite of information taken from Hong Heping and Tian Xia, "Head to the New Century," *Zhongguo Kongjun* [*China's Air Force*] 1996-5; and Wen Guangchun, ed., *Jidong Zuozhan Houqin Baozhang*. This is one of six books under the title *Gaojishu Tiaojian Xia Jubu Zhanzheng Houqin Baozhang* [*Logistics Support for Local Wars under High-Tech Conditions*] that the General Logistics Department commissioned the National Defense University and all logistics organizations to compile in 1995.

4. The PLA adds guerilla operations as the third mode for its ground forces.

5. Teng Lianfu and Jiang Fusheng, eds., *Kongjun Zuozhan Yanjiu* [*Air Force Operations Research*], Beijing: National Defense University Publishers, May 1990, p. 187.

6. Paul H.B. Godwin, "Change and Continuity in Chinese Military Doctrine: 1949-1999," a paper presented at The Center for Naval Analyses Corporation's 1999 conference on PLA Warfighting. Harlan W. Jencks provided a detailed critique of this strategy in "People's War Under Modern Conditions: Wishful Thinking, National Suicide, or Effective Deterrent," *The China Quarterly*, No. 98, June 1984, p. 305-319.

7. The *PLAAF Dictionary* defines air strategy as "The overall plan and guiding plan for air force building and combat. It is part of a country's military strategy and consists of three interrelated parts: air force strategic objectives, air force strength, and air force strategic employment." Zhu Rongchang, ed., *Kongjun Da Cidian* [*Air Force Dictionary*], Shanghai: Shanghai Dictionary Publishing House, September 1996, p. 6.

8. Chengdu Military Region Campaign Training Office, *Jituanjun Yezhan Zhendi Fangyu Zhanyi Kongjun de Yunyong* [*Air Force Utilization During the Campaign to Defend Group Army Field Positions*], February 1982, p 1. This ground force domination is not surprising, since every PLAAF commander and deputy commander until the late 1980s had their roots in the ground forces. It was not until 1973 that the PLAAF had its first aviator as a deputy commander, and 1985 until the first aviator became the commander. Even so, the Army still selects the PLAAF senior officers, and there are no air force general officers in any of the four PLA general departments (General Staff, Political, Logistics, and Equipment Departments).

9. Hua Renjie, Cao Yifeng, and Chen Huixiu, eds., "Kongjun Xueshu Sixiang Shi," [*Air Force Art and Thought History*] Jiefangjun Publishers, Beijing, 1991, p. 294-331.

10. Teng Lianfu and Jiang Fusheng, eds., *Kongjun Zuozhan Yanjiu*, p. 261.

11. *Ibid.*, p. 186.

12. *The Republic of China 1993-94 National Defense Report*, Taipei: Li Ming Cultural Enterprise Co., Ltd., 1994, p. 65-66.

13. *Republic of China: 1998 National Defense Report* (Taipei: Li Ming Cultural Enterprise Co., Ltd., 1998, pp. 30-31.

14, *Republic of China: 2000 National Defense Report*, Taipei: Li Ming Cultural Enterprise Co., Ltd., 1998).

15 Briefing from Ministry of National Defense, December 2000.

16. *http://www.fas.org/nuke/guide/china/facility/airfield.htm*. There are 6 military airfields within 400 kilometers, 11 more between 400-600 kilometers, and 19 more between 600-800 kilometers.

17. Interviews in Taiwan, December 2000.

18. In late 1999, the PLA began a program of training called the "three defenses and three attacks," including attacks against stealth planes, cruise missiles and armed helicopters, and defense against precision strikes, electronic jamming, and electronic reconnaissance and surveillance.

19. Hong Heping and Tian Xia, "Head to the New Century," *China's Air Force,* 1996, No. 5, p. 4-7.

20. *Ibid.*

21. The timing of Liu's comments on an offensive capability came as he took over the commander's position in December 1996 and as Taiwan began final preparations to receive the first squadron of 150 F-16s and Mirages in April 1997.

22. Sun Maoqing, "Make Efforts To Build Modernized People's Air Force: Interview With Air Force Commander Lieutenant General Liu Shunyao," Beijing *Liaowang*, April 14, 1997, No 15, pp. 20-21.

23. Yu Xiao, Tai Yang, Fu Song, and Wang Jianyun, "We Must Win the Next Battle: Two Fighter Division Commanders' Views of Simultaneous Offensive and Defensive Capabilities," *China's Air Force*, 2000, No. 2, pp. 4-8.

24. *Air Force Dictionary*, p. 30. The PLAAF's units (*budui*) includes divisions, brigades, and regiments. The regiment is the lowest level for logistics management. Below the unit level are elements (*fendui*), which include battalions, platoons, companies, and squads. Aviation troop equivalents of battalions and platoons are groups (*dadui*) and squadrons (*zhongdui*), respectively. *Fendui* consist of the troops that actually carry out the logistics work.

25. *Logistics Support for Mobile Operations*, Chapter 1.

26. *Air Force Dictionary*, p. 274.

27. Yao Jun, ed., *Zhongguo Hangkong Shi* [*A History of China's Aviation*], Zhengzhou: Dajia Publishers, September 1998.

28. Kenneth W. Allen, *People's Republic of China's Liberation Army Air Force*, Washington, DC: Defense Intelligence Agency, 1991, Section 7, p. 5.

29. *Ibid.*

30. *Air Force Dictionary*, p. 165. Composite depots are *zonghe ku*, and specialty depots are *zhuanye ku*.

31. In May 1976, the Aeronautical Engineering Department (*hangkong gongchengbu / konggong*), which had been downgraded to a second level department in 1969, was re-established as the fourth first level department and changed its name to the Equipment-Technical Department (*kongjun zhuangbei jishubu*) in November 1992. Following the April 1998 creation of the General Equipment Department, the PLAAF changed the name of the Equipment-Technical Department to

the Equipment Department (*kongjun zhuangbeibu/kongzhuang*). According to interviews with PLA officials, the Headquarters Department transferred its second level Equipment Department and Scientific Research Department (*keyanbu*) to the Equipment Department, so that its responsibilities matched those of the General Equipment Department. *Air Force Dictionary*, p. 146; *Shijie Junshi Nianjian 1999* [*World Military Yearbook*], published by PLA Press, Beijing, p. 103.

32. *Air Force Dictionary*, p. 276.

33. The difference between material (*wuzi*) and air materiel (*hangcai*) is that the former consists of items such as lumber and concrete for the entire PLAAF, and the latter consists of items only for the aviation branch's aircraft and aviation troops. The four other branches (AAA, SAM, radar, and airborne) and specialized support elements (communications troops, etc.) do not use air materiel.

34. Interview with PLA officials. The same situation now exists at the military region headquarters, where the Joint Logistics Department is responsible for general purpose supplies and the Equipment Department is responsible for special purpose supplies and all maintenance.

35. *A History of China's Aviation*.

36. *Air Force Dictionary*, p. 70-71.

37. Oliver Chou, "Air Force Building Projects Take Off in Past 5 Years," *South China Morning Post*, April 17, 1999.

38. The term command post is sometimes confusing, since the PLAAF has also created several air corps level command organizations called command posts. Beginning in 1993, the PLAAF changed the names of six of its seven existing command posts to bases (*jidi*)—Dalian, Tangshan, Xian, Shanghai, Wuhan, and Kunming. Apparently the Lhasa Command Post did not convert to a base.

39. Title unknown, General Logistics Department document, June 1979, p. 35.

40. *Logistics Support for Mobile Operations*, Chapter 3.

41. *Air Force Operations Research*, p 157.

42. *Ibid.*, p 152. Wang Houqing, Zhang Xingye (ed.), *Zhanyi Xue* [*The Study of Campaigns*], Beijing: National Defense University Press, May 2000, p. 346.

43. *Ibid.* The Chinese is *Kongjun zhanyi, you kongjun zhanyi juntuan dandu huo zai qita junbingzhong peihe xia shishi de zhanyi.*

44. Li Man Kin, *Sino-Vietnamese War*, Hong Kong: Kingsway International Publications, Ltd., 1981, pp. 33-35. The PLAAF deployed F-5, F-6, and F-7 fighters, plus Il-28 bombers, to the border. At that time, the Vietnamese Air Force was equipped with MiG-21s, plus U.S. F-5As and A-37s left over from the war. The Vietnamese also had SA-2, SA-3, SA-6, and SA-7 SAMs plus the formidable ZSU-57-2 self-propelled AAA.

45. *Dangdai Zhongguo Kongjun* [*China Today: Air Force*], Beijing: China Social Sciences Press, 1989., p. 638. Since the nearest point from Nanning was 110 km and the farthest was 280 km, each helicopter trip took 2 to 4 hours. During most sorties, the helicopters could not turn off their engines or refuel at the pickup points. It was not until 1986 that the PLAAF turned almost all of its helicopters over to Army Aviation.

46. *China Today: Air Force*, p. 638.

47. Information on the PLAAF's activities during the 1979 conflict come from a General Logistics Department document, [Title Unknown], June 1979, pp. 35-37.

48. King C. Chen, *China's War With Vietnam, 1979: Issues, Decisions, and Implications*, Stanford, CA: Hoover Institute Press, 1987, p. 114.

49. Wang Hai's autobiography published in January 2001 does not even mention the 1979 conflict. Wang Hai, *Wang Hai Shangjiang: Wode Zhandou Shengya* [*General Wang Hai: My Combat Career*], Beijing, Zhongyang Wenxian Chubanshe [Central Literature Publishers], February 2000.

50. On August 1, 1960, the Kunming MRAF CP (*Kunming junqu kongjun zhihuisuo/Kunzhi*) was formed and was responsible for controlling PLAAF units in Yunnan Province. The Chengdu MRAF was not established until 1985, at which time the Kunming MRAF CP became subordinate to it. The Kunming MRAF Command Post was renamed the Kunming Base (*Kunming jidi/Kunji*) sometime after 1993.

51. *China Today: Air Force*, p. 311.

52. Yuan Zhong and Hong Heping, "Air Force Completes Joint Tactical Training Base, First of Its Kind, To Provide Simulated Battlefield Environment for Combat Exercises Between Various Arms of Service," *Jiefangjun Bao* [*Liberation Army Daily*], April 13, 1995.

53. Zhao Xianfeng and Zhang Jinyu, "Lanzhou MR Air Force Improves Logistics Support for High-Tech Air Battles," *Liberation Army Daily*, December 6, 1995.

54. This same bomber regiment, which is most likely the 48th Air Division at Leiyang, Hunan Province (identified by Rick Kamer), has conducted several "first time" exercises over the past 2 years. In October 1999, the division's airborne refueling B-6s were part of the flyover of Tiananmen for the PRC's 50th anniversary. In October 2000, one of the division's regiments conducted "a 4-hour integrated long-range mobile exercise under unknown conditions, covering a distance of more than 2,000 km across four provinces. The raid was led by division commander Yu Jijun." In December 2000 or early January 2001, the same division conducted a 10-hour mobility exercise. In March 2001, the same division conducted its "first exercise involving bombers and tankers flying together in a combined task force (*huncheng biandui*). The task force implemented new campaign methods (*zhanfa*), including conducting a transregional flight with stopovers at several unfamiliar airfields and live bombing." In May 2001, the division implemented another "first" by conducting a division-scale reconnaissance and bombing exercise. An undetermined number of aircraft from the division conducted yet another "first" by flying a mobility exercise during the second half of the night. All of these articles stressed that the exercises were conducted during poor weather conditions. Wang Dinghua and Niu Yingfu, "Guangzhou Region Air Force's 'Bomber' Regiment Conducts Maneuver Exercise," *Liberation Army Daily* (Internet), December 5, 2000; Yang Mingde, Wang Dinghua, and Tang Baiyun, "PRC Guangzhou Bomber Regiment Conducts 'Long-Distance' Bombing Flight Drill," *Zhongguo Xinwen She* in Chinese, January 5, 2001; Wang Dinghua, "A Certain Air Division Forges Large Aircraft Assault Capability," *Liberation Army Daily* (Internet Version), August 22, 2001; Wang Dinghua and Fan Haisong, *Liberation Army Daily* (Internet), September 8, 2001.

55. *Logistics Support for Mobile Operations*, p. 191-193. Zhao Xianfeng and Zhang Jinyu, "Lanzhou MR Air Force Improves Logistics Support for High-Tech Air Battles," *Liberation Army Daily*, December 6, 1995. Several *Liberation Army Daily* articles have stated, "The PLAAF has set up a rapid mobile emergency support regiment with centralized command organization, to practice 11 special wartime support tasks such as rush-repairing bombed runways, extinguishing

aircraft fires, giving first aid to injured pilots, and repairing bombed oil pipelines."

56. Yang Yang, "Training for Logistic Support Units Viewed," *Liberation Army Daily*, December 29, 1995.

57. *Kongjun Bao [Air Force News]*, April 3, 2001.

58. *PLA Pictorial*, January 2001.

59. *China's Air Force*, 1993, No. 1, p. 49.

60. Zhao Xianfeng and Zhang Jinyu, "Lanzhou MR Air Force Improves Logistics Support for High-Tech Air Battles," *Liberation Army Daily*, December 6, 1995.

61. Interview with Ministry of Defense officials in New Delhi, May 1999.

62. "The Security Situation in the Taiwan Strait," Report submitted by Secretary of Defense William Cohen to the U.S. Senate as directed by the FY99 Appropriations Bill, February 17, 1999.

63. "China reportedly to transport troops by civil aircraft to attack Taiwan," *British Broadcasting Corporation*, *Ming Pao* (Internet), September 26, 2000.

64. Tan Jun and Li Yundou, "Chief Military Officers of a Certain Unit of Hubei-based Airborne Forces Carries out first Military Drill," *Wuhan Hubei Radio* (Internet), April 24, 2001. The airborne forces also paradropped pieces of light artillery, boxes of ammunition, combat vehicles, and logistics supplies.

65. "Large-Scale PLA Airborne Opex In Central China," *Liberation Army Daily*, July 21, 1999.

66. Lu Wen, *Lianhe Zhanyi Zhanlue Houqin Zhiyuan [Strategic Logistics Support in Joint Operations]*, Beijing, National Defense University Press, April 2000, p.153. The paper did not identify which aircraft were being described as comparatively advanced (*bijiao xianjin*), but most likely it is the F-8 and/or Su-27.

67. *Logistics Support for Mobile Operations*, p. 196.

68. *Air Force News*, December 11, 1999.

69. Lian Juntao and Zhang Jinyu, "Chi Haotian Watches Air Force Logistic Exercise Aimed at Promoting Scientific and Technological Training and Large-Scale Stage Opera 'Matsu' in Nanjing," *Liberation Army Daily*, April 14, 2000.

70. *Logistics Support for Mobile Operations*, pp. 197-199.

71. *Ibid.*, p. 214.

72. *Air Force Dictionary*, pp. 195-196, 234-235.

73. Sergey Sokut and Ilya Kedrov, "War in Europe: Yugoslavia: 78 Days Under Missile and Bombing Attacks: NATO's Limited War Was Uncompromising," Moscow *Nezavisimoye Voyennoye Obozreniye, FBIS*, No. 25, July 2-8, 1999, p. 2.

74. Nick Cook, "War of Extremes," *Jane's Defence Weekly*, Vol. 32, No. 1, July 7, 1999.

75. Sokut and Kedrov.

76. Mark Hewish, "Waging War with Weather," *International Defense Review*, Vol. 32, No. 12, December 1, 1999.

77. Nick Cook, "War of Extremes."

78. Kenneth W. Allen, Glenn Krumel, and Jonathan D. Pollack, *China's Air Force Enters the 21st Century*, Santa Monica: RAND, 1995, p. 130. Examples of flying hours are as follows: *China's Air Force*, No. 2, 1993, p. 43, identifies a PLAAF regiment commander who entered the military in December 1970 and had flown 1600 hours, equating to an average of 123 hours per year. *China's Air Force*, No. 6, 2000, p. 31, identified four young pilots in the Nanjing MR who averaged 150 hours per year in the new F-7-3 (identified as the 29th air division by Rick Kamer). Two pilots were squadron commanders and two were deputy group commanders. *China's Air Force*, No. 5, 1993, p. 53, identified a second-grade deputy group commander pilot in the Chengdu MR who joined the PLAAF in 1982 and had flown 900 hours, for an average of 80 hours per year.

79. Robert S. Dudney, "Fifteen in a Row," *Air Force Magazine*, No. 25, April 1999. Unfortunately, figures are not readily available for other Asian air forces.

80. *China's Air Force*, No. 4, 1994, pp. 30-31. Rick Kamer identified the unit based on a photo of one of the unit's aircraft.

81. *Air Force Dictionary*, pp. 276-277. The PLAAF uses the term *changci* to rate the logistics support for flying—excellent, good, and bad. According to an interview with a PLA official, the term is also used to describe the number of flying days or missions per year, based on two "flying days" per 24-hour period—one daytime and one nighttime. The 1992-2 issue of *China's Air Force*, p. 48, provides another example of the use of *changci*, the August 1st Aerobatics Team, which is the PLAAF's "Thunderbird" equivalent, conducted 180 *changci* (demonstrations) from 1962-1992 for 58 countries and 149 delegations. This equates to six demonstrations per year.

82. Mo Qiang, Liang Weitong, and Zhang Lianfu, "Leizhou Bandao Shangde Youliao Bing" [Leizhou Peninsula fuel troops], *China's Air Force*, 1995-5, p. 32. The unit identification was made based on information from Rick Kamer from photos in *China's Air Force*, 1993-3, p. 24. The 2nd Air Division began receiving the PLAAF's second regiment of Su-27s in 1996. The 3rd Air Division at Wuhu received the first regiment in 1992.

83. Ramesh V. Phadke, "People's Liberation Army Air Force (PLAAF): Shifting Air Power Balance and Challenges to India," paper written for the Center for International Security and Cooperation, Stanford University, September 2001.

84. A B-6 bomber must have its airframe overhauled after 800 flying hours. PLAAF Aeronautical Engineering Department, *Hangkong Weixiu* [*Aviation Maintenance*], No. 10, 1988.

85. "Chinese Exercise Strait 961: March 8-25, 1996," briefing presented by the U.S. Office of Naval Intelligence at a conference on the PRC's military modernization sponsored by the Alexis de Tocqueville Institute, March 11, 1997.

86. Lo Ping, "It Costs China 3 Billion Yuan to Make a Show of Its Military Strength," *Cheng Ming*, Hong Kong, April 15, 1996. Steven Mufson, "China Masses Troops On Coast Near Taiwan," *The Washington Post*, February 14, 1996.

87. State Department Briefing with James Rubin, *Federal Information Systems Corporation, Federal News Service*, August 3, 1999.

88. Victor Lai, "PRC Jets Twice Cross Taiwan Strait Center Line," *Central News Agency*, August 10, 1999. According to this report, about 340 international flights and 730 domestic flights fly over the Taiwan Strait every day.

89. Sun Maoqing, "PLA Commander on Modernizing Air Force," Beijing *Liaowang, FBIS-CHI*, April 14, 1997. The PLAAF's definition of flying in "weather conditions" is divided into "three weather conditions" (i.e., day and night visual flight rules [VFR], and day instrument flight rules [IFR]), and "all-weather" or "four weather conditions" which adds night IFR flights. Although this particular reference does not mean being able to fly in poor weather conditions, some reference to flying in weather conditions does mean exactly that. The exact meaning is usually clear.

90. *China's Air Force*, 1999-6, p. 15.

91. Huang Xing and Zuo Quandian, "Holding the Initiative in Our Hands in Conducting Operations, Giving Full Play to Our Own Advantages To Defeat Our Enemy—A Study of the Core Idea of the Operational Doctrine of the People's Liberation Army", *Zhongguo Junshi Kexue* [China Military Science] in Chinese, No 4, November 20, 1996, pp. 49-56. Senior Colonel Huang Xing and Senior Colonel Zuo Quandian are research fellows of the Academy of Military Science.

92. Liu Xuejun and Zhang Changliu, "Study of Measures To Counter Unmanned Aerial Vehicles," *Guoji Hangkong* [Flight International], March 1, 1996.

93. Xu Xiangdong, Gu Gang, and Yang Jun: "Mobilize Local Information Warfare Resources to Participate in Anti-Air Raid Combat," *Beijing Guofang*, December 15, 2000, pp. 7-8.

94. Chengdu Military Region Campaign Training Office, *Jituanjun Yezhan Zhendi Fangyu Zhanyi Kongjun de Yunyong* [*Air Force Utilization During the Campaign to Defend Group Army Field Positions*], February 1982.

95. *Logistics Support for Mobile Operations*, pp. 194-195.

96. "The Aviation Unit Under the Air Force of the Nanjing Military Region Takes a New Step Forward in Tactical Training," *Liberation Army Daily Internet Version*, October 8, 2000.

97. *Logistics Support for Mobile Operations*, pp. 194-195.

98. "Air Force Opens 71 Airports for Civilian Flights," *Xinhua*, January 18, 1996

99. Oliver Chou, "Air Force Building Projects Take Off in Past 5 Years," *South China Morning Post*, April 17 1999.

100. *Hangkong Zhishi* [*Aerospace Knowledge*], November 1989, p. 3.

101. *China's Air Force*, 1999-6, p. 20. Rick Kamer helped identify the unit as the 1st Air Division.

102. *Logistics Support for Mobile Operations*, pp. 229-230.

103. Wang Jinyuan and Jin Zhifu, "A Certain Jinan Air Force Unit Focuses on New 'Three Attacks and Three Defenses' to Explore Wartime Emergency Support—Warplanes Do TOL's on Expressways," *Liberation Army Daily*, May 8, 2000.

104. *Liberation Army Daily*, May 15, 1997.

105. *Ibid.*, September 26, 1999.

106. *Guangming Daily*, November 22, 2000.

107. Interview with John Frankenstein, Research Associate, East Asia Institute, Columbia University.

108. AFSC Pub 1, *The Joint Staff Officer's Guide*, 1997, Government Printing Office, Chapter 6.

109. No aircraft were used during the 1962 border conflict with India or 1969 with the Soviet Union.

110. "Air regiment holds transregional night maneuver," *Air Force News*, November 23, 2000.

111. *Logistics Support for Mobile Operations*, pp. 189-190.

112. Zhao Bo, "Seven Days and Nights of Exercises in the South China Sea: Revelations as Guangzhou Military Region Air Force Military Transportation System Conducts a Comprehensive Support Exercise under Modern Conditions," *Liberation Army Daily*, August 5, 2001, (Internet Version).

ABOUT THE CONTRIBUTORS

KENNETH W. ALLEN is a Research Analyst at the CNA Corporation's Center for Strategic Studies. Previously, he was a Senior Analyst at TASC, Senior Associate at the Henry L. Stimson Center, Executive Vice President of the US-Taiwan Business Council, and served 21 years in the U.S. Air Force, including assignments in Taiwan, Berlin, Japan, Headquarters Pacific Air Forces, China, and the Defense Intelligence Agency. He has written extensively on China's airpower. He received a B.A. from the University of California at Davis, a B.A. from the University of Maryland in Asian Studies, and an M.A. from Boston University in International Relations.

ANATOLY V. BOLYATKO joined the Far Eastern Studies Institute in 1992 and is Director of the Center for Asian Pacific Studies at the Russian Academy of Sciences. He is a Professor of International Affairs, Doctor of Sciences (military) and Academician at the Russian Academy of Military Sciences. Retired Soviet Major General Bolyatko also served as Deputy Chief of the Treaty and Law Directorate of the Soviet General Staff and the head of the Military Delegation during the negotiations that led to the conclusion of the Soviet-American Agreement on Prevention of Dangerous Military Activities (1989). Later, as head of two Soviet military delegations, he developed similar agreements with Canada and Greece. He also took part in the creation of the START-1 and CFE Treaties. After a long and distinguished career in the Soviet military, he retired in 1992. His most recent publications include *The Negotiations on the Prevention of Dangerous Military Activities* (1991) and articles on problems of international security in academic journals. In 1996 his monograph titled *On Regulating Military Activities* was published in Moscow.

DAVID M. FINKELSTEIN is the Director of "Project Asia" at the CNA Corporation's Center for Strategic Studies. He is a retired U.S. Army Foreign Area Officer for China with extensive joint political-military assignments at the national level. Among these assignments, he served as the Director of Asian Studies, Joint Chiefs of Staff, J-8 and Assistant Defense Intelligence Officer for East Asia and the Pacific. A long-time student of Chinese security affairs, Dr. Finkelstein holds an M.A. and Ph.D. in Chinese history from Princeton University and studied the Chinese language at Nankai University in Tianjin. Dr. Finkelstein has written many articles on Chinese security issues and the People's Liberation Army. His 1993 book-length study, *Washington's Taiwan Dilemma, 1949-1950: From Abandonment to Salvation*, was hailed in a *Presidential Studies Quarterly* review as "blazing a new trail" and should "take an important place in the literature of U.S. Chinese relations in the mid-20th century."

HIDEAKI KANEDA retired from the Japan Maritime Self Defense Force with the rank of Vice Admiral in 1999. He is currently a Senior Research Advisor for National Security, Mitsubishi Research Institute, Inc. He also serves as Special Research Advisor for the Okazaki Institute and a member of the Policy Proposal Committee for the Japan Forum for Strategic Study. During the 2001-2002 academic year he was a Senior Fellow at the Asia Center and J. F. Kennedy School of Government, Harvard University. He is the author of a number of books and articles about security, including "International Consensus in National Defense of Japan," *World and Japan*, Tokyo, Sep. 2000, "Changing Situation of China's and Japan's National Security," *World and Japan*, Tokyo, Sep. 2001, "Proposal for Maritime Coalition in East Asia and West Pacific Region," *IMDEX*, Germany, Nov. 2000, " Introduction to BMD," *The Okazaki Institute*, Tokyo, Nov. 2000, and " Role of JMSDF in Peace Time," *Securitarian*, Tokyo, Aug. 2001. Admiral Kaneda graduated from the National Defense Academy in 1968, the Maritime War College in 1983, and the U.S. Naval War College in 1988.

TAEHO KIM is a senior China analyst at the Korea Institute for Defense Analyses (KIDA), Seoul, Korea, and a nonresidential research associate of the Mershon Center, Ohio State University. He is also a co-editor of the SSCI-listed *The Korean Journal of Defense Analysis*. Dr. Kim is the author and co-author of over ten books, policy reports, and monographs, including *China's Arms Acquisitions from Abroad: A Quest for "Superb and Secret Weapons"* (with Dr. Bates Gill, Oxford University Press, 1995), *The Dynamics of Sino-Russian Military Relations: An Asian Perspective* (CAPS, 1994), and *The ROK Defense Policy after the ROK-PRC Normalization* (KIDA, 1993). His most recent English articles include "A Testing Ground for China's Power, Prosperity and Preferences: China's Post-Cold War Relations with the Korean Peninsula" (forthcoming in 2001), "Sino-ROK Relations and the Future of Asian Security: A Developing Continental Power Balance?" (2000), "Strategic Relations Between Beijing and Pyongyang" (1999), "Korean Perspectives on PLA Modernization and the Future East Asian Security Environment" (1998), "A Reality Check: The 'Rise of China' and Its Military Capability toward 2010" (1998), "Korean Views on Taiwan-PRC Relations and the Japan Factor" (1997), and "China and Virtual Nuclear Arsenals" (1997). His research interests are Sino-Russian military cooperation, Chinese arms acquisitions, and China's relations with Northeast Asian countries, including Sino-North Korean relations.

JAMES R. LILLEY was born in China, educated at Yale University, and served for a number of years in Southeast Asia. He was the Director of the American Institute in Taiwan from 1982-84, the U.S. Ambassador to the People's Republic of China from 1989-91 and to the Republic of Korea from 1986-89. He served as Assistant Secretary of Defense for International Security Affairs from 1991-93 and is presently Senior Fellow at the American Enterprise Institute. Ambassador Lilley is the co-editor of *Beyond MFN: Trade with China and American Interests* (AEI Press,

1994), *Crisis in the Taiwan Strait* (NDU Press, 1997), and *China's Military Faces the Future* (M.E. Sharp, 1999). He has written extensively on Asian issues.

ERIC A. MCVADON, retired U.S. Navy Rear Admiral, is a senior consultant on East Asian security affairs for Areté Associates, the Center for Naval Analyses, and several other organizations, and Director of Asia-Pacific Studies for National Security Planning Associates, a subsidiary of the Institute for Foreign Policy Analysis. He was defense and naval attaché at the U.S. Embassy in Beijing, 1990-92. His Navy career included extensive experience in airantisubmarine warfare and politico-military affairs, including service as the NATO and U.S. Sub-Unified Commander in Iceland, 1986-89. His recent undertakings include work on the People's Liberation Army, the China-Taiwan problem, Chinese attitudes toward regional security, and diverse issues involving the Korean Peninsula. He writes and speaks widely in North America and East Asia on security and defense matters. Admiral McVadon's publicly available writings include an article on China and the PLA in the Autumn 1996 *Naval War College Review* and chapters in the 1997 National Defense University book entitled *Crisis in the Taiwan Strait* (published in English and Chinese in the 1999 RAND book, *The People's Liberation Army in the Information Age,* and in the 1999 AEI-M.E. Sharpe, Inc ., book, *China's Military Faces the Future*).

SUSAN M. PUSKA is a colonel in the United States Army Ordnance Corps. She has served as the U.S. Army Attaché, Beijing, People's Republic of China (PRC) since January 2001. During 1996-1999, she served as a China political-military officer in the Office of the Deputy Under Secretary of the Army, International Affairs. In 1992-94, she was assigned as an Assistant Army Attaché in Beijing, PRC. She is a graduate of the U.S. Army War College, and the University of Michigan, where she was awarded an M.A. in 1988. Her publications include *Peoples' Liberation Army After Next* (editor, 2000), and *New Century, Old Thinking:*

The Dangers of the Perceptual Gap in U.S.-China Relations (1998), both published by the Strategic Studies Institute, U.S. Army War College.

ANDREW SCOBELL joined the Strategic Studies Institute (SSI) in August 1999 and is SSI's specialist on Asia. Prior to this he taught at the University of Louisville, Kentucky, and Rutgers University, New Jersey. Since 1988 Dr. Scobell has published articles in such journals as *Armed Forces and Society, Asian Survey, China Quarterly, Comparative Politics, Current History,* and *Political Science Quarterly.* Recent articles and monographs have focused on China-Taiwan relations, China's military modernization, and Chinese strategic culture. His book *China's Use of Military Force: Beyond the Great Wall and the Long March* will be published by Cambridge University Press next year. Dr. Scobell earned a Ph.D. in Political Science from Columbia University.

MARK A. STOKES is Country Director for the People's Republic of China (PRC) and Taiwan within the Office of the Secretary of Defense, International Security Affairs (OSD/ISA). He is the author of *China's Strategic Modernization: Implications for the United States* published by the U.S. Army War College, Strategic Studies Institute, in 1999. Lieutenant Colonel Stokes has served as a signal intelligence and electronic combat support officer in the Philippines and West Berlin. He served as an assistant air attaché at the U.S. Defense Attaché Office in Beijing, PRC, from 1992-95. Before his assignment to OSD/ISA, he was the Asia-Pacific regional planner within the Headquarters U.S. Air Force Operations and Plans Directorate from 1995-97. He holds graduate degrees in International Relations and Asian Studies from Boston University and the Naval Postgraduate School. He received his formal Chinese Mandarin language training from the Defense Language Institute in Monterey, California, and the Diplomatic Language Services in Rosslyn, Virginia.

LARRY M. WORTZEL is Director of the Asian Studies of the Heritage Foundation and a member of the U.S.-China Security Review Commission. He retired in November 1999 as a colonel in the U.S. Army after 32 years of military service. During his military career, he served in infantry and intelligence positions in Morocco, Korea, Thailand, Singapore, and China. Dr. Wortzel also served in the Office of the Secretary of Defense, the U.S. Pacific Command, and on the Department of the Army staff. His last position before retiring was as Director of the Strategic Studies Institute at the U.S. Army War College. Dr. Wortzel is the author of two books on China and has edited and contributed to two other books as well as many journal articles and monographs. Dr. Wortzel earned a B.A. from Columbus College, Georgia, and an M.A. and Ph.D. in Political Science at the University of Hawaii.